T R A V E L E R S '   T A L E S

THE
BEST
TRAVEL
WRITING
2006

TRUE STORIES
FROM AROUND THE WORLD

TRAVELERS' TALES

THE BEST
TRAVEL WRITING
2006

TRUE STORIES
FROM AROUND THE WORLD

Edited by
JAMES O'REILLY, LARRY HABEGGER,
AND SEAN O'REILLY

Travelers' Tales
Palo Alto

Art Direction: Stefan Gutermuth
Interior design and page layout: Melanie Haage using the fonts
Nicolas Cochin and Granjon.

Distributed by: Publishers Group West, 1700 Fourth Street,
Berkeley, California 94710.

ISBN 1-932361-31-6
ISSN 1548-0224

First Edition
Printed in the United States
10 9 8 7 6 5 4 3 2 1

*I stand under a Connemara sky slashed with rain
and ask the old farmer the nettled question, while
leaning against the old drystone wall, "Where does this
road go?" He leans against the clabbered stones, and
whistles for his sheepdog to follow him home,
then replies, "To the end, lad. To the end."*

—PHIL COUSINEAU, *The Book of Roads*

Table of Contents

Publisher's Preface

THE VIRTUES OF TRAVEL HAVE LONG BEEN TOUTED, and we are all familiar with the clichés. Travel broadens the mind, dissolves dogma, rattles the cage, brings new vigor to the step. It is hilarious, romantic, life-threatening, enlightening, toxic to weak relationships, invigorating to the strong. Travel is tedious and soporific, exhilarating and addictive. It is expensive because evanescent, cheap because the traveler is forever rewarded with memory and story. You wish you were home, you wish you never had to go home. All of these things are true, and if you are lucky you may well experience each of them on the same trip.

I saw the Dalai Lama recently at the annual American Himalayan Foundation dinner in San Francisco, and he underscored what seems to me the most important of all the very good reasons to travel. The others on stage with him (former President Jimmy Carter and Dick Blum, Senator Dianne Feinstein's husband) were talking in the usual generalities, politician-style, about the importance of education, when His Holiness added in his wonderful guttural Tibetan-accented English: "Education yes very important. But brilliant mind linked with negative emotion...very dangerous. So—what we need also is education of warm heart." And of course the way he said it, everyone in the room got it. Talk about communicating a powerful idea that washed away all prattle!

So without further ado, let me just say that here in these pages, in stories from all over the world, lies such an education.

James O'Reilly
Palo Alto, California

Introduction

HERBERT GOLD

BEHOLD, HERE IS A MAN DOING BATTLE IN HIS KHAKI-clad peripatetic soul to overcome impulses toward jealousy as he reads accounts by Bob Guccione Jr. (Vatican City), Alain De Botton and Rozalia-Maria Tellenbach (Switzerland), Laura Resau, Peter Heller, and Marianne Rogoff (Mexico), Bill Belleville (Galapagos), Constance Hale (Italy), Pankaj Mishra (Venice), Jeff Greenwald (Israel), and Phil Cousineau (San Francisco), all places he has traveled to and written about. Hey, editors, what for do you need these other writers? Just collect my collected and uncollected sublime words.

But now comes a reluctant confession. Even as a veteran traveler, I found new revelations here, entertainment and depth in the perspectives of writers who are, to their eternal credit, not me.

Vladimir Nabokov, asked who were his favorite contemporary American writers, answered, "Several."

"Who?"

He shook his head. "Anonymous praise hurts nobody."

I have a few favorite stories in this book, but I'll only mention that I chose to read Bill Belleville's "A Million Years of Memory" first because Galapagos is one of my favorite destinations. I found this observation: "They tell me reptiles don't dream.... But I wonder: Do they even need to, out here in an enchanted place that is still part dream itself?" In a personal nose-to-nose staredown with an iguana, I was almost smart enough to have Mr. Belleville's excellent think; I salute him for having it.

Many times in this book I came on observations that brought past travels back vividly to mind or made me want to see if I had enough frequent-flier mileage to head off to a new place, boots packed and old Banana Republic shirts stowed. (Also, don't forget vitamins and Pepto Bismol.)

Most of these narratives offer an occasion for the blessed *a-hah* reaction, as in:

A-hah! Now I see—taste, hear, experience—something I would not otherwise have known. In a few cases, I had the less blessed *Oh no!* reaction, as in: What were the editors thinking of? But that's part of the fun of a collection, just as part of a successful host's party comes during the ride home: Why did he invite *that* one? We measure our taste against that of another. We take pleasure in perspectives we did not choose ourselves. It's another form of *a-hah*. Armchair traveling is a way of discovering both the magic of evocative words and, more practically, where we might want to go next vacation time.

As a crazed Haiti addict, my eyes, ears, and even my brain become more alert if someone reports visiting the Caribbean. Once I asked a couple home from a cruise: Did you stop in Haiti?

The husband turned to his wife: "Was that Number One or Number Two?"

The travel writers in this book are not folks who stop only long enough to buy the t-shirt, the mahogany salad forks, the bottle of rum.

Another gentleman on an airplane, recognizing that

I had written about Paris and France, wanted to know where I ate when I was in Paris, "the capital of misery and the paradise of hope." I tried to answer: cafés, bistros, markets, brasseries, even restaurants. He wanted the names of the best ones, plus star menu attractions. I tried to say that I looked for comfort, affability, art, and adventure, not four-, five-, or nine-star cooking. "You mean you don't go for the cuisine?" No, there's cuisine everywhere now. The conversation ended with mutual sullen silence, his because he felt I was keeping the great cuisine for myself, mine because I tend to be sullen anyway.

As the wheels were lowered to land, I recommended to my seatmate that he buy a copy of George Orwell's great book, *Dining Out in Paris and London*.

The writers in this book are not offering recipes to sample. They are travelers, writers, deep in the state of anecdotage. They go where they go (quoting a French beatnik who came to San Francisco to learn to speak American) in order to "dig ze scene." They discover the compensations for jet lag and conniving cab drivers. They are making the scene and reinventing it for us.

An underappreciated benefit of travel is jet lag, which administers educational doses of melancholy, regret, night-wandering, and nostalgia; and then, when it lifts, the ardent visitor appreciates life in his or her home place or designated destination with the fresh eyes of recovery. Once, pre-melatonin, I wrote an article in praise of time zone-leaping jet lag, arguing that the best remedy is just to relax and enjoy it. Anyway, like most marriages, eventually it ends.

The letters home of good travelers like those in this book are personal confessions of rediscovery of the world as a wise child discovers it, all new, filled with possibility. When I took my children one by one to Haiti, their obligation was to write every day in the blank journals we bought as we left. ("Dad," recently complained my ten-year-old daughter, now more than ten, "why didn't you stop me from writing about Haitian kittens?" But "The Kittens of Haiti" account is a record of her concerns at age ten, which may be why there are no ten-year-old essayists represented in this collection.

My only objection to this admirable anthology, full of playfulness and insight, novel perspectives and quirky charm, is that there is no adventurous report on that bewildering stepchild of the Western world, Haiti. I happen to know just the writer for the job. He has a gray and grizzled face which has seen too much sun and stares back at me in the mirror when I brush my sharp and expensively-tended teeth. Home office phone number will be supplied upon request.

❧ ❧ ❧

Herbert Gold is the author of Haiti: Best Nightmare on Earth; Bohemia; *and many novels, including* Fathers *and the forthcoming* My First Murder.

~≈ ~≈ ~≈

Music of the Storm

Do you know what you are looking for?

"**D**ON'T EXPECT TO BREEZE YOUR WAY ONTO A Bugis schooner. The crews earn enough from cargoes and can do without you and your paltry fare," cautioned my guidebook on Indonesia. But the moment I strayed into the glaring sunlight on the docks at Parepare, I discovered that this advice wasn't meant for women. As I walked alongside the row of schooners, eager shouts hit me like volleys of gunfire, from one crew after another. No woman traveler, not even a fortyish one like me, could be said to lack for willing takers.

I had no intention of going for a schooner ride. The Bugis sailors of Sulawesi Island had practiced piracy for centuries—still did, according to the stories I'd heard in my six months in Indonesia. It was the Bugis who had inspired our word "boogeymen." If I let a crew get me out to

1

sea, my Indonesian friends had warned, the sailors would rape me. Then they would slit my throat, help themselves to my moneybelt, and toss my carcass overboard.

Retreating from the men's shouts, I stumbled into a dockside eatery that smelled of the clove-flavored cigarettes popular with sailors. I rummaged in my pants pockets for a handkerchief to mop my streaming face and glasses. The place was empty. Although the sticky-sweet tea they drink in Indonesia always makes me perspire more, I sat down and ordered a cup, glad to be out from under the direct gaze of the sun and the sailors. Thank goodness I wasn't going to set foot on any schooner. No. Certainly not. Lovely though it might be to see one of those wooden ships open its seven sails to the wind, I wasn't crazy.

All I wanted, I told myself, was a second look. I'd fled the docks too soon to really see the boats. What harm could there be in going back to the docks just once? And if I should happen to meet a crew that seemed nice . . . What if the stories about the Bugis weren't true? What if . . . ?

As I waited for my tea, I lapsed into a flow-state that frequently happens when I travel, letting my mind drift, decisions seemingly made without conscious volition. Sometimes I feel as though an inner pilot takes over where my guidebooks leave off, and maneuvers me, willy-nilly, where she wants me to go. Not that I'm easily hustled into anything. I often will loiter at the edges of a new adventure for weeks, wading in, retreating, studying the dangers and obstacles, mentally testing this or that way, all the while reassuring myself that it's only speculation—of course I won't do it—as I drift out too far to come back.

That morning in Parepare, though, I didn't get to dawdle as usual. Scarcely had my tea arrived when I saw a man closing in on my table. After a perfunctory cough or two, he offered in Indonesian to help me find a schooner. I invited him to sit, neither of us taking his offer seriously. For him, it was just an excuse to meet the new foreign woman in town; for me, a way of finagling an escorted tour of the docks. Abbas, as he was called, appeared boyish at first, all arms and legs and tousled hair, until I noticed a tiredness about his eyes. He had an anxious way of pushing back his forelock whenever he alluded to his three ships at sea. When he mentioned that he owned a fourth, the *Sumber Murni,* moored nearby and preparing to sail south along Sulawesi's coast to Ujung Pandang at its southernmost tip, I asked to see her.

I liked her instantly, though I knew nothing of ships. Fifty feet long, she had a well-rounded belly, a long sharp nose that tilted upward, and two masts. Her hardwood sides creaked and sighed. I had read that the Bugis still built schooners evocative of *Treasure Island* and *Peter Pan,* and I had seen pictures before, yet one long gaze at the *Sumber Murni* lying there at anchor, with the waves slapping against her hull, almost took my breath away.

We went aboard and I met the captain. To judge from his evasiveness when I asked about the cargo, he was probably smuggling something. Barely twenty, he wore his hair in long dark curls and walked with a swagger. None of the crew looked over thirty, and two were about twelve. Except for one hulking Ambonese, they seemed slight, almost waiflike. They're adventurers, I thought, just boys who ran away to sea. Born on little islands flung here and there throughout the archipelago, they must have grown up watching the ships come and go, dreaming of what lay beyond the reef or across the strait, until one day they left home to see for themselves.

Like them, I had run away. Six years earlier, I'd left a husband and career in San Francisco to knock around Asia and Oceania. Everywhere I went, local families took me in. I'd stay with them awhile, learning their ways, but inevitably grew restless. I hungered for the next island, the valley just beyond the next mountain range; I wondered what kind of people lived there, what language they spoke, whether they would welcome me with smiles or fall on me with spears. Before long, I'd be off again.

I always wanted the opposite of whatever I had. One night I'd be sleeping on a canopied bed in a maharajah's palace, waited on by turbaned servants; the next, on a cow-dung floor under a thatched roof, the guest of a poor family. If I had safety, I wanted risk; if I found love, I craved freedom; in community, I longed for isolation. Once, alone in the New Guinea jungle, ill with malaria and near death, I protested bitterly against my fate, refusing to die at the very outset of the adventure I'd waited for all my life. My unsatisfied hunger willed my body to get well.

Now, standing on the creaking deck of the *Sumber Murni,* I ran my eyes up and down her high rigging and thought of impossible quests, islands with no names, daggers, duels, and the wind in my face. To let her sail off without me was unthinkable.

After he'd shown me his ship, Abbas took me to a restaurant overlooking the harbor. He was a worrier. All through the first two courses of our lunch, he fretted about his business—about the monsoons and tides, the price of timber and rice, things in general. By the third course, he was fretting about my safety. Midway through the fourth course, a fish stew, it dawned on him that I might actually accept his offer of a schooner ride. He leaned forward and crammed his forelock back with both hands. The worry-lines over his brow deepened.

"Don't go," he urged. "Those are rough men. I won't be with you. I'm just the owner and I have no control over what they do at sea."

But it was no use. I was ready to sail. The more Abbas tried to dissuade me, the more I insisted on going. Something about the way he spoke of his four ships reminded me of a mother who can't rest easy until all of her brood has come home, and this made me believe I'd be safe. Besides, I was besotted with the *Sumber Murni*. Abbas's sensible warnings struck me as slurs on her fine-crafted perfection, and on her name, which meant "well of purity."

Even so, I took precautions. When he saw he couldn't change my mind, Abbas took me to register with the harbor police as well as the city police, using his influence to speed the procedures. Lest my backpack, watch, and camera present a temptation to the crew, I sent them overland to Ujung Pandang with an Indonesian friend who was going there. And Abbas made a point of mentioning to the captain that my friend would be waiting for me at Ujung Pandang and that the police there had been informed.

It was nearly dark when I told Abbas goodbye and negotiated the narrow gangplank. The captain had no schedule, so I slept on deck to make sure he wouldn't leave me behind. In the night, I was awakened by shouts and saw the dark shapes of men scrambling up the rigging. A fair wind had come up, and it was time

to depart. As the crew struggled to raise the huge sails,
I tried to make out their faces, to discern whether they
really meant to slit my throat. But the shifting lantern-
light revealed scarcely more than a shoulder here and a
knee there. They sounded intent on their labor, grunting and chanting in unison.

"A free girl. I like that!" It startled me to hear English
spoken. Mohtar, the big Ambonese whose voice had
dominated the chants, flopped down at my side.

"Where in America do you come from?"

He was a bronzed Goliath, and he was sitting too
close.

"San Francisco," I replied and scooted back a little.

"I was there two years ago. Working on a modern
freighter. I saw San Francisco, Yokohama, Amsterdam,
Singapore . . ."

"How did you like San Francisco?"

"Hard to say. I went in bars and nobody talked to me.
But a free girl! You go around the world and you are
fantastic. People see you. They talk to you."

I felt wary. In my experiences in Southeast Asia, the
men who jumped on me as soon as we were alone usually started by calling me "free." They'd seen enough of
my culture to know that American women were freer
than their women, but not enough to understand that
we had rules, too.

Just then a shaft from the lantern lit up Mohtar's nar-
rowly spaced eyes. Though I usually liked Ambonese
men for their easy banter, Mohtar's eyes had none of the
twinkly good humor I expected. They were too intense.

I asked him why he'd quit the freighter.

For a minute, he was silent. Then he lapsed into
a gravelly Indonesian: "Something happened. And I

haven't been able to get married after that. But I regret nothing. I take the bad with the good."

I was curious to know what he meant, but didn't ask. Twice in my travels, I'd unintentionally become engaged to a man by saying the wrong thing, so I'd learned to stay off the topic of marriage when I didn't know the culture well.

"Since I left Ambon as a kid," Mohtar continued, "all I've wanted is a life of adventure." Then, with a quick jab to my ribs: "You and I are two of a kind!"

I resolved to keep away from Mohtar, to the extent that you can avoid anyone on a small boat. Conveniently, the captain admonished him to get back to work. Soon I heard the sails flap overhead like wings of a giant raptor, and the harbor slid away behind me.

Not long after sunrise, the shoreline dropped from view. Then the wind died. There wasn't much to do. The captain made a half-hearted show of consulting a nautical chart of the Strait of Makassar and pointed out where we were on it, but he did this mainly for my sake; these men scorned compass and sextant and navigated by the stars. In the long-boat lay an old tin that housed our cooking fire; one sailor passed the time by blowing on it through a tube of bamboo. Mohtar and several others tried to catch fish, but I didn't look in their direction, not wanting Mohtar to get ideas. Instead, I sprawled on the hot deck along with the rest of the crew, fanning myself and waiting for a breeze.

Out of the blue, the mate nudged me and asked, "What's the verb 'to be' in Latin?"

"I need a six-letter Japanese word for 'teacher,'" said another sailor.

Soon five of us were poring over stacks of Indonesian-language crossword-puzzle books someone had brought up from below. I realized that without me, these "pirates" would be hard put to fill in some of the foreign terms. My throat seemed safe. Yet I felt a little disappointed to realize that nowadays pirates don't swashbuckle anymore. At least these ones didn't.

Still, I kept clear of Mohtar, who never joined in the puzzle solving. I was frequently aware of him looking at me and took care to cast my eyes elsewhere.

If we'd had a wind, or an engine, we could have reached Ujung Pandang by afternoon. But we were still at sea when the first, tentative stars of the evening blinked overhead and a dark cloud reached up toward them. Suddenly, it snuffed them out. The sea turned choppy.

The captain ordered me below, but I sat cross-legged on deck for a long time, not out of defiance, but because I couldn't take my eyes off the waves. From about eight feet high, they steepened to thirteen feet, then eighteen. Peaks and crevasses appeared. When the wind picked up, it was dazzling to see those ink-black peaks go white and crash like avalanches of snow, throwing cold spray over the deck.

For an instant, they looked like a Himalayan landscape, and I remembered a solitary game I used to play. When I was seven or eight, I would pretend to be an explorer who'd lost her way on Mount Everest. Eventually, too tired to go on, I would fall asleep in the snow, never to wake up. Whatever dream happened to flit through my mind at the moment my body froze would also freeze. If I died dreaming I was a yeti, I would turn into a yeti. If I died visualizing a dandelion, I would turn into a dandelion. I was fated to live forever inside my last thought.

All at once, a shrieking wind reminded me where I was, and I gripped my glasses. Our little *Peter Pan* boat was pitching hard. The sky roared, and rain crashed down. Everything went black. I couldn't tell whether the water sloshing into my lap was from waves or rain. Then lightning flashed, and suddenly I saw sailors running after crates of cargo floating about the deck, and other men crawling up the rigging, straining against the wind. Though the captain opened his mouth to shout at them, I could no longer hear him, or distinguish the thunder from the roar of breaking waves.

Despite the din, or maybe because of it, from somewhere inside my head came a snatch of music that I couldn't identify, the melody of a folk song I'd heard once and forgotten, or of a medieval hymn perhaps, each note distinct and pure. I felt too happy to leave. There I sat, still absurdly cross-legged, immobilized by the power of it all—the foaming seas, the rain and spray, the wind bent on prying my glasses out of my hands, and in the center of the storm, those clear, true notes. I was too lost in the music to care when a wave broke over me from behind and hurled me to the opposite side of the deck. I barely registered standing up, trying to find something to hold onto. The short trek across the lurching deck, to reach the door of the hatch and go below, was like slogging through deep snowdrifts. My hand on the door handle at last, I paused, exhausted, and another wave swamped me.

Then I was truly lost. I gripped the handle, my legs sailing across the deck, and strong arms pulled me into the hold. I lay down in pitch-blackness on a bamboo mat, though I could no more sleep there than on the back of a racing camel. With every roll of the ship, my feet seesawed over my head and I felt sick to my stomach. Once, I flew clear off the mat. All during the night I could hear hurried footsteps of sailors descending and going up again into the howling gale. One of the men fed me a cup of tea, holding the rim to my lips as if I were a child. Afterwards, he washed my face, handed me a fluffy towel, and said, "Go ahead and vomit on this. Really, it's nothing. I'll wash it later."

I passed the whole night as one instant. Just at the moment when the second wave swamped me, my thoughts froze. My last sensation before starting below had been joy at hearing those strange, sweet notes inside of me, a sensation I've never experienced before or since, and somehow, as I was being pulled into the hold, one of the notes elongated, trilling and swelling like a concert of cicadas, drawing me into itself.

By morning, the storm had subsided. To my embarrassment, I saw that I had vomited and urinated on my clothing. My face was damp with tears. A familiar voice—it belonged to the man who had given me tea in the dark—asked how I was. Looking up, I saw Mohtar. For the first time, I noticed that his left shirt-sleeve was hanging limp and empty by his side. He had only one arm.

Thinking back to our earlier conversation, I realized he must have been injured while working on the freighter, and this was why he had given up on marriage. I recalled an afternoon several weeks earlier on Ambon Island when I'd overheard two village women gossiping about someone who'd had part of his arm bitten off by a wild boar in the forest; the women seemed to assume losing a limb made a man unmarriageable. Now I was beginning to grasp what Mohtar meant about regretting nothing, about taking the bad with the good.

Later, as I knelt on the deck in clothes I'd borrowed from him, washing his towel and my soiled garments in a bucket of sea water, a school of dolphins romped by. I could die now without regret, I thought. In the storm, I had lost some of my old hunger for living life at full tilt, for seeking the opposite of what I had, because the thing I'd wanted most, without knowing it, was simply to hear the music inside of me.

It makes no sense, I know, to say I went inside a note that night, or to say the note held an ocean within it, an ocean bigger than the one battering our ship. But from the moment my thoughts froze, I could neither speak nor move, much less form a rational idea. I felt only the one note, felt it pierce me with a delight that verged on pain, pulling me under, dragging me down to the bottom of a sea where it seemed very cold, yet the heat seared me. My ears rang, yet I heard nothing but silence. And I dwelled in that note until morning.

Of course, I was conscious of being on a Bugis ship in the Strait of Makassar; I was conscious of my fear and nausea and the slow passing of the hours, of the sailor who fed me tea, though his voice seemed to come from a great distance. I didn't sleep a bit.

In the morning, I wondered what, if anything, there was left to do. I toyed with the idea of going home, maybe having babies or getting a respectable job. Devoting the rest of my life to the poor? But I knew I would do nothing of the sort. I would keep traveling. Before that night on the *Sumber Murni,* I'd half-expected that my travels would eventually transform me into a different, wiser person who'd be ready to settle down. Now I knew I was never going to change that much. I was still me.

Fifteen years later, I'm wandering still.

Travel has a way of confounding your expectations. Board a pirate ship hoping to see swordplay, and you may find wordplay instead; ascend a holy mountain in search of enlightenment, and you may be lucky just to find a place to go to the bathroom; run away from home thinking to purge yourself of your restlessness, and you may spend your whole life on the road.

For me, travel is like breathing. True, as I've grown older and physically worse for wear, it's gotten harder not to have a permanent home, but travel has also become less a hunger, more a disciplined art. Perhaps what I'd been craving all along was less the opposite of whatever I *had* than the opposite of whatever I *sought*—the confounding of my expectations. Nowadays I try to go with whatever happens, riding the waves and remembering there is music in everything. In everything.

❧ ❧ ❧

Judy Copeland teaches creative non-fiction and composition to undergraduates in the writing program at Richard Stockton College of New Jersey. "Music of the Storm" originally appeared in the Water~Stone Review *where it won the 2004 Brenda Ueland Prose Prize.*

❧ ❧ ❧

To Lhasa

Unlikely companions journey to the holy city.

I T WAS 5 A.M. AND PITCH BLACK AS I STOOD BY THE SIDE of Golmud-Lhasa highway. At intervals headlights bore down on me, their beams flashing across my waving hand. They pointed toward the Kunlun Mountains which rose like a steel wall across the southern horizon.

Sooner or later, someone was bound to stop and offer a lift. I was going to the holy city of Lhasa—and going *my* way. No Tibet permit, no travel agent, no set itinerary, no insipid airport greeter, no bus windows between Tibet and me, no government-issued tour guide. Damn the Chinese and their damn regulations. I wanted a sacred pilgrimage, not a plastic package tour.

Two years before I had tried this trip and failed miserably—couldn't find a truck driver willing to take the risk of carrying me. Maybe the police twigged to my plan and put the word out. Maybe there was something political happening and a crackdown on unauthorized visitors. Maybe my companion, a man, looked like too much trouble to the drivers. Or maybe my Chinese was just too awful to persuade them. Anyway, I couldn't find a ride then, and after a week of trying I gave up and went elsewhere.

Now, I was back. My Chinese was better, Lhasa was calm, and I was alone. This time, for sure.

At length a groaning Jiefang truck, heavily laden, wheezed to a halt a dozen paces up the road. The driver, a slightly built Chinese Muslim, looked down from his high perch. "*Nali qu?*" he queried, though the answer was obvious—where else did this road go? "Lhasa," I replied. He leaned over to open the passenger-side door. Hefting my backpack on the seat in front of me, I climbed aboard.

The sun rose late on a brisk October morning. We climbed a tilted landscape of barren scree toward a high, rocky plateau. The driver, surnamed Ma, was not a talker. He was alone, which is unusual for travelers on the Golmud-Lhasa highway. Setting off on that road is like starting across the Atlantic in a rowboat. You're on your own against the elements, and they can be ruthless. I imagined Ma was glad to have a companion, even if only a useless female foreigner.

As I watched the Kunlun Mountains edging past, I congratulated myself for finding a ride on this forbidden road. A couple of hours later we halted behind a long line of trucks. I craned my neck to see the cause of the holdup: a police checkpoint.

Oh God. Shrinking rapidly, I melted down below the level of the dashboard for a sudden, feigned nap. Ma grabbed some papers stuck above the sun visor, banged open his door and shuffled off toward the front of the line. Papers duly stamped, he returned to his seat.

Does he know it's illegal to carry foreigners here? I hadn't asked for fear of losing my ride, but now, crouching behind the dashboard, the possibility of getting us both arrested made my heart pound.

Several minutes later the trucks in front moved off. Ma nudged the beast into first gear, and we slid past the checkpost. We were five miles down the road before I dared to lift my head.

Yahh! The sun was coming up, a hurdle had been crossed, and the land was buck-naked gorgeous. We drove and drove and drove. Another checkpoint appeared, which I finessed just as before. On we went, spinning pavement beneath us on the long, high, desolate roadway across the Roof of the World.

The old Jiefang "liberation" trucks are extremely simple in design. They break down often, are easy to fix, and can run on an engine held together with baling wire and gaskets cut from bits of cast-off rubber. Each one carries a big iron crank to turn the engine over when, as often happens, the electric starter fails. Ma's Jiefang was eleven years old, and heavily overloaded. On uphill sections I thought I could probably go faster by walking. Of course there was no radio. The windows didn't seal, so a sub-zero breeze constantly cooled the cab, but there was no heat either. Despite layers of down, fleece, and Gore-Tex, I still shivered; but the stalwart Ma clad in a flimsy polyester jacket didn't even bother with his overcoat.

In late afternoon the fuel tank was running low, so we halted in the middle of nowhere to gas up. Ma had a spare drum lashed to the top of his load, such precautions being usual on a route where fuel is expensive, hard to find, and often dirty. But Ma's rubber hose wasn't quite long enough to reach from the drum to the tank. A lot of petrol splashed on him before I jumped out to grab the free end.

When Ma got back into the truck, the smell of gasoline from his fuel-soaked gloves was strong. As we got under way, I watched him peel off the gloves, drop them on the dashboard, then pull out a cigarette and light up.

Nothing happened. The gloves remained on the dashboard, eerily quiescent as Ma drove along, slowly smoking his cigarette to a stub. I was just beginning to breathe again when he finished the smoke, tossed the butt out the window and re-donned his gloves. Then he lit up another.

POOF! Suddenly bright orange flames were rising serenely from Ma's gloved hands.

The truck was barreling down the highway at no great speed, but with incredible momentum.

I don't remember if Ma was shouting, and if so, what he might have said. All I know is that I reared up from my seat and tried to smother the flames with my Gore-Tex-clad arms. But Ma wouldn't let me; he pulled his hands out from under my arms, and began to blow on them. He blew hard. The flames grew larger.

Again I tried to paw down his hands beneath mine to smother the flames; again he pulled them out, blowing all the more frantically. The flames grew larger still.

We scrabbled this way for perhaps half a minute. Meanwhile Ma was stepping on the brake. An eternity later the Jiefang shuddered to a stop. In a flash he was outside, threw down his burning gloves on the ground, then stripped off his polyester jacket, which had also ignited. He stamped on the jacket to put out the fire. A minute later we were standing next to a pile of smoldering rags in the middle of a silent, empty plateau.

When he was sure the flames were out, Ma pincered the jacket between a couple of unburnt fingers and gazed at it wistfully.

Never mind the jacket! "Show me your hands," I told him.

He stepped up mutely, and held out his scorched appendages. The left hand had an orange-sized charcoal lesion covering the palm. Blackened skin was already separating from the flesh beneath. His right hand was tomato-red and blistering.

"It's nothing," he said.

Words formed calmly and surreally in my head: *get your first aid kit*. I went back to the truck where my backpack was lying across the seat, and pulled out my pitiful collection of Band-Aids, amoxicillin, and Pepto Bismol. No burn cream of any kind, but I did have antiseptic ointment and a clean bandanna to put on his wound.

When my doctoring was done and the worst burn covered, I began to think of what lay ahead: 500 miles of inhospitable terrain. The only way to get out was to drive. How could he do it with his scorched palm? And if he couldn't, would I have to pilot this dinosaur all the way to Lhasa?

"Do you want me to drive?" I asked, hoping feverishly that he would say no.

He hesitated. "All right."

Damn! Wishing I hadn't asked, I climbed into the driver's place behind that behemoth of a steering wheel. He showed me how the controls worked: the gigantic gear-shift lever that needed careful nuance coordinated with brute force to engage, the high-beam switch hidden on the floor among tangled wires, a knob that had to be pulled to get the engine even started. Ma's Qinghai dialect was hard to understand, but the controls were pathetically simple. When he was done, I pulled out the choke with trepidation and jiggled the key in its slot.

The engine gurgled to life. I eased the gearshift lever, and as if by magic the highway began moving. As I shifted, we picked up speed, and I felt a moment of exhilaration. Hey, this isn't so bad. I can handle it.

The sky was growing gray as the sun dropped. After about five minutes we met an oncoming truck, and I was seared with sudden panic. How wide is this truck? How wide is the other one? How wide is the road? How close to the edge do I need to go? There was forty-five degrees of play in the steering wheel. Heart in my throat, I steered to one side, and the oncoming vehicle roared safely past. Whew. Sweat pricked my skin; Tibet suddenly didn't seem so cold anymore. *Omigod here comes another one!*

After the fifth truck there was a breather, and I glanced over at Ma huddled on the passenger seat. He looked utterly miserable, suffering from the material torment of his scorched hands and the spiritual torment of my inept driving. We had gone barely six miles but already I was a wreck. I began to think that it might be better to give him back the wheel, and a short while later, I did.

"Shall we stop here for the night, or keep on driving?" It was 10 p.m., and we had just arrived in Tuotuohe, a tiny outpost some 14,700 feet above sea level. The indomitable Ma, shifting and steering deftly with the unburnt half of his right hand and a few functioning fingers of his left, was still going strong. He was ready to keep on all night.

I said, "We need to find a doctor to look at your hands."

Ma shrugged. "Not necessary. Let's keep going."

We argued fruitlessly until I declared that he could go on without me; I would find another ride in the morning. At that dire threat, he backed down, and took us to a wooden shack where there was a simple restaurant operated by his fellow Muslims. After a bowl of spicy beef noodles, I was escorted to a room in back. I unrolled my sleeping bag on a thinly padded bed, dragged the cotton comforter over me, and surrendered to sleep.

Two hours before dawn, in the bone-cracking cold of a Tibetan October night, Ma was up and outside working on his truck. In the yard I found the Jiefang standing with its enormous hood open. Ma was warming up the engine with a blow-torch—standard equipment for the Golmud-to-Lhasa run. When that didn't work, he got out his tools and began tinkering. I helped by turning over the engine with a big iron crank, and by holding the flashlight while he worked. Two hours later the truck still wouldn't start, so he petitioned another driver for a tow. At last we were off and running. We had eaten no breakfast, but it was too late to worry about that now. Warmed by yellow heat from the rising sun, we started on the remaining 430 miles to Lhasa.

The Qinghai-Tibet highway crosses some of the bleakest terrain on earth. Since leaving the city of Golmud we had seen little more than rock, gravel, and

snow. Yet the worst was still ahead: the formidable
Tangula Mountains, which gird the plateau and separate Qinghai Province from Tibet Autonomous Region.
Grinding up to the 17,000-foot pass took four hours.
Then we descended into a comparatively hospitable
region, where grass grows thinly and nomads dwell in
widely scattered tents. Yet we were less than half way,
and had more hills to climb ahead.

The hours dragged by. We passed the town of Amdo,
stopping just long enough for a bowl of noodles. I insisted on changing the dressing on his hand, which was
pussing and sloughing off burnt skin. When darkness
fell, Ma asked if I wanted to stop. By now I knew that
his fifteen years on this run had hardened him to driving all night. Besides, I had the Lhasa itch. I said: let's
go on.

So we did. Dozing in my seat, I was little aware of the
hours that passed, until about 3 a.m. when I was awakened by a sudden silence. Ma had pulled off the road for
a nap, for after seventeen continuous hours at the wheel,
even he was beginning to crack. I asked if he would like
me to take over, and he said yes.

Driving that lumbering truck certainly woke me up,
especially the jolt of fear that came with each oncoming
car. Ma lay in a snoring, insensate heap on the seat beside me. After about twelve miles I noticed some sparks
down by my left foot where by day I had seen crudely
taped-together wires. I joggled his shoulder. His eyes
opened for a fraction of a second. "*Bu yao jin,*" he muttered: Don't worry! and a waving hand dismissed me. I
kept on driving.

Slowly, we ground up to a pass, went over the top,
then began to descend. Before long we were plung-

ing into a canyon and the truck was gathering speed. I stepped harder on the brake. At this moment, there was a blinding flash and the headlights went out.

I was now blind, and piloting a multi-ton cannonball down a perilous mountain road. I was not calm this time, but I steered straight, braked hard, and prayed in all of God's languages. Somehow I avoided hitting the rock wall or going over the edge.

Ma took it all, I thought, rather calmly. After the smoke had cleared from the cab, he got down and re-twisted the wires that had come apart. Then he took the wheel.

It was dawn when, at long last, we rolled into Lhasa. He dropped me off in front of the Potala Palace just as sunlight was gliding down its blazing white walls. Feeling like a footsore pilgrim who had trekked a thousand miles to the Holy City, tears of gladness came to my eyes as I walked the final blocks of my journey.

≈≈ ≈≈ ≈≈

Pamela Logan's writing has appeared in periodicals including The Los Angeles Times, The Christian Science Monitor, *and* Far Eastern Economic Review. *Her photography has been featured in* National Geographic, Newsweek, *and* The New York Times. *A fourth-degree black belt in Shotokan karate, Logan is the author of* Among Warriors: A Woman Martial Artist in Tibet, *a* New York Times *Notable Book of the Year in 1998. She is the founder and president of the Kham Aid Foundation, a nonprofit agency that supports monastery conservation work and other Kham-related projects, including assistance for Tibetan schools, environmental protection, and economic development.*

❧ ❧ ❧

Sex, God, and Rock 'n' Roll

An unlikely Catholic visits the temporal
headwaters of his religion.

THE FIRST TIME I WENT TO THE VATICAN, I DIDN'T
get in. I turned up just as they were closing. The
second time, a year later, I missed again, once more
cutting it too close. I have a chronic lateness problem.
But twenty years later, on a typically hot Roman day,
under an eye-wateringly blue sky, I arrived at the visitor
entrance at a quarter to nine in the morning, before it
opened, and finally made it inside.

I am a practicing Catholic, sometimes generously
mistaken for a devout one, and believe me it is a mistake.
Yes, I go to Mass regularly and know and respect the
covenants of the faith, but I break most of the command-

ments—and might break the rest if those sins weren't against my own moral code, which I have to admit is not telephone-book thick. I'm also that awkward kind of Catholic, like so many, many others, who over the years has come to separate the formalities and obligations of the Church from a belief in God.

But the Vatican is the epicenter, spiritually and physically, of Catholic orthodoxy—all the more so now, as Pope Benedict XVI, by all accounts an unbending theological conservative, has taken office. For a visitor like me, the question is how to square the grandiose certitude of the Vatican with my own more subtly shaded spiritual beliefs. I don't claim to have the answers, and here I was in a place that specializes in providing all of them.

The Vatican may be the world's greatest museum. In fact it's a museum of museums. I swear they have museums they've lost, as you or I might lose keys. When I was there, my guide, looking to take me to the Sistine Chapel by a shortcut, stumbled across a vast plain of a hall, part of which was closed to the public. On one side was a wide stairway leading down to a dimly lit space—a great room filled with Chinese and other antiquities, marble lions, statues, and tall-as-a-person vases, some millennia old. Many of these priceless works of art and invaluable markers of history had been given as gifts to various popes over the years—and sometimes not so willingly given.

Yet the Vatican seems curiously sterile, and lacking in human scale. In its museums and public spaces a ponderous silence carries fragments of visitors' conversations like dust on a beam of pallid sunlight. A lifeless, institutional reverence wafts through halls that now chronicle the history they once contained, halls wallpapered with art. Even the magnificent St. Peter's Basilica, breathtaking when first seen upon approach, overwhelming when entered, seems bereft of spirituality. Its awesome marble statues; serene, gold-laced caskets of popes and saints; and huge, brilliantly rich paintings of biblical scenes and figures are polished and illuminated to advantage. The giant cupola is so high above the ground that the sunlight is weak by the time it hits the floor, washing the Basilica in a sober, blue-gray light.

Mass takes place with all the passion of an art installation projection: I see it, it's engaging—it might even be riveting—but, improbably, I just don't *feel* it. I'd been warned that for a devout Catholic, entering St. Peter's can precipitate a profound religious experience, but for me the overall effect was of a giant arena with the seats removed. (All the missing pews are returned for Masses celebrated by the pope.) It's as if God, like Elvis, has left the building.

I was raised a Catholic, sort of, in the sense that my father, having given me his full name and ethnic heritage and, he presumed, everything else worthwhile, decided he might as well throw in his religion, which was then like an old sweater he didn't wear anymore. I don't mean this cynically; he personally had no use for religion but meant well: he knew it was a good influence, and England's Catholic schools in the 1960s provided a better education—and were far stricter—than other schools. Around the same time, my father started *Penthouse* and began building it into one of the world's largest privately held magazine empires. For thirty years he was a prime target of religious extremists (which only added to his allure and success) and an evergreen lightning rod for right-wing fund-raising.

At eleven I became an altar boy, by accident—I thought I was joining the church soccer team. An hour into the indoctrination I was still oblivious, and when the priest passed a saint's relic (a finger) to each one of us to kiss, I thought, *Boy, they must really take winning seriously.* But no soccer balls appeared and I was getting a little antsy, so I asked the priest when did we start practicing and where exactly was the field? He looked at me with a disgust that seemed to be evenly divided between my idiocy and his, in having accepted me.

Nonetheless I became a diligent, devoted, and even record-setting altar boy, serving so many Masses a week that I was eventually told I needn't come quite so often. I was virtually trolling the sacristy, looking for priests who might be about to say Mass. In my early teens I shook off Catholicism like rainwater, and thought no more about it until my late twenties, when one day in New York I walked into a church to pray privately, found there was a Mass going on, and stayed for it and reconnected. More important, I chose it—voluntarily—and realized that nothing I'd ever felt about religion or gotten from the church had ever left me. I picked up where I'd left off, like a great book put down, in this case fifteen years before. A couple of years later I went to confession—the most profound and humbling act a Catholic can perform: telling a complete stranger everything you've spent most of your energy lying to everyone else about. I started with the required admission, "Forgive me Father for I have sinned, it's been about seventeen years since—" but he stopped me, saying, "You don't have to tell me how long it's been; we haven't said that for thirteen years."

It was around that time I started *Spin*, the music magazine that, though not dedicated solely to hedonism, was open to the argument that it was not altogether a bad idea. When people found out I was an active churchgoer they were invariably shocked. Which, in the beginning, shocked me, until I realized that I wasn't fitting either stereotype—rock-and-roll editor or religious person. I was both. More accurately, I was striving to be either in any kind of meaningful way. One Sunday in the early eighties, I stopped by my father's house in Manhattan, and he asked me where I was coming from. I told him I had just been to Mass. "That's good," he said, "one of us has to go." He sounded not quite sad, but resigned, like a man suddenly remembering a land long ago left.

"Faith is not meant to replace reason, but is for those things which reason cannot explain," said St. Thomas Aquinas. Indeed, faith—that leap into the unknown and unknowable—is the price of admission for any religion. The embrace of mystery is both humbling and liberating, embodying as it does a recognition that there is more to life than the literal. But at the Vatican, the physical grandness of the Church can feel awfully literal, and indifferent to the ineffable value and emotional nourishment of my faith. Indeed, as I walked through the Vatican's spectacular halls and gardens, I didn't get as much a sense of the glory of God as the glorification of the planet's alpha church. I was glad to have seen the art and precious objects on the walls, in cabinets, and even on the ceilings, but all that beauty did not, in my mind, honor the humble Christ so much as flatter the vanity of the institution.

I did have a profound spiritual experience, but it came three weeks after my visit to the Vatican and hundreds of miles to the south, in Sicily. There, on a backstreet in Palermo, on a pole and behind glass, lit by three electric candles, I saw an icon of the face of Christ in his agony. The street was dark, soundless, still, and Christ was frozen in eternal suffering and mystery, and I realized it is the preservation of mystery, not answers, and humility, not exaltation, that allow us to live with our imperfection and fears.

≈≈ ≈≈ ≈≈

"Most Catholics have tried to reconcile the perfect order of the Church with the imperfect world in which we live," says New York-based magazine entrepreneur and practicing Catholic Bob Guccione Jr. "There's no virtue in befriending only priests—Christ hung out with tax collectors and prostitutes. Not to be too flippant, but Christ was the original rock star." Founder of Spin *in 1985 and publisher of the now-defunct* Gear, *Guccione also writes for the* U.K. Independent.

❧ ❧ ❧

Japanese Tattoo

The author learns the history of an art form
straight from the master.

"*AKEBONO DESU NE,*" I SAID, POINTING WITH A FORE-finger at a patch of gray: *dawn.* A grunt and a curt nod of affirmation. It was a conversation we had had before. His English was limited to a few words—*herro, bye-bye, gullfriend-o*—and my Japanese was little better. Still, I wanted to talk about it. Dawn.

"*Beta,*" he pronounced, indicating a patch of black, oily beneath a slick of capillary blood. Literally the word meant *all over* but, in this context, *without gradation* or, more precisely, an area densely charged with thick *sumi* ink. *Akebono:* dawn. *Beta:* darkness.

"*Sakura desu,*" he continued, playing the naming game appreciated alike by small children and adults with limited vocabulary. He pointed at a cuneiform

motif in brilliant vermilion with a saffron center and
foils of beetle green. Cherry blossom: fragile, evanescent.
"Sakura, sakura, sakura," he repeated, pointing at a succession of blossoms, some partially obscured by clouds of
gray and black.

"Sakura wa kirei desu ne," I ventured, and the tattoo
master laughed. It was a good-natured laugh. He understood the difficulties of language, and he understood
that I wanted to talk about it. It was my skin, after all.
It was my life: interludes of color between the darkness
and the dawn.

Years before, I had become entranced with *irezumi*,
more elegantly known as *hori-mono*, the Japanese tattoo.
Yet I had known, from its first vague awakening, that
my interest somehow lay deeper than my skin. Then, as
now, the result was of little consequence to me. Rather, I
sensed that in essence a Japanese tattoo was more than a
picture. It was a decision, an act of existential willfulness,
not only unnecessary, but ill-advised, an act the effects of
which were irreversible, and that to pursue such an action,
fully cognizant that pain would be involved, as well as
some degree of risk, was nothing short of sublime—a feat
of grace. I resolved, one day, to do it. But my resolution
entailed certain stipulations: it must be done in the traditional way, and it must be done at the hands of a master of
the art. A dozen years passed, during which I experienced
no inclination to have myself otherwise tattooed. And
then, during an eight-month sojourn in Japan, with some
difficulty—for in Japan tattoo is, as it has always been, a
mysterious and clandestine art—I contacted an *irezumi*
master.

Our first meeting was a preliminary that precedes
every compact between a master and his client. The

master evaluates the client's sincerity and character in much the same way that the client evaluates the master's style and virtuosity, for the master believes that once he has put needle to flesh, not only does the client become the bearer of his design, but of his honor, as well, and an earnest master will not commit either his skill or his reputation to one he deems unworthy of its custody.

Tea was brought. *Meishi* (the ubiquitous business cards) were exchanged. Polite questions were asked regarding family, credentials, and status. Akasaka, whose working name signifies an ascending path, exhibiting mild amusement at the notion that a *gaijin* should want traditional tattoo, made jokes at my expense that, innocuous though they were, nevertheless caused faint blushes among the several apprentices who had gathered around. I presumed I was only being tested—which, perhaps, was itself the objective of the test—and therefore remained composed.

All the while Akasaka worked *kiku*, chrysanthemum flowers, upon the shoulder of a young man who ground his teeth and clenched his fists against the mat on which he lay. Our eyes did not meet, except as they were locked upon this common object of our attention, the tattoo revealing itself in a blossom of blood from beneath the skin of that young man. Then, suddenly, Akasaka looked up and spoke to me directly. An apprentice translated for my benefit: "Teacher Akasaka say he think he can make tattoo that will be please to you."

I had settled into a tidy four-and-a-half tatami room in Minato-ku, a few blocks from Tamachi Station. The elevated Shuto Expressway ran past the front of my grimy apartment bloc and, in the rear, a saltwater canal flowed by beneath my window, home to egrets, cor-

morants, crabs, and square-shouldered, bobtailed alley
cats. An arching bridge spanned the canal to the north,
across which working men marched toward the docks
each morning in a silver light, reminding me fancifully,
if unoriginally, of Hiroshige. Noodle sucking Japanese
inhaled their breakfasts in noodle stands along this path,
and gangs of workmen, uniformly dressed in khaki,
with white plastic helmets and close fitting *jika-tabi*,
split-toed canvas work boots, performed calisthenics to
amplified plink-plonk Romper Room ditties. Grave,
gray-clad schoolgirls made their way toward a nearby
private high school and blue-suited salarymen and prim
office women strode to their office buildings. Ambling
in the direction of the train station, an outlandish round-
eyed head bobbing like a beach ball upon a sea of raven-
haired congruity, I daily breasted this purposeful crowd
and left it astonished in my wake.

One day, wandering among houses with arching tiled
roofs and gardens of bonsai delicacy, a striding, smoke-
breathing monster confronted me. Not Godzilla, but a
fifty-foot billboard of the Marlboro man. In the summer
of 1995 *Waterworld*, the time that land forgot, was big
in Tokyo. Kevin Costner, exuding fair-haired American
charm, appeared on talk shows ad nauseam. But, by far
the most insistent, the most gleaming, the most awesome
star writ large by Japanese television in the summer of
'95, the fiftieth anniversary of the leveling of Nagasaki
and Hiroshima with atomic bombs, was *Enola Gay*, the
B-29 that delivered them, demonstrating once and for
all that, in Japan, America was larger than life—that,
in Japan, America somehow loomed larger than death
itself. Was it love, or was it mere fixation, the unwitting
daydream of a Freudian aspiration?

At first I found it hard to reconcile this improbable crush. At that time I considered the America I lived in to be cynical, self-indulgent, and derivative. Yet, as I grew to know Japan (however imperfectly), I realized that what Japan found irresistible about America was not different in principle from that which my own naïve blue eye, in its unblinking optimism, had found irresistible about Japan. Thus, even as Japan, like a smitten teenager, pursues the buxom fantasy of its American sweetheart, a romance of furtive gropes and fumbling, so its sophomoric advances are awkwardly returned, as when an American friend, enamored of the Land of the Rising Sun, had a pair of *geta*, wooden platform sandals, custom made for his size thirteen feet, in which he looked like nothing so much as a man standing on a matched set of small coffee tables.

The evening of my first appointment with Akasaka, I took the Keihin-Tohoku rail line to the outlying suburb where he kept his studio. Arriving early in order not to be late, I sat outside on the street corner to await the precise moment for a timely appearance since, in Japan, timeliness is important, and premature arrival is as indefensible as tardiness. The neon lights of love hotels winked and hummed beneath a harvest moon, and black bicycles rattled by, uniformed high school girls standing erect in slouching knee socks and loafers upon the rear hubs, hair and skirts flying. Their small, white hands lay like smudges of powder beside the high tunic collars of their lean, furiously pedaling boyfriends.

At exactly seven o'clock I entered the small studio through a discreet door. Several apprentices and their clients acknowledged my sudden appearance with alarmed expressions, a common greeting for foreigners who materialize in places where foreigners are never seen. One wonders if one has inadvertently trespassed, a thought shared by both parties. The senior apprentice, a man tattooed from his neck to the koi that swam upon the tops of his feet, rose hastily and disappeared up a narrow flight of stairs. I waited until he reappeared, beckoning me with a fluttering of the fingers that in the West means *shoo*.

Akasaka was seated on the floor soldering together bundles of needles. As it happened, Akasaka-*sensei* was one of the most venerated tattoo masters in Japan, a two-time world champion. I did not know this when I had first sought him out. I had merely seen a picture of him and had been impressed by his sober demeanor. Being forty-four, I would have guessed his age to be fifty-four. He was unbendingly dedicated to his art. He was a hopeless English student. There was no vestige of piety about him, a man of the world who loved *enka*, the proletarian soul music of Japan, luxury automobiles, girls, all the simple pleasures of the flesh. He ate *o-bento* from the convenience market, smoked, and drank. Yet when once I asked him about a photograph in his studio of a man silhouetted against the backdrop of the Taj Mahal, he pointed at his own nose and told me about having visited. Finding the paving stones strewn with leaves and dust, he had asked for a broom and had swept them himself in the fast belief that a monument of such age and distinction should be tidy.

I bowed.

He dipped his head and shoulders, returning to his work while I removed my shoes and coat and sat down on the *zabuton* that the apprentice had positioned, just so.

O-cha, green tea, was served. I waited.

The apprentice kneeled beside the master.

We waited.

At length, Akasaka made a noise in his throat, a sort of *uhn* that means...I do not know what it means, but in Japan it is ubiquitous and addictive and I, myself, still fall into the habit of it from time to time. He looked up and a smile divided his face. He nodded and gestured toward the mat laid out on the floor before him. I removed my shirt and positioned myself in front of him so that my knees touched his knees. He drew deeply on a cigarette (Hope brand, from a packet placed and perpetually replaced within reach by his attendant), tilted his head, and squinted through the smoke at my chest and shoulders. Then, with the tip of a *sumi* brush, he drew the first strokes of his design upon my skin. And I realized that thereafter nothing in my life would be quite the same.

It is usual for the *irezumi* master and his client to negotiate the iconography of the tattoo. This is in part a matter of aesthetics, design, and in part a question of signification, for the tattoo must mean something, must say something profound about the person upon whose skin it is inscribed. Japanese tattoo is an unforgiving medium that does not make allowances for duplicity or self-deception. The tattoo is, after all, not an investiture that can be sloughed off like a business suit, a uniform, some hip ensemble. It is as real as flesh. It is the very skin of truth. I had selected a classical motif called *sakura-fubuki*, literally "cherry blossom storm." At Akasaka's behest we added *ryu*, the Japanese dragon, accompanied, as always, by *taifu*, typhoon, the divine wind. In the Japanese arts, cherry blossoms, which survive in splendor for a day or two only before being blown to the ground, symbolize the transitory nature of life. *Ryu*, a water motif related to the naga of Southeast Asia and invested in the ancient cosmologies of Hinduism and Buddhism alike, symbolizes the force that compels being and nothingness to issue one from the other. To my mind, the dragon is neither good nor evil, neither dark nor light, but is responsible for the *tendency* of all things simply to be or not be. Dragon and typhoon, cherry blossom and storm. Being and nothingness, and that which arouses them to issue one from the other. It was an elementary dichotomy, yet for me a symmetrical one that fit with equal aplomb the analogous nature of my mind and the reflective congruity of my body, the right side and the left side which, meeting, comprised the center.

Traditional Japanese tattoo is executed following a two-fold process. The outline is inked in first. It may be drawn using an electric needle (the single, electrically-driven needle is utilized only as a time- and cost-saving device, and while it is not scorned by the master, apprentices—in the way of students—will occasionally speak of one-point, or American style, tattoo with thinly masked derision), but if it is incised in the traditional way, it is done with no more than two or three *hari*, needles, bound together and mounted in a wooden grip. The coloring of the design comes later, one hue at a time—more or less, as the tattoo master usually works areas of the design defined by the contingencies of time: the length of the appointment, the depths of the client's pocketbook, the limits of the client's capacity for pain. Coloring is considered to be the most important part of the work, and is strictly the domain of the master. Indeed, if any part of the tattoo is colored by anyone other than him, the master will disavow it.

Broad areas of color are charged with as many as ten needles mounted together in a wooden handle. The master spreads the skin of the area to be colored between his thumb and forefinger. The wooden handle rests across the thumb and is worked by the other hand in prodding strokes. Each stroke pushes the inked tips of the needles into the lower epidermis rapidly and accurately. Lighter tones are effected with a shallow infusion and a sparse pattern, while intense color is injected deeply, in a dense pattern. One learns to associate luxuriance with the sharply rising curve of pain, and with the alarming rhythmic sound, not unlike velcro being pulled apart, of ripping flesh.

Pain is the cornerstone, the mystical heart, of traditional Japanese tattoo. Another name by which tattoo is colloquially known in Japan is *gaman*, meaning patience, and a word one often hears softly spoken in the course of tattoo work is *ganbaru*: bear it. An American scholar of Japanese culture, who had written a book about *irezumi*, once asked me to describe the pain involved in Japanese tattoo for, in spite of his close affiliation, none of his Japanese correspondents had been willing to talk about it. Form, a sort of unspoken code of honor, prohibits those initiated into the mysteries of Japanese tattoo from admitting to the pain involved. The client who never flinches, who never grimaces or grits his teeth, will win the master's heartfelt respect. Of course, such forbearance is sometimes nothing more than macho posturing but, given the depth of the pain, one can only sustain one's disingenuousness for a relatively short period of time. The person who genuinely seeks to take possession of his pain steps forth boldly to meet it and, having done so, discovers that it is less frightening than he had expected. It is a relative condition, not unlike pleasure, though at the opposite end of the scale that can be experienced with or without tolerance lightly or profoundly, hedonistically or profitably, depending upon the focus of one's attention. The experience of pain, just one of the body's many ecstasies, is ironically the truly enduring mark of traditional Japanese tattoo, for it becomes engraved upon the soul, just as pictures are engraved upon the flesh, and the deeper memory of it relentlessly wakes the bearer from his unrepentant slumbers, reminding him, and often him alone, to know *all* the moments of his brief existence.

Japanese tattoo was conceived in shadow, and it abides in shadow today. Yet, in the course of its long and obscure history, it flourished. It is one of Japan's high arts and is widely recognized by the rest of the world as the pinnacle of the craft, though it has been disowned in its native land. Its vague early history consisted in a nebulous medley of poignant marks that little resembled the complex, decorative designs of the art in its maturity. There were tattoos that identified criminals. There were tattoos assumed as indelible pledges of love, the beloved's name inscribed upon the flesh of the lover with the ideograph for *inochi*, life. There were tattoos that inveighed religious piety. There were tattoos that rendered marginalism precise.

The decorative pictorial tattoo evolved gradually during the Edo period, hand in hand with *ukiyo-e*, the popular woodblock print. Some of the great masters of *ukiyo-e* were also tattoo designers, and their iconographies and sense of style survive to this day in the designs of Japan's traditional tattoo artisans. Even the gestures inherent in the creation of traditional tattoo are remarkably similar to those of the woodblock designer and carver, and the word *hori*, itself, from which the name *hori-mono* is derived, articulates the motion of digging or gouging or carving.

The most assertive single influence upon the development of the decorative tattoo in Japan was the eighteenth century translation and publication of the classic Chinese novel, *Shui-hu Chuan* (in Japanese, *Suikoden*), variously rendered into English as *The Water Margin* and *All Men Are Brothers*. This hugely popular work recounted the exploits of Sung Chiang and his rebel companions during the years 1117 to 1121. Outlaws and brigands, they nevertheless were men of honor, and each section of the book tells of one man's exploits in revolt against a corrupt government. Significantly, a number of these champions were tattooed, and were so depicted in accompanying illustrations by Hokusai, and later by Kuniyoshi, in the Japanese editions. What is historically incongruous, yet noteworthy, about this novel was its overwhelming popularity during the reign of the Tokugawa, a regime whose indelible totalitarian mark upon the Japanese people is undeniable to this day. It is an epic rife with personality and rebellion, and its favor bears witness to the alter ego, albeit reserved, of a people whose extraordinary passion would, and will, not be snuffed by the blank hand of bureaucracy, even when that hand is its own.

The proletarian classes of Edo embraced the virtues of Sung Chiang: virility, honor, and self-determination. The full body tattoo provided this circle of working men, in ostentatious imitation of their heroes, with a means of subsuming values they admired while, at the same time, and in an explicitly Japanese way, pledg-

ing their *nakama*, their insiders' clique, all members of
which would bear similar tattoos. Predictably, it was
not only honest working men who found the qualities
attributed to Sung Chiang and his band of outlaws ap-
pealing.

In Akasaka's studio I often encountered formal
Japanese wearing—or at those moments not-wearing—
clothing of questionable taste, with full body tattoos in
various stages of completion, who revealed not (except
in their too perfect concealment of it) the slightest surprise at the appearance of a tattooed foreigner among
them, maintaining a prim indifference and never speaking to me directly, yet with respect to whom Akasaka
would archly say, gangsta', cocked forefinger pointing
at my chest like the barrel of a gun, upon their departure. Akasaka's connection with *yakusa*, the Japanese
underworld, was a given, though unspecified. In Japan,
the traditional tattoo is the mark of a gangster, and
Akasaka's position in the guild made an alliance inevitable. That he was, himself, a *gangsta'* seemed entirely
unlikely. Nevertheless, he commanded perfect obedi-
ence and loyalty of his students, a pervasive, if archaic,
Japanese ethic that is ardently revered but is nevertheless
comparatively ephemeral in modern Japan outside the
strictures of such conservative *nakama* as the *yakusa*. One
of Akasaka's apprentices, a young man from Kobe, even
wore the tattooed *kanji* characters for *Akasaka family
member* in a prominent line down his belly.

Centuries ago, criminals were tattooed beneath the
arm, and the decorative tattoo, according to legend
(although not necessarily in accordance with historical fact), evolved as a means of concealing such marks
within the depths of its fantastic iconography, the deco-

ration absorbing the aberration as the criminal vainly
hoped he would himself be reabsorbed into the dense
enigma of his culture. It is supposed that the convention of leaving the underarm unmarked proves that the
bearer of traditional tattoo is not a criminal. In modern
Japan, however, the traditional tattoo no longer conceals,
but is itself concealed, and it is virtually impossible for
the post-War generation to dismiss the stigma of tattoo from its consciousness. Even I, a *henna-gaijin* (crazy
foreigner), of whom virtually all transgressions were
forgiven—and in Japan the number of possible transgressions that one may wittingly or unwittingly commit
are uncountable—with great sadness lost several friends
to their prejudice.

The fear and loathing that most Japanese adults feel
toward *irezumi* is more than simple prudery. Traditional
tattoo provokes a resonant abhorrence (and concomitant
titillation—historical books on *irezumi*, for example, are
consigned to the back rooms of Japanese porno empo-
ria) in Japan. It is like the mark of Cain, only relatively
more serious. The *yakusa* correlation was cited by every
Japanese person I asked as the reason they believed tattoo was morally wrong. I accepted this, though it was, I
felt, at once the root and far from the root of the issue.
The root itself, in the nature of roots, diverges intermi-
nably. One must ask why and why and why again. Why
does the association of tattoo with the underworld make
tattoo bad? Because the underworld is frightening. It is
unpredictable. But most people who have borne traditional tattoo throughout its long history have not been
affiliated with the criminal element. Even today tattooed
people are not necessarily lawbreakers. Why are *these*
tattooed people bad? Because they are different. They

have set themselves apart. Is this wrong? Is it not their
choice to do with their body what they will? No, it is not
their choice, because their body does not belong to them.
A person's flesh is indistinguishable from the flesh of his
parents, or of his parents' parents. By indelibly tattooing
the flesh of one's body, one sets apart, and thus dishon-
ors, the flesh of one's ancestors.

In 1996 I returned to Tokyo to do some work for a
major museum, work that occupied my days with the
same frantic (but nevertheless regulated) precariousness
that propels Japanese people headlong down the corridors of their lives. I filled the nights with appointments
at Akasaka's small studio. After two weeks, on the evening before my departure, I arrived at the studio for a
final visit. Akasaka's apprentices were seated downstairs,
and we exchanged greetings. I sat down in my coat and
looked meaningfully in the direction of the senior apprentice. The formalities had been dealt with and I was
ready, if not a bit impatient. But he avoided my glance
and uncomfortably lit another cigarette. What's all this,
then? I thought to myself.

Eventually he rose from his seat and ascended the
stairs, soon to return. Teacher Akasaka had confirmed
that there would be no appointment that evening.
Betraying no emotion, I replied, *"Ah, so desu-ka."* Not
an insistent *why*, the plaintive demand of a Westerner,
but more politely: *oh, is that so.* The other apprentices
had fallen silent. Nervously, the senior apprentice
explained to me that Akasaka-sensei had decided he
would like me to accompany him, as his guest, to an
onsen, a natural hot spring, at a resort in the mountains
north of Tokyo.

Fully aware that tattooed men were banned from public baths in Japan (the international pictograph for "no tattoos allowed," decorated limbs with a canceling diagonal slash, is prominently displayed), I realized that this would be a special *onsen* and that its patrons would therefore, on this occasion, undoubtedly all be tattooed. I was stunned. I was, after all, *gaijin*, a foreigner, an outsider, and the *nakama* of men bearing traditional tattoo was so private, for obvious reasons, as to be virtually invisible. Surely Akasaka was joking?

No, we would leave in half an hour.

We took one of Akasaka's plush vans, detouring to pick up my belongings, as we would spend the night at the resort, from which I would be driven the four and a half hours back to Narita Airport in the morning. The young apprentice from Kobe was my chauffeur. He demonstrated for me the van's satellite navigation system, and then we talked until conversation had exhausted itself (and me). Eternally solicitous of my needs, real or imagined, he then switched on the miniature television set mounted to a swiveling bracket beside the steering wheel and commenced a running commentary of the game show to which it was tuned while I quietly dozed off.

Having stopped only for a quick meal at a roadside *tonkatsu-ya*, we arrived at the *onsen* at about eleven o'clock. Akasaka and several of his younger apprentices including, unusually, a young woman who was presumably also his mistress—a different one from the girl I had met the year before—were just arriving. To my great happiness, Akasaka had brought his kit with him and proposed that we accomplish some tattoo work before partaking of the hot springs. We arranged ourselves on the tatami mats in my room, switched on the *televee*, unpacked the beer, and were soon riding high upon waves of cross-cultural hilarity. Outside the somber confines of the studio, it was the young peoples' opportunity to let their hair down a little, and they asked frank questions about my person and my profession. My judicious answers only provoked further and more candid lines of inquiry, and soon they were scrutinizing the snapshots of girlfriends in my notebook and pressing me for details concerning my love life. Akasaka worked industriously on my tattoo. He had asked me what part I would like him to finish that night, and when I had chosen the dragon, he had nodded his approval.

Eventually, cued by a glance from his teacher that did not escape my notice, one of the apprentices asked, "How long can you stay?" Momentarily confused by his ambiguous English, I hesitated, and as I did so I saw the young man's brow furrow and his eyes flicker in the direction of his master's face. In that instant the subtext of his question became clear to me: Akasaka was fatigued, but good manners forbade him from saying so. "I'm tired," I said, "can we stop now?" An audible sigh made a circuit of the room, and we all smiled.

A tattoo appointment is always properly followed by a hot bath, the pangs of which are exquisite. In addition, the steaming bath is the best venue for seeing tattoo, as well as for being seen, since the skin's surface dryness is quenched and the heat produces a flush that intensifies the colors and, as the blood rises, transfuses and enlivens them. Gathering in the large tub, we examined each other without pretense, appraisingly. I was surprised to discover that Akasaka, himself, was only sparsely tattooed, and that his calves, like those of his apprentices, were a cacophony of random marks, mere scribble boards for testing colors and experimental configurations. The only woman among us, Akasaka's student mistress, also tattooed (but whose tattoos we would have to scrutinize in imagination only), called to us over the wall that divided the men's bath from the women's side, making the boys laugh and fidget with unrequited emotion.

Then, because it was seemly and decorous, and also because it simply pleased him to amuse himself in this way, Akasaka instructed his youngest disciple to wash me. As we stepped from the bath and I seated myself on a low plastic stool beside the faucets, the poor boy's discomfiture provoked roars of laughter from the others who, undoubtedly, had themselves been subjected to similar mortifications. All I could do to save him was to maintain a straight face and allow him to proceed. With a pleading look in his eyes, he pointed questioningly in turn to my arm, my leg, my back, chest, stomach, and from his perch on the edge of the great, steaming tub, his master invariably acknowledged his inquiries with single firm nods. I have, I must admit, never been so intimately soaped up and scrubbed down by a young Japanese boy.

I had been honored, but was still, as I had been from the beginning and would ever be, the object of Akasaka's harmless little jokes. Yet, some nights before, as I had lain on the familiar mat in his studio, I had allowed my eyes to examine, object by object, the trappings of the room. All the larger accouterments, the samurai armor, the swords, the Buddhist saints and deities, all the knickknacks, the equipment, the small toys, were in their places. The nattily framed photographs on the wall all were familiar from the previous year, but one.

During a break I walked over to examine it more closely. In it Akasaka bent over a recumbent form, working assiduously. The outline of the client was both familiar and unfamiliar to me, but I recognized the tattoo's motif. *Sakura-fubuki*. Cherry blossoms, some obscured by clouds of gray and black.

≈ ≈ ≈

Dustin W. Leavitt contributes articles and essays on subjects including travel, social commentary, and art criticism to books and periodicals. Much of his travel writing visits Asia and the Pacific, where he has lived, worked, and wandered at various times in his life. He teaches at the University of Redlands, near Los Angeles. "Japanese Tattoo" first appeared in print in Kyoto Journal.

❧ ❧ ❧

Sahara Unveiled

The world's biggest mystery lies in the human heart.

WE'D BEEN DRIVING FOR DAYS — TEASING OURSELVES along the border of Algeria—the desert tantalizing and beckoning. Trans Sahara, trans Sahara—the words resounded in my head like a familiar mantra. Although conjuring up all my tightly held romantic desert fantasies, the voice of reality spoke of something far different—and undeniably dangerous. The borders were closed. The Tuareg, the beautiful and bold blue men of the desert, were killing people—rampantly, or so we were told. All the southern borders had been shut down—Morroco, Mali, Mauritania, Algeria.

I had just begun my year-long solo backpacking and camping sojourn across the great continent of Africa, and as my fifth week unfolded before me, I felt the itch to strike out to a place where there would be no tracks but my own. The Sahara seemed the perfect, pristine canvas. Days earlier, while dining in a quaint café in Casablanca with a strikingly handsome German overland driver, I revealed to him my plan of crossing alone, of my intention to disguise myself as a boy. He listened without emotion as I laid my scheme before him, my bravado belying the apprehension that had taken up permanent residence in my heart. With the disquieting demeanor of a predator he leaned forward, taking my arm in a painful grip to quiet me, and began to speak in a low and hushed tone. His description was vivid and graphic—the surprise attack just north of Tammarraset, the furtive convoy of camels and men. Using the cover of night they killed passengers, tortured the driver, and spirited the vehicle away, leaving the remaining party to fend for themselves in the wilds of the biggest desert on earth. Some of them died. Most lived, the visible scars worn as badges of courage while the unseen burrowed deep into the soul and remained unspoken.

The blond handsome man told me not to go, not to attempt it, I would surely die. Five days later, I found myself driving day after day along the western fringe of the Sahara—the desert taunting me like a beautiful dancer shrouded and mysterious in her layers of veils. I was in the company of a rag-tag group of adventurers I had come upon in the marketplace of Marrakech. I discovered they had a vehicle converted for desert travel—they liked the danger and intrigue of my plan for an illegal crossing. Over sweet mint tea in the medina we struck an agreement—we would join forces. I was the only woman among them. And now we had arrived. Careening along the deeply rutted dirt roads of Morocco under a cloudless, unforgiving sky, it was decision time. Did we dare to cross the border on our fat tires and brave hearts—could we do what we had come for but was so forbidden?

Using no roads, leaving no tracks, waiting for dark, like thieves we crossed—and found ourselves alone, in the desert. I will never forget that first night. The flat, hard packed, ancient sand—holding untold secrets—the playful gypsy moon that accompanied me as I left camp and the warming fire in search of the best vantage point for the sunrise. Bedded down on the desert floor, looking up at the impossibly starry sky, I smiled to myself . . . I was here . . . I was not afraid . . . I was ready for the next challenge.

It came in the form of a snake just before dawn. I was vaguely aware of various creatures crossing over my body in the night on their determined march across the cool sands—a beetle, a lizard, it mattered not—I was deep in my dreams of the desert and nothing could disturb me. But the snake had a message to deliver and when I sensed its lithe body sliding by far too close for comfort, I bolted upright, the false sense of security that had lulled me to sleep only hours before shattered. I arose, pulled on my clothing—strangely cold—and found myself walking toward the biggest dune that lay before me. The dark sky seemed cavernous and endless above me, holding no decipherable hint as yet of the imminent dawn. I whispered past the sprawled, sleeping forms of my traveling companions and began the long and arduous climb. The Saharan sands licked at my ankles, my feet sinking into the comforting warmth that had survived the chill of the night. Clawing my way to the very top, I arrived moments before the sun showed its cunning self—rising big and hot and bold before me. As the first rays of light lit my face, I closed my eyes and paid silent homage to the desert—to all that lived upon and within her and to the gift of life she gave. I celebrated my aloneness, my unwavering sense of self—the hint of danger that always seemed to surround me and enhance these moments of my life.

As if on cue, I became aware of an eerie uneasiness settling over me. It hung in the air, waiting to be acknowledged. I turned to look behind me and noticed a pink, angry cloud on the horizon. Not above me, but before me, it rolled with raucous abandon across the landscape. A thunderstorm? Not so easy, this was a sandstorm . . . the realization hit with sickening reality. My mind raced, trying valiantly to remember everything I had ever heard about this phenomenon—people die, people get lost and never found. Do I stay still and wait for it to pass? Or do I defy it and run headlong down the dune to the safety of camp and my companions who surely must wonder what has happened to me by now....

It arrived so fast; I had no time for action. I simply sat and waited for it to hit. As the sand began to whirl around me, I noticed a vague outline of something approaching me—something big. I could not conceive of what this might be—in the Sahara, on top of a dune, in the middle of a sandstorm. The outline slowly became clearer; the shapes defined . . . camels, and men . . . like a dream they materialized before me. There were four of them, Tuareg clearly—the famous indigo turbans wrapped tightly around their heads, obscuring all but their dark and penetrating eyes. It seemed as though they were not surprised to find me here—an American woman, alone, in the desert.

They bid the camels to lie down and silently they did—as though they too knew this was not the time to complain or argue. One of the men approached me with a swath of cloth and began to wrap it around my head and face. He was so gentle, careful to cover my mouth, my nose, my eyes, my ears; leaving a small breathing hole to insure I would have air and live. Time was short; unburdening the camels, the Tuareg made a circle around us with the saddles and supplies—all without a word exchanged. It was a well-orchestrated and rehearsed routine, they moved swiftly and confidently—instincts guiding every move, knowing what must be done. A small bowl of water was placed before me; two of the Tuareg arranged my body on my side, arms crossed over my face. A blanket was expertly wedged around my prone form—just as the sandstorm hit full force.

I clamped my eyes shut and steeled myself for the ordeal to come. The sand quickly became like tiny shards of glass, penetrating the protective cloth and invading my eyes, my nose, my mouth. It was impossible to breathe. I curled my body tighter and tighter—taking shallow, gasping, desperate breaths. The winds howled without abate and it felt as though nothing could stop the fury of the gods in the desert that day.

Hours, minutes, days, I had no comprehension of the time that passed. My senses had all shut down and there was nothing but the vastness of that moment. At times I was acutely conscious of where I was and what was happening, at other times, I found myself lapsing into strange and surreal hallucinations—thinking this is what it must feel like to go mad. Then, as suddenly as it began, it ended. All was silent and still, yet I could not bring myself to emerge—I remained tightly curled in my desert womb, waiting for the relentless wind to continue its assault.

A gentle hand on my shoulder brought me back to life. I slowly pulled myself upright from beneath the weight of the sand that had entombed me. My new-found friends seemed incredibly untouched by the furious storm—I was battered and wounded and weak. They laughed at me; my bowl of water was full of wet sand and untouched. A goatskin bag passed from hand to hand—I drank gratefully. One of the men approached me, wet the end of his turban with the precious water, and began to wash the sand from my cheeks. Stunned by the care and comfort these men were giving a complete stranger, I looked at him in wonder; he looked steadily back at me as though he knew my thoughts.

The men pointed down the dune to my camp—I could see the truck in the distance, small black dots that must be my companions. I wondered what they were thinking—if they were looking for me—or packing up to leave me behind. My Tuareg friends rousted the complaining camels and burdened them once more with the goods they were carrying to market. We began the descent to camp, my unsteady legs giving way in the deep new sand. The sun was low on the horizon and I found myself momentarily disoriented and confused until I realized I was seeing the sunset. I had been on the dune for an entire day.

We emerged into camp through the curtain of sand that still hung heavily in the air—my startled companions staring as though we were a desert mirage—seeing, yet not believing. Recovering quickly, they offered tea and bread while throwing out countless questions—verbal spears that pierced my fragile countenance. The Tuareg hunched down around the fire, loudly slurping the sweet, thick, liquid.... I had nothing to say. I was still in the sandstorm dream, with my tribal men and their camels—I was not yet ready to return.

The Tuareg stayed. They would not leave. My companions were feeling the need to move on, yet the four tribesmen remained by my side and would not depart. Night descended, the sky vast and clear, stars seeming inches above my head. I reached out again and again expecting to touch them, so real and deep and dark was this night.

We sat by the fire while I told the story of the storm, the unexpected arrival of the camel caravan, the gentle respect I was shown by these strange, silent men. More tea, more bread—all the while the Tuareg sat quietly watching me. I was not intimidated by their intense observations of me, the mystery of their eyes and mystique of their nomadic existence was powerful and intoxicating. I found my mind returning again and again to those hours on the dune. The moon was fully up now and I was spent and weary. I rose and gathered my things, taking a precious bowl of water with me for my nightly cleansing ritual. As I began to escape into the flat, quiet night, I heard footsteps, turned, and there were the Tuareg, padding softly behind me. I waved them back to camp but they would not go—I could hear my traveling companions laughing by the fire, yet no one came to rescue me—they were clearly my men and I must deal with them on my own terms. I desperately needed to relieve myself—I made motions of disrobing, washing—they clearly understood, yet they made no move to allow me privacy. Finally I shrugged, turned back into the desert and walked resolutely into the dark. Away from the light of camp, I stopped. The Tuareg surrounded me, waiting to see what I would do next. I began to dig a hole with my heel, there was nothing left to do but simply continue. No coyness now, my body called.

As I began to loosen my trousers, the tribesman I took to be the youngest gently touched the top of my head to get my attention. I looked up to see him raise his flowing robe in one fluid movement—it floated off his strong body like a soft white cloud—the other three catching the sides of the garment and smoothly bringing it down over my head. Each corner was then drawn out by one of the tribesmen, to make a tent of sorts—my own private desert boudoir. Amazed by their ingenuity, I disrobed with total abandon and began to cleanse my body of the sand that had invaded every fold and crevasse. The water ran in rivulets down my back, making me shiver with the contrast of its coolness against the heat of my skin. I was thankful for this simple pleasure, thankful for the gift of water in this harsh and dry land. I quickly relieved myself, redressed, and as I rose, the robe was casually tossed off and back onto the young tribesman. We walked solemnly back to camp, the four of them in a protective circular formation around me.

They slept next to me that night. I, in the center, tucked into my sleeping bag, the new moon beaming down upon me; they, sprawled on their blankets—one to the north, one to the south, one west, and one east. I pretended to sleep, but lay awake for hours, just listening to them breathe—enraptured by their presence and the gentle force of their guardianship.

They left me the next morning, my Tuareg warriors. Each one approached individually, looked me in the eye, and with a nod of respect turned and disappeared into the desert landscape. Such dignity. The last man, my young warrior of the night before, stepped up before me, his eyes locked onto mine. Slowly and deliberately he unwound his indigo blue turban and gently wrapped it around my head. I could smell his sweat—it was clean and sweet—it was of the desert. He touched his heart and offered his hand palm up, I returned the gesture and gently pressed my own palm to his. With the grace of one who has known many partings, he turned and walked away without looking back—his camel in tow and my heart in his hand.

❧ ❧ ❧

Dar Robertson continues her forays into wild places, with an undying passion for the deserts of the world. Working when she must, pursuing her love of wildlife when she can, and traveling in between—she divides her time between planning and executing major international events (the work part) and her affiliation with the only privately licensed meerkat sanctuary in North America (the love part) located in the high desert of California.

❧ ❧ ❧

Blinded by Science

The universe called, and she came.

ABOUT AN HOUR OUT ON THE LONGTAIL BOAT TO Phranang, I feel a sudden, stabbing reminder of those six cups of tea. They'd gone down in a teahouse in the seaside town of Krabi, while I was chatted up by a Thai love prince who had emerged in the center of my karmic field. With a ritual softness he'd poured cup after cup of jasmine-scented potion, while from his lips tumbled pearls he'd gleaned of my language: You, me, go. I wanted to respond in kind—what more needed to be said?—but I was quiet. He was a man, and I was in recovery from just such an affliction. Even my shrink had advised a moratorium on all things male. My lovely contraband watched me for signs of melting, his eyes watering with such a tragic thirst that despite my resolve, I suffered chest pains when I heard the boatman's call. I departed forever from the idea of him, the bursting forth of its many possibilities. How easily one can forget—wavering between intention and impulse—to attend to one's physiological details.

The boat is slim, its end curlicued like the proboscis of an exotic insect. There are about twenty of us in various stages of heat-induced delirium, traveling on Thailand's Andaman Sea. About half are foreigners, there purely for the experience—to my left is a robust blonde with a German flag sewn to her backpack and an alarming tropical disease on her leg. When I squirm away from her on the narrow plank seat, the boat rocks, eliciting scowls from the tourists and smiles from the Thais.

I consult my English-Thai pocket dictionary. "*Law diou*," I say to the boatman, and point towards the shore. He looks through me as if gazing into the horizon. I'm not yet desperate enough to resort to pantomime, so to distract myself I follow the movements of an elderly Thai lady seated to my right, cool and content under an immense lampshade hat. She takes out a wooden box, removes several ingredients—a green leaf, a white nut, some black paste—bundles them together and stuffs the whole package into her mouth. In seconds she has it chewed down to a manageable wad.

The lady feels me watching. She projects a gob of saliva six feet past the side of the boat, turns and motions that I ought to try some. I politely decline with a nod, the way I'd seen Thais do. I'd read that betel nut chewing is a respectable pastime of older Thai women, yet don't think I've quite come of age.

I am twenty-six, and I'm here in Thailand to study its effect on my brain. A research project to replace the one

I'd abandoned back in California, where I'd been living in my car and collecting raw data on every man I could.

Men. I was cataloguing their qualities, measuring hardnesses and protrusions. Eyes, and where they traveled. Hands, how they moved and what they insinuated. I observed variations on ugliness, on beauty, how one morphed into the other, transformed by a laugh or a sneer. The psychotropic effects of saliva. The lubricating properties of sweat.

I conducted my research in restrooms, in storage rooms. In the back rows of movie theaters. In dirt, sand, water. Dozens of cars. There were men whose names I never recorded, men who'd strike out from the sloth of domesticity, busting into my badness. Over time I discovered that certain conditions were favorable to my study. Like heat. Beer. Stars. I noted the seizing up I'd do in a man's presence, how the universe tilted to ensure we collide. I'd estimate the torque of his muscles in the dark, a man who wouldn't look at me in the light of day, or would—like he'd look over a used car.

On visits to my shrink, I'd review the data I'd collected over the past week, and he'd always respond with, "So what have you learned from this?"

I learned how to sweeten my voice. How saying yes is easier than saying no. I considered writing a thesis on the transparency of ultra-thin condoms. On the density of loneliness as compared with the lightness of being alone. I came to this conclusion: When organism A and organism B begin the process of merging, a sleeping spore lies patiently in the shadows. It waits for a soft, pink underside to unfurl, for the rare condition of love. When this occurs, the spore awakens, ravenous. It seizes on love's tender bud, rots it from the inside. I labeled this spore Shame. No matter how careful I was, I could not eradicate it. Shame tainted everything I touched.

One day, a picture of Asia came from somewhere and invaded my mind. It lit up like a glorious cancer, like the curve of jaw on a man I'd met once while standing in line to pay for gasoline. For months I slept alone, the wash of my dreams spiked with Buddhas. I decided to go to Thailand, where I hoped to be purged of my bad science, wash my sluttiness off into the sea.

I arrived in Bangkok at night, was dropped by a sullen taxi driver at a flophouse. I abided by the sign near the door—No Shoes—without guessing its prophetic meaning. The hassle of hustling up new shoes the next morning was worth the view from the flophouse roof, a sleek plane of beige smog, Bangkok's golden pinnacles piercing through. That first day, I was pulled into the city by the crooked finger of an invisible *phi*. The Buddhas in the temples slurped me into their ears, better to hear the chants of the monks, the calls of noodle-hawkers and lotus-sellers. The Bangkok streets were redolent of diesel, incense, rotten food. Children dodged buses and three-wheeled *tuk-tuks*. Radios blared. People heaped so many smiles upon me that I thought I would collapse under their weight.

Hungry, I bought some fruit from a street merchant who kept his table in the shadow of three billboards: an icy Coca-Cola pouring into a thirsty mouth, a movie scene of people being blown to oblivion, and the Marlboro Man riding off into the sunset. The merchant's wares were arranged into Buddhist temple shapes. I tried to dislodge a mangosteen without sending nirvana rolling to the dirt.

I was the fruit fated to roll, the betel nut chewed, savored and spat out. Every encounter I had on the

Bangkok streets was pregnant with undetonated karma. There was the curry at a roadside stand that incinerated my taste buds, after the proprietor asked, "White-boy hot or Thai-boy hot?" and I was determined not to be a *farang*. Then, the Floating Market, where I bought a lotus flower: As I bent to inhale its fragrance, a scorpion staggered out like a piss-drunk cowboy, brandishing his stinger. When I almost blew off my finger with a firecracker I'd been handed at a street festival—where the various gunpowder-filled concoctions had names like Hen-Laying Egg, or Bright-Minded Ball—I figured it was time to meander south, bringing me to this present state of consciousness where my bladder and I have become one.

Lesson learned in Thailand: Avoid excessive hydration while traveling by lollygagging longboat. The gentle lapping of the river against the boat's hull is like the voice on a self-help CD: *Relax, let go*, it whispers. *Allow every part of your body to become heavy, verrry heaavy, releasing anything you are holding on to.*

I do not relax. I double-cross my legs, recruiting about twelve different muscles in a team effort to barricade my bladder. How I will later stand and exit the boat is a bridge I will slosh across when the time comes.

We near the Phra Nang shore. Only later am I fully able to appreciate the massive rock formations jutting out of the water, like giant elephants lumbering across the sea. Right now I have my eyes locked upon a little structure next to the pier. I can just make out two letters painted on its door: W.C. I stare at it as if it were a sacred mandala.

I am the Buddha under the Bodhi tree, as Immovable as a Mountain.

The Thai lady takes a tea kettle out of a basket.
I am a Fortress, a Locked Trunk buried in the earth.
She pours some tea into a glass—
I am a Frigid Housewife. A Dead Whale.
—and holds it out to me.
Dang.

I dare not shake even just my head. I have reached a pinnacle upon which I teeter, a dilemma that has followed me throughout my life: I must choose to either keep my dignity or cut the ties that bind me, between the discipline of holding back forever and the flagrant flinging open of the gates to freedom.

I waver. I try not to wobble. I hold on for a life-altering moment while mumbling something to the German girl about keeping an eye on my stuff. I can't hear her response because I am diving into the sea, relief spreading through my body before I even hit the water.

When I surface, I have been reborn under a lucky star. I swim, victorious, toward the fabled white sands of Phra Nang, just another American fool, slogging out of the water and over to where my new German friend waits, pissed off, with my pack. *"Danke schöen,"* I say, as she stomps away. I decide to sit on the beach and dry off a bit before I look for the night's bungalow.

A breeze teases a fringe of palms as the last jigger of daylight drains into the sea and stars sidle out, one by one. The smell of coconut and kaffir lime beckons from an outdoor café. The me of yore would have planned ahead, would have snatched up that tasty little treat back at the teahouse with whom to conduct an experiment, say, on the effect of a tropical climate on the libido—but this very, very, very, *very* good girl is as unaccompanied as a clam.

I'm watching the waves, and there are sparkles floating on the surface, as if handfuls of heavenly bodies had
been flung across the sea. Then, an iridescent humanoid
form rises up from the water. I frantically pat myself
for outgrowths of dementia. Is that a narcotic rush I'm
feeling? Could it be possible that back in Krabi, that
Thai boy toy sprinkled some upcountry opium in my
tea? The last time I'd tripped was during a peyote ritual
gone awry, one that had manifested a ten-thousand-fold
hallucination of my high school algebra teacher, Sister
Ursula. She'd sprouted undulating arms, with millions
of chubby hands each grasping chalk and a great omnipresent mouth that bespoke: *There are Vastly Compelling
Reasons to find the Roots of Unity.*

The sparkle-clad figure is heading my way. I leap to
my feet and run like the dickens, an instinct that has
served me well when I've listened to it. I run along the
beach, toward a rocky outcropping. I find a cave. The
fragrance of incense and a soft, flickering light beckon
me into its recesses.

Well, I'll be danged!

Scores of wooden penises are wedged, stacked, glued
with melted wax to the surface of a candle-lit altar.
These are the most alert save-the-race likenesses I've
ever seen, their angles of repose ranging between 45 and
90 degrees—a sort of *Kama Sutra* lesson in geometry.
Some are decorated with squiggly Thai script. Others
are rather banged up, evidence of past abuse. I spy a
contingent of thumb-sized red guys with black helmet
heads, all lined up in military formation, led by a log-
sized member. As humongous phallic shadows waltz
across the walls of the cave, something inside me churns.
I break out in a sweat. My breathing becomes shallow.

"Penises!" I say, a little loudly. The word just slips out of my mouth.

"Sorry?" a voice answers behind me.

I jump. It's a man. A Brit, by the sound of him. He's dripping, must've just come from an evening swim. He wears the teeniest, tightest cutoffs I've ever seen on a man—Is it a Euro thing? I wonder—has hazel eyes, a dark tangle of curls. He smiles and holds out his hand.

"I'm Noland," he says. "I saw you running, figured you were another Yank who'd fallen off her trolley. Or perhaps you've come to place an offering on the altar?"

"Melinda," I gasp, and shake his warm, wet hand. "I'm afraid I don't have a, um, penis with me," almost whispering the p-word. "Do you have one I could use?"

Noland laughs. "The Thais call this the Princess Cave," he says. "The local fishermen pile these little beauties in here to honor the sea goddess, hoping for good fortune at sea. And in the bedroom, of course. Thai legend has it that she gave birth to a man, whom she created to be her lover. He would come down to the water to meet her and they would frolic in the waves."

I shiver. "I could've sworn I saw somebody, *glowing,* in the water—"

"'Twas I!" Noland says. "Covered in phosphorescent plankton. Dinoflagelletes, specifically, with flagellating tails."

"Flagellating tails?"

"Like sperm," he says, rubbing a thumb and forefinger together in a circular motion. "A bit slimy, yet kind of tacky."

He's looking at me intently.

"The dinoflagellates, I mean," he says.

We talk some more. Noland tells me he is an anthropologist, taking a break from field work in Malaysia. Came to Phra Nang to do some writing.

"About life in the bush?" I ask.

"Poetry," he says. "Letting all the smells and tastes and everything I've absorbed for the last eight months float up to the surface, burst out of me and onto the paper."

"I know what you mean," I say. "I think some of those dino-numbers got into the drinking water. I've been sending home cryptic postcards about being brainwashed by squids, Buddhas and Thai beach boys."

"Lovely!" says Noland.

And he is. Lovely. Especially lit by candles and surrounded by penises, which I stare at to avoid flagellating into his eyes. But it's too late. Vast populations are fluttering in my bloodstream: dragonflies and butterflies and golden honeybees of love. Before I can find a cold shower somewhere, pheromones are gushing from my every pore. My heart throbs as ecstatically as a rave dancer, replicating itself in all the errant places of my body that I've been trying to ignore for the last several weeks. That little emergency vial of rationale I keep on the top shelf of my mind, the one that comes complete with a subliminal tape-loop of my shrink's voice, which to listen to is equivalent to wearing a chastity belt—I feel it explode from the high-voltage current coursing through me.

As my last few shreds of decency and restraint take flight, I'm desperate. I've got to think of something fast, anything to get me off this Love Train before it leaves the station. How about . . . a compilation of phallus terminology! Yes! It will be my life's work. I immediately get started on a mental list: Peter, Prick, Rod, Demon Stick, Dong, Manhood, Boner, Tool, Schlong, Old Betrayer, Tumescence—

"Would you fancy a swim?" Noland says, vaporizing my data. But a swim is a sportingly grand idea. The reformed me (struggling to climb back on the wagon) knows I must get out of this penis palace, spit spot, before I do something rash. Swimming in the sea has got to be safer than dicking around with a scantily-clad lad in a cavern of one-eyed snakes.

"Aye," I say.

I take deep breaths, reminding myself of all the unsexy things that (according to my shrink) lie in wait for me if I don't change my sexy ways: Loneliness. Alienation from society. Bad credit forever (though I'm still puzzling over its connection to sex). "Deviance is a symptom of self-hatred," he'd once said ominously. Why, then, does the deviance factor make the consequences seem so sexy? So outré? Why do I so love this feeling of hating myself?

We walk down to the water's edge. I'm not wearing a bathing suit but my underwear and bra could pass as one. Though it's dark, I duck behind a palm tree. Unbuttoning my shirt and my fly in front of a man is just too suggestive. For the first time ever I'm not trying to whip myself into any more of a lather than I am in already.

The sea is warm and calm, the glowing clouds of plankton creating a magical soup. I wade in hesitantly, shy. Shy-like. Noland grins at me from just beyond, bobbing on the surf. A fetching merman. But before I am forced to try to stop my legs from morphing into a matching mermaid tail, I feel the sting of tears. Inevitably I am reminded of this wreckage that I drag around, of all that has been worn away, never to be recovered. Gone is the softness of naïveté, even the mid-grade texture of limited experience. Just who do I think I'm fooling? I know it all, and the knowledge pulls me down, no matter how hard I try to throw it off. No floating lotuses, no deadpan Buddhas, no juke joint of Johnsons can help me.

When I was a little girl—long before I'd tossed off my virginity like last year's phone book—someone had loved me. He was one of my mom's boyfriends. I remember an outing near the ocean, where I'd gotten gum in my hair, and he'd borrowed a knife and cut it out. I remember his wrinkled brow. How his hand shook. Afterwards he'd picked me up and called me Sweetheart, though I was too big to be carried. I didn't want him to put me down. Not long after, he disappeared. Though I missed him at first, eventually I forgot him.

Many years later I ran into him on the street. Though I was grown he recognized me. Let me tell you a story, he said, and talked about that day by the sea. How he'd carried me until the feeling left his arms. He'd kept the lock of my hair with the gum stuck to it to remember me by. He asked about my mother, and gave me his phone number. Call me sometime and tell me what you're up to. When I finally called, his number had been disconnected.

"Look at this," says Noland.

He shows me something he'd learned on a trip to West Africa, how to play a water drum. He splashes a Congolese rhumba while I attempt water ballet. We discuss scholarly topics, such as the mating dances of the Trobriand Islanders. After a while, we stop talking and listen to the surf's rise and fall. Inhale, exhale. Diastole, systole. I look down at myself. I'm shimmering. I glance over at Noland and he is, too, and suddenly his sparkles and mine seem to be calling out to each other, our own little emissaries, our polite diplomats. *Hello! I see you!* they say. *I see you too!* then bowing to each other, *Thank you* (bow). *Thank you!* For a long time, Noland and I just float, side by side, as tiny alliances are formed between us.

Then Noland mentions he is leaving. He's taking the late boat out of Phra Nang in a few hours, back to Krabi to catch an all-night bus to Singapore.

"I was wondering," he says, "if you'd fancy coming along?"

On rare, perfect days I move through space as if propelled by a benevolent force. No matter where I turn, it is all so crushingly gorgeous, and my one true purpose is to dip into each shiny poppy bowl and suck nectar like a butterfly, see myself reflected in everything with wide-eyed familiarity. This, according to my shrink, is evidence of a narcissistic disorder run so amok, it has its own House of Mirrors. "I am not a narcissist!" I cried, as he nodded and scribbled into his notebook. "What would you say, then, is influencing your behavior?" he queried. I thought for a moment. "I'm blinded by science," I said. He gave me that inscrutable shrink look. I wanted him to understand. "Can't you see?" I said. "All that is good inside me is inspired to divide and multiply, a gazillion cells of beneficence splitting off into infinity."

Noland and I sit under a palm tree, dripping single-celled organisms, while I debate whether or not to abandon the enchanted inlet of Phra Nang, which haven't even seen by the light of day. I remind myself that the tsunami wave of lust roaring in my veins is not a sane reason to catch an all-night bus to Singapore with a man I'd just met in a penis cave. I counter that it has to do with expanding the perfection of the experience, increasing its chances of staying fixed in my memory, without some streak of bum luck busting in and taking over. Like being eaten alive by flophouse bedbugs. Or getting the runs. Or running into those three Aussies in Bangkok, whose vacation pastime is to go from village to village, sampling and comparing prostitutes. If I loiter about this penis voodoo cave much longer, I will likely end up as an instrument of the sea goddess, my sole purpose being to beget more lovers for her enjoyment. Or find myself addicted to the love sparkles in the water, forgetting who I am and where I came from and never, ever be able to leave.

Armed with a dozen rationalizations, I leave at 9 p.m. to catch the all-night bus for Singapore.

I could report how Thais like to watch machine gun videos on buses that take mountainous turns at 45-degree angles, threatening to pitch themselves into the lush gorges below. I could explain how two people in the back of a bus can share a blanket and observe the chemical reaction taking place. I could hypothesize how lust isn't a nasty thing. Or maybe it is. Isn't it about being a pilgrim of the flesh, making devotional offerings to the molecules of another? Molecules that—like those throat singers in Tuva—chant your name and the name of the universe, multi-tonally, so they sound as one?

It's a theory, anyway, that Noland and I will thoroughly test.

❧ ❧ ❧

Melinda Misuraca's work has appeared in Salon.com, Natural Bridge, The Thong Also Rises: Further Misadventures from Funny Women on the Road, *among others. She hides out in Northern California.*

CHRISTOPHER COOK

≈ ≈ ≈

Full Moon over Bohemia

The Czech countryside—at night,
in the dead of winter—is no place for solitude.

THE FULL MOON HOVERS MIDWAY DOWN THE SOUTHERN sky, a platinum sphere afloat in a black sea of stars. I glance back at the cottage, at the small quarter-paned window aglow with firelight, the wood smoke curling off its rooftop chimney, then thrust both poles into snow and slide away down the slope toward the distant treeline.

Southern Bohemia, the remote countryside, on a wintry December night. The temperature hovers just below freezing. Fresh snowfall blankets the rolling fields and spreads under thick stands of conifers. The landscape spreads pale white and shadowed in gray, just right for a cross-country trek on skis by moonlight. After months of living within the urban confines of Prague, surrounded by too many people and too much noise, I need this solitary adventure.

I'd arrived earlier in the day with two friends after an hour's drive from the city. The paved road off the main highway had given way to a paved lane undulating through snowblown hills fringed in trees. Sturdy farmhouses and stone cottages dotted the hills, an occasional frozen pond. Then another turnoff into a smaller lane, which might have been paved or not—one couldn't tell for the drifting snow—and there eventually appeared a remote cluster of houses. Past them the lane abruptly stopped. There we parked and unloaded, piled our gear onto a sled and plunged across the fields toward the isolated cottage. It was a hard slog, thigh deep in snow, and before long we were sweating, stripping away our outer coats.

The cabin itself was either a weekend *chata* or *chalupa* (the latter is usually larger), and it seems almost every Czech family owns one. This one belonged to my friend Vaclav, who'd spent years working on it, improving it, maintaining it, a never-ending project. The single large room downstairs with a living area and kitchen felt cheerfully rustic, the two bedrooms upstairs cozy and snug. But then, Czechs seem to value comfort above all else. Between the latest electronic gadget and a comfortable pair of house shoes, I do believe they'd choose the slippers. They often remind me of hobbits.

Having finally arrived, we threw open the cottage doors and aired it, cut firewood, built a fire in the stove, sat down to bread and sausage and beer. Following a brief rest, we strapped on our skis and set off for an afternoon trek through the surrounding countryside. Afterward, more food, more beer. Conversation by the stove's warmth, dozing into a nap. Contented. As I say, a hobbit's existence. Very pleasant.

By evening, though, the cabin had begun to feel claustrophobic, the friendly chatter noisy and intrusive. I needed to get away, outdoors, alone. This pressing need for solitary time seems peculiar to Czechs, the most sociable of peoples. But they are very tolerant, too, so they smiled when I quickly explained myself and ducked out the door. Those crazy, restless Americans!

This is true, at least in my case. I've felt skittish lately, more than a little off-kilter. Fenced in. A Texan by birth and upbringing, I'm accustomed to open spaces, wide skies, and large distances, and the Czech Republic, like most of Europe, often feels cloistered and crowded to me. Yet altogether civilized, and charming. I can't imagine Americans living so compactly without social catastrophe. Even as it is, the sheer stress of daily life in the States seems to erupt in anger, in routine violence. But not here, though by comparison this country is poorer. It was the same when I lived in Mexico: so much poverty, so many smiles . . . well then, so much for the correlation between wealth and contentment. Quality of life cannot be measured with money. Convenience will never replace joy.

These thoughts pass through me scarcely noticed as I skim over the moonlit snow, my skis sliding down the gentle slope toward the treeline. The cold air gathers around me, encloses me in frost. My breath, at first ragged, falls into a rhythm. I move across the open field under a wide arc of scattered stars, headed into mystery, leaving everything extraneous behind, forgotten. Just me and the starry night and the snow slipping past underneath, as smooth as dreamless sleep. Lost in reverie beneath a Central European sky.

Reaching the treeline, I come to a slow halt, pause for a searching look. My eyes trace the deep shadows for an entry point, a trail. There it is, scant, twinned grooves almost covered in new snow. The towering evergreens loft over me, and beyond the first of them moonlight falls downward through the branches in small ragged splashes, reveals the surface of snowfall only dimly here and there. Beneath the thick canopy of the forest, I will have to see with my skis, an edgy prospect. I push off all the same, and enter.

The beauty of cross-country skiing is not found in what one sees so much as in what one does not hear. Snow subdues sound, absorbs and smothers it. Inside the woods, the stillness is profound. Such silence. What is left is emptiness. And that absence of things heard becomes uncanny, mystical. Like the nothingness of Zen. Except for my own quiet suspiration, the world no longer exists.

But trees certainly do, as I soon discover. Here in the murky forest, where the meandering trail is less seen than intuited, I find sudden, sharp, invisible declines fairly teeming with trees. I hurl downward, waving my ski poles wildly, frantically, bumping into low branches, finally smashing into a sturdy trunk, full stop, expelling a most unZen-like *harrumph*. Sprawled ungracefully, with snow down my collar, I think: A forest threadbare in moonlight is lovely, but perhaps not such a good idea.

An hour later, I finally find myself through it, emerging from its far side into another open field. I am a bit lost now, but if I turn left and travel far enough, I think I can circumvent the trees and circle back into fields near the cottage. At least it seems so. But of course the immediate way is uphill. And quite a long, steep hill at that, a real effort. It will cost something to climb a hill like that on skis more willing to slide down than up. But one does what circumstances require, one must. This is a lesson, I tell myself. This is the adventure. Any bold exploit teaches us something, unwanted or not. And it does not come free.

So off I go. Halfway up, I calculate the cost, and it seems very high. The temperature has plummeted, the air biting cold, but beneath my coat, my sweater, I am drenched in sweat. And tired, out of breath. I stop to take a rest, doubled over. The silence settles over me again. The emptiness. Now there is nothing in the world but my fatigue and this hill. For some reason, the notion that my life has come down to this, a simple but perfect metaphor, seems depressing. What could be worse?

The answer promptly rises through the silence, cuts through it like a knife: distant howls. Eerie, unearthly, hair-raising howls. But very much of this earth, I gather, and of these woods. Wolf howls. Or wild dog howls. And not one, but several. This is not a sound I wished to hear. It is not even a sound I thought might exist here. But it does, undeniably so, and it is coming my way.

There are moments in all our lives when we wonder at our own capacity for creating dilemmas. Not just ordinary dilemmas, but absurd ones. Outrageous ones. The sort of predicament that could make a fine story, if we survive it. And if we don't, well then, no one will ever know just how foolish and wretched we felt in those final forsaken moments. This is not reassuring, to realize the options are so extreme: a fine tale that becomes more comical with each retelling versus, for example, an ignominious end being ravaged and devoured by wild dogs.

This notion—not just an idea, mind you, but an actual image, and a gut-wrenching sensation in my belly—spurs me into action. My fatigue is palpable, but so is the fear, and what muscles won't accomplish is assisted by adrenaline. I move upward, gaining the slope, and when the skis seem to be holding me back, I rip them off and climb with my boots, plowing the knee-deep snow like a machine. My heart is thumping, my breath flushing raucous clouds of exhaust like a steam engine. The metaphor of the hill now seems trivial. It is nothing compared to the mythos of the wolf, the wild dog archetype, of the primeval canine predator that terrorized our prehistoric ancestors and still lurks forgotten within the marrow of our bones.

The howls have come much nearer, are circling now. They rise from the woods, echo through the trees. The dogs—for this is surely what they are; wolves must have been killed out of these parts a hundred years ago, because after all this is Europe, the Czech Republic, not Montana, not the Yukon . . . right?—these dogs must be tracking me by smell, downwind. But staying out of sight, a good sign. On the other hand, perhaps they simply haven't found me yet. But they're looking.

I push on through the snow, clothes soaking wet to my skin. Thinking they probably aren't wild dogs anyhow. Most likely, they are farm dogs. Pets, really. Though of course, when you get a pack of them running together . . . well, we've all seen what humans can do in packs, much less dogs. People use guns, bombers, nuclear warheads. Then pretend afterward they didn't enjoy it. Whereas dogs suffer no such guilt. They just rip with their teeth, go for the entrails, growling, snarling their primordial pleasure.

At the top of hill, I quickly lower the skis off my shoulder and refasten them to my feet, shove off down the slope aiming toward a place, just discernible, where the treeline seems to come to a point in the moonlight. The freezing air whips past my eyes, turns tears into thin strings of crusted ice down my cheeks. Behind the near treeline, the howling paces me. This is the closest they've been yet. I can practically feel them there, briefly believe I see their loping eyes. I drive the poles into the drifting snow, pushing hard, thrusting forward, no longer thinking—or at least I'm unaware if I am. It's down to me and them in a race, and while they're faster, I have more to lose than they have to gain. If it comes to that, I can bite, too. And scream. In Canada once, I had a black bear come into my tent and when I screamed it scrambled out quick. It couldn't get away fast enough. Recalling the incident now, I smile. It has over the years become a fine story, a staple for late nights over a beer with friends in this tavern or that.

And this escapade will, too. I feel almost certain of it. But first . . .

Reaching the bottom point of the treeline, I turn the skis to skirt it and see in the distance across a wide rolling expanse a small flickering light. A golden twinkle set against a squat silhouette. The cottage, its window. My friends. I strike out for them, moving more steadily now. From the woods behind me rises a tumultuous chorus of howls. It ascends in what seems to me a bitter, keening complaint, as if even nature can prove unjust. The hair at my neck stands on end and I shudder.

Half an hour later, I lean against the cabin steps and remove my skis, prop them against a wall and stand watching the dark line of trees beyond the luminous snowfield. I listen closely. From inside the cottage, a murmur of voices. But from the distant forest, nothing. Over it hovers the Bohemian night with stars like diamonds strewn across a black velvet cloak. The wide lucid moon reaches down the sky.

After a while, I walk up the steps and open the cottage door, go inside. My friends look up from their chairs beside the stove, their expressions both welcoming and surprised at once. They're wearing flannel pajamas and big cozy house shoes.

"*Tak, dobry ve er*," calls out Vaclav. Well then, good evening. He holds out a Pilsner in my direction. "How was the skiing?"

"It was great," I reply, taking a seat, "a real adventure. Want to hear about it?"

They both smile. Yes, of course. Why not?

~ ~ ~

Christopher Cook is the author of two award-winning books, the novel Robbers *and the short story collection* Screen Door Jesus & Other Stories. *Both books appear in international translations and have been adapted to film. His work also appears in the Houghton Mifflin series of* Best American Mystery Stories. *A native of Texas, during the past decade he has lived in France, Mexico, and now the Czech Republic. He resides in Prague.*

≈≈ ≈≈ ≈≈

The Discreet Charm of the Zurich Bourgeoisie

Or, as Huey Lewis sang, "It's hip to be square."

THE MOST SINCERE COMPLIMENT YOU COULD PAY Zurich is to describe it as one of great bourgeois cities of the world. This might not, of course, seem like a compliment—the word *bourgeois* having become for many, since the outset of the Romantic Movement in the early nineteenth century, a significant insult. "Hatred of the bourgeois is the beginning of wisdom," felt Gustave Flaubert, a standard utterance for a mid-nineteenth-century French writer, for whom such disdain was as much a badge of one's profession as having an affair with an actress and making a trip to the Orient. According to the Romantic value-system which today still dominates the Western imagination, to be a bourgeois is synonymous with laboring under an obsession with money, safety, tradition, cleaning, family, responsibility, prudishness, and (perhaps) bracing walks in the fresh air. Consequently, for about the last two hundred years, few places in the Western world have been quite as deeply unfashionable as the city of Zurich.

Attractive girls born outside Switzerland are particularly against going to Zurich. Such girls (and modern science has proved this) prefer L.A. or Sydney. Even if they are looking for something protestant and homey, they chose Antwerp or Copenhagen instead.

I've always tried to interest girls in Zurich. I've always thought that a girl who could like Zurich could like important recesses of me. But it's been hard. I recall a trip with Sasha. She was an artist, she was beguiling, she was tricky. We'd have furious arguments, often in the middle of the night. Sometimes the argument went like this:

> SHE: You don't like intelligent women, that's why you're disagreeing with me.
> HE: I do like intelligent women, but sadly you're not one of them.

Neither of us came out of this sort of thing very well. It's a reminder (were one to need it) that lovers practice a form of rudeness that is generally impossible outside of open warfare.

One weekend, Sasha and I flew to Zurich (we lived in Hackney in London, we were bohemian, we had views, evolved ones, about Habermas). I tried to point out how exotic Zurich was. Trams were exotic, as was the "Migros" supermarket, and the light gray concrete of the apartment blocks and the large, solid windows and the veal escalopes. We normally associate the word exotic with camels and pyramids. But perhaps anything different and desirable deserves the word. What I found most exotic was how gloriously boring everything was. No one was being killed by random gunshots, the streets were quiet, everything was tidy and, as everyone says (though you don't see people trying) it was generally so clean you could eat your lunch off the pavement.

But Sasha was bored. She wanted to go back to Hackney. She couldn't bare the tidiness. On a walk through a park she told me she wanted to graffiti insults on the walls—just to shake the place up a bit. She did a little mock scream, and an old lady looked up from her paper. Her boredom reminded me of my friend Gustave Flaubert, who'd grown up in Rouen, which is perhaps a little bit like Zurich minus the lake. "I am bored, I am bored, I am bored," Flaubert wrote in his diary as a young man. He returned repeatedly to the theme of how boring it was to live in France and especially in Rouen. "Today my boredom was terrible," he reported at the end of one bad Sunday. "How beautiful are the provinces and how chic are the comfortably off who live there. Their talk is of taxes and road improvements. The neighbor is a wonderful institution. To be given his full social importance he should always be written in capitals: NEIGHBOR." Sasha was bored of Flaubert (she'd tried *A Sentimental Education*, but got bored half way), but she and Flaubert at least agreed on how boring it is to live in a boring place.

However, as mother tends to tell you near the end of the school holidays, it's mostly boring people who get bored—and I began to lose patience with Sasha's boredom. I wanted someone interesting enough inside not to ask of a city that it also be "interesting"; someone close enough to the well-springs of passion that she wouldn't care if her city wasn't "fun"; someone sufficiently acquainted with the darker, tragic sides of the human soul to appreciate the stillness of a Zurich weekend. Sasha and I weren't an item for much longer.

But my attraction to Zurich continued. What most appealed to me about Zurich was the image of what was entailed in leading an "ordinary" life there. To lead an ordinary life in London is generally not an enviable proposition: "ordinary" hospitals, schools, housing estates, or restaurants are nearly always appalling. There are of course great examples, but they are only for the very wealthy. London is not a bourgeois city. It's a city of the rich and the poor.

According to one influential wing of modern secular society, there are few more disreputable fates than to end up being "like everyone else"; for "everyone else" is a category that comprises the mediocre and the conformist, the boring and the suburban. The goal of all right-thinking people should be to mark themselves out from the crowd and "stand out" in whatever way their talents allow. But the desire to be different depends on what it means to be ordinary. There are countries where the communal provision of housing, transport, education, or health care is such that citizens will naturally seek to escape involvement with the group and barricade themselves behind solid walls. The desire for high status is never stronger than when being ordinary entails leading a life which fails to cater to a median need for dignity and comfort.

Then there are communities, far rarer, many of them imbued with a strong (often Protestant) Christian heritage, where the public realm exudes respect in its principles and architecture, and where the need to escape into a private domain is therefore less intense. Citizens may lose some of their ambitions for personal glory when the public spaces and facilities of a city are themselves glorious to behold. Simply being an ordinary citizen can seem like an adequate destiny. In Switzerland's largest city, the urge to own a car and avoid sharing a bus or train with strangers loses some of the urgency it may have in Los Angeles or London, thanks to Zurich's superlative tram network— clean, safe, warm, and edifying in its punctuality and technical prowess. There is little reason to travel alone when, for only a few francs, an efficient, stately tramway will transport one across the city at a level of comfort an emperor would have envied.

There's something faintly embarrassing about loving the Dutch seventeenth-century painter Peter de Hooch deeply, so deeply that one would include him among one's favorite painters of all time. Of the hundred and seventy works assigned to him, most are plain mediocre, overly coarse in the early years or mannered in the later ones. He is operating in a minor genre, his pictures are too pretty and yet not quite pretty enough, not as pretty as a Raphael's or Poussin's, and compared to his countrymen, he lacks the inventiveness of van Steen, the grace of Vermeer, or the density of van Ruisdael. His morality can appear reactionary, a celebration of the most banal human occupations: delousing and cleaning the patio. He doesn't even paint people very well, look closely at his faces and they are no better than sketches. And yet I've long loved him for reasons very similar to why I love Zurich: because he understands and celebrates bourgeois life, without sentimentalizing it. The world he paints, despite the differences, seems in essence identical to the Zurich I grew up in.

De Hooch is often described as fitting into a tradition of Dutch art and literature which sermonized about the virtues of domesticity. Although de Hooch's paintings do look positively on domestic pursuits, although one would be unlikely to come away from them emboldened to break up one's marriage or leave the kitchen dirty, it seems unfair to label him a crude moralist of domestic virtue. He never tells us that it is important to love one's children or keep the house tidy, he merely provides us with such evocative, moving examples of maternal love and ordered rooms that we would be unlikely to disagree.

Furthermore, his art has none of the smug tone of much overt propaganda of domestic virtue. The simple pleasures of home come across as highly vulnerable achievements. Critics might argue that de Hooch was not painting seventeenth century Holland the way it really was, they could point out that many women were abused by their husbands, many houses were dirty and primitive, there was a degree of blood and dirt and pain that de Hooch chose not to represent, idealizing matters instead. And yet his art is never sentimental, because it is so infused with an awareness of the darker forces liable at any point to vanquish the hard-won serenity. We don't need to be told that the whole of Holland was not spotlessly clean, we have enough suggestion of it through the many windows at the ends of corridors in de Hooch's canvases. We don't need to be told that the order achieved by women in their homes might be destroyed by war or feckless husbands, we can feel the danger too.

In *A Woman with a Young Boy Preparing for School*, a mother butters some bread for her son, he stands dutifully beside her, a little man holding his hat, dressed in a neat gray coat and polished shoes. If the scene is both unsentimental and moving, it is because we are made to feel the evanescence of these intimacies of mother and son. To the left of the canvas, a corridor leads to an open door and out to the street, where there is a large building marked Schole. The boy will soon disguise his debts to his mother who has over the years buttered him loaves and checked his head for lice.

De Hooch's art helps us to recover positive associations of that word with which we may have deeply ambiguous relations: bourgeois. It seems laden with negative connotations, it can suggest conformity, a lack of imagination, stiffness, pedantry, and snobbishness. But in de Hooch's world, being bourgeois means dressing in simple but attractive clothes, being neither too vulgar nor too pretentious, having a natural relationship with one's children, recognizing sensual pleasures without yielding to licentiousness. It seems the embodiment of the Aristotelian mean. His works perform the valuable task of reminding us of the interest and worth of modest surroundings, quelling vain ambitions and temptations to disengage snobbishly from ordinary routines: the evening meal, the housework, a drink with friends. By paying attention to the beauty of brickwork, of light reflecting off a polished door, of the folds of a woman's dress, de Hooch helps us to find pleasure in these omnipresent but neglected aspects of our world.

Some seventy years before Peter de Hooch painted his greatest works, in a passage in his *Essays*, Michel de Montaigne expressed thoughts that appeared to capture in words some the atmosphere of de Hooch's art—and in turn, the qualities upon which the greatness of Zurich is in my view founded. Seeking to remind his readers of the adequacy of ordinary lives, Montaigne wrote: "Storming a breach, conducting an embassy, ruling a nation are glittering deeds. Rebuking, laughing, buying, selling, loving, hating, and living together gently and justly with your household—and with yourself—not getting slack nor belying yourself, is something more remarkable, more rare, and more difficult. Whatever people may say, such secluded lives sustain in that way duties which are at least as hard and as tense as those of other lives."

Unfortunately, the point keeps getting lost. We keep forgetting that buttering bread for a child and making the bed have their wondrous dimensions. Sir Joshua Reynolds clearly didn't understand. Writing of Jan van Steen in the next century, he remarked that though van Steen's work was wonderful, "he would have ranged with the great pillars and supporters of art" had he been able to live in Rome, the greatest city in the world for artists, rather than Leiden, a depressing Zurich-like backwater. In Rome, he would have been inspired to paint really great canvases, he would not have had to limit himself to beggars and merchants, provincial towns and the clutter of daily existence. It is one of the glories of Dutch seventeenth-century art that it proves Sir Joshua Reynolds conclusively wrong. Alongside van Steen and Vermeer, Peter de Hooch and his housewives cleaning the patio deserve much of the credit.

Zurich's distinctive lesson to the world lies in its ability to remind us of how truly imaginative and humane it can be to ask of a city that it be nothing other than boring and bourgeois.

⊱ ⊱ ⊱

Alain de Botton was born in Zurich and educated in Switzerland and England. He is a philosopher and author of seven books including The Art of Travel, How Proust Can Change Your Life, *and* Status Anxiety. *His works have been translated into twenty languages. He lives in London.*

~❧ ~❧ ~❧

The First Kiva

The journey gives all, even when
the destination is elusive.

IT IS THE MOST SACRED SITE IN AMERICA, AND IT IS A secret. It exists on no maps, no brochures, not even a website. There are no guidebooks that tell how to find it. In fact, it is forbidden to visit if you are not of the tribe.

The place is Sipapu, somewhere concealed in a tributary corridor of the Grand Canyon. It is a travertine dome, looking something like earth's navel. Some have said it may be the legendary fountain of youth. The Hopi believe it is the center of the cosmos, the umbilical cord leading from Mother Earth, and the place of mankind's emergence from the underworld. There is no place more sacred to the Hopi, the oldest carriers of ancient Indian beliefs and practices. The 10,000 Hopi, who live in the arid highlands of northern Arizona, have inhabited the same place for a millennium, far longer than any other people in North America. They are not only the oldest dwellers in this land but are considered to have a wisdom, a knowledge of things, beyond average comprehension. Peace-loving and knit tightly together by clan relationships, they are intensely spiritual and fiercely independent. Their religion, deep and all-pervading, is a many-stranded cord that unites them to their stark and beautiful environment. Sipapu is their tabernacle, and their secret.

A quarter century ago I was an untutored river guide on the Colorado River through the Grand Canyon. On most trips we would stop for a snack and a swim at a major southside tributary that ran with the blue-green brilliance of Navajo jewelry on a bolo tie. Once I asked the senior guide what was up the turquoise tributary, and he told me about Sipapu, describing a twenty-foot-high carbonate cupola about five miles up the tributary canyon. There was a pit in the center of the dome that bubbled with pale green water. The water served as a lid, so that ordinary humans could not see the magical things going on beneath the surface. He said the Hopi believed that beneath the pit was the end of a rainbow. It was a bridge to the gateway to this world, the Fourth World, Tuwaqachi, World Complete, from the pre-emergence place. He also said it was forbidden for whites to visit. Though he had never seen it, he knew of another guide who had. Soon afterwards the guide who visited Sipapu was piloting his raft through one of the biggest rapids of the Colorado, and he capsized. He quit the river, and was never heard from again.

For seven seasons I rafted the Colorado, and each time I passed the azure tributary, which I learned the

Hopi called Paayu, I wondered about making the pilgrimage hike. And then thought better of it.

Now, a score and five years later, with a ripened perspective, I thought I could at last make the journey. I had spent years stealing across international borders in search of adventure and stories, and had long ago twisted the word "forbidden" to mean "invitation." I also knew there is little on the planet that has not been abundantly examined, and this was one. I imagined hiking into this hidden place, and photographing, recording, videoing, and writing about Sipapu, staging a journalistic coup for sacred places.

But there was trouble from the outset. I well knew the Hopi had withstood the unraveling effect of white man's society more successfully than any other Native American culture, and that their mytho-religious ceremonies were often off-limits to outsiders. But back when I was a guide the Hopis were conducting bus tours through their reservation, and seemed keen to earn monies through tourism. Hoping the allure of tourodollars would entice the Hopi to allow a journalistic showcase of Sipapu, I called the Hopi Cultural Preservation Office in Kykotsmovi, Arizona and asked for a guide and interpreter. The rebuff rumbled through the phone. Nobody would guide me; nobody would speak to me; I would not be allowed to see it. There would be no photographs. They did not care about tourism potential. Stay away, was the resounding message.

That just fueled my resolve. So, I called Tom, an old friend and fellow ex-guide in Flagstaff. He said he and his wife had hiked down the Hopi Salt Trail from the Canyon rim to Sipapu twenty years ago with an idea to offer tours, but when they got back from the outing his marriage fell

apart, and he never went back. But, he did have his map
and some crude directions he would lend me.

So I teamed up with an ace multimedia producer, who
could capture video, stills, and sounds of the site, while
I did the writing. Then, after weeks of planning, the
morning of departure my multimedia guy cancelled, re-
cruited to go to St. Louis and cover Mark McGwire's attempt to break the season home-run record. Undaunted,
I grabbed my trusty camera and headed to the airport.
At least there would be images and words.

In Flagstaff Tom gave me background on the ancient
Hopi Salt Trail, which was the path from the rim to
Sipapu and beyond to a series of natural sodium chlo-
ride seeps. Since prehistoric times, people made the
precarious journey to the salt mines near the sacred site,
returning with the precious crystals to be used for sacred
ceremonies. Today, since salt is readily available at the
trading post or convenience store, it was rare for a Hopi
to make the journey, and few whites had ever found the
way down this trail.

Tom lent me his old map and directions, and after
buying fresh film and supplies, I headed north to the
Hopi reservation. I hoped by meeting in person some
of the key tribal members they might reconsider my
proposition. Driving north up Route 87 from Winslow
I entered the 4,000-square-mile Hopi Reservation.
Flat-topped red and brown mesas loomed, and overhead a few plum-colored clouds followed like kachi-
nas (the revered spirits of ancestors and creation, and
the carriers of rain) watching my journey. I drove up
to Second Mesa, and stopped at the first curio shop
to ask directions. I asked the shopkeeper if she knew
anything about Sipapu. With the darting, lateral eyes

of a hunted species she said no, and vanished into the back room.

A few miles down the road I came to the Hopi Cultural Center, a flat-roofed sprawl of mortared sandstone. Inside I introduced myself, and asked if anyone might be around who could help with my proposed journey to Sipapu. Everyone who might help was away, I was told by the receptionist. She didn't suggest I return later.

I wandered into the museum, and asked the curator about Sipapu. But he claimed ignorance, and tried to sell me a picture book. I had lunch at the adjacent restaurant, where the young Hopi waitress sat me in the only booth with broken lights, though the place was empty. After ordering the *piiki* (Hopi blue-corn-flour bread), and *noqkwiwi* (a traditional lamb-and-corn stew), I asked her what she knew of Sipapu. Her dark marble eyes locked into mine as she said the young people did not really know about the ancient ways, and then she turned away.

It was getting late, and I hoped to get to the trailhead by dark, so I drove east across a bleak terrain of crumbling yellow sandstone, shored by ship-like geological remains, flat-topped and forbidding. I crossed the Navajo Reservation through Tuba City, across the Painted Desert, and up to The Gap, named for a huge break in the Echo Cliffs overlooking Route 89. The cliffs had the appearance of a muddy sea frozen in the midst of a storm. The setting seemed from an old Western film, and in fact it was . . . the classic westerns, *The Last Frontier* and Zane Grey's *Heritage of the Desert* were filmed here.

According to Tom's map, The Gap was just a mile from the turn-off towards the trailhead. I filled up at the gas station, and asked the Navajo attendant what he knew of Sipapu. His deeply etched mahogany-colored face gave me the look of a puzzled sheep, and said, "Never heard of it."

"But that's impossible . . . the turn-off is just a mile from your gas station."

He just spun his back to me, and went about his business.

I walked across the street to The Gap Trading Post, and bought final supplies for the hike, including two gallon jugs of water. At the register I asked the woman attendant if she knew about Sipapu. She nodded no, and gave me a cryptic smile, looking very much like a bemused Marilyn Whirlwind in *Northern Exposure*. I asked again, prodded by her smile, and she said, "Well, I have driven to the trailhead . . . it's a long ways . . . you should be careful. Do you have rain gear?" When I said no, she offered me a garbage bag to use as a poncho, and as I left I saw her spectral face hanging like a lantern in the dark room.

A mile up the road I turned west, off road, into the vast tan desert of the Coconino Plateau. The sky was darkening, clouds gathered like bruises, and a couple of satiny-black ravens flew in front of my windshield, looking very much like Hopi thunderbirds. I followed Tom's directions . . . left at the stone hogan, right at the corral, follow the dry washbed, straight past the red sandstone cairn . . . but I quickly got lost. I was stuck in a puzzle in a maze, a latticework of dirt roads, scratching across the desert like claw marks on the back of the land. I wrestled the wheel of the Ford Explorer like a captain in a typhoon. The dirt tracks created clumsy and confusing impositions on a terrain that did without for millions of years, and may do so again. There was no logic to these roads. They took sudden detours around rocks, split off in two or three erratic directions at once, then convened again like participants in a square dance of the mad. Often only a tremor of human instinct told me whether I was still following the track or had veered off on an illusion, or worse, toward one of the craterlike fissures caused by erosion that opens twisted mouths in the earth and waits for a catch.

I wandered for two hours, utterly lost, and when night pitched its black tent, I pitched my own in a *cabine de lux*, a roofless abandoned stone hogan on a hill, above any flashflood paths. It stormed all night, a ceaseless bucket rain with no quality of mercy, unlike any I had seen in my years of guiding. Rain is the scarcity here, and a driving force of the Hopi religion. When rain came, their prayers were being answered. Forks of lightning, like illuminated nerves, and thunder like gunfire tore apart the night, making sleep impossible, and torturing me with thoughts that the gods were speaking in disapproval.

I awoke savoring the pure, sweet pellucid smells of the wet desert plants and rocks. The rain had waned to a drizzle, but the skies were still smoking billows in malignant violet, dense as wool. I waded through the mud to fetch my old reliable Minolta for a shot of the sunrise, but my camera seized. Even with fresh batteries and film, it wouldn't advance. Though the Hopis had steadfastly refused to allow any photos of Sipapu, I refused to see this for anything more than it was . . . a freak breakdown of the only chance for image coverage of my quest. Of no further relevance was that my watch was suddenly also broken. I dumped all the wet and mucky gear in the back of my rented truck, and took off to the southwest, a Hopi cardinal direction, abandoning Tom's useless instructions, and using only the compass as my guide.

In minutes I came to the end of the road, the blunt edge of a great canyon. With a sweep of my head I could see high buttes, mesas, table mountains, cathedral spires, stone minarets, tortuous towers, and palisades that seemed to tear the sky. And with some orienteering, I could see that the Salt Trail canyon spilled into the ditch a couple miles to the northeast. Trundling overland, I found a trailhead, shouldered my pack, and headed down 3,000 feet into this Paleozoic pit, every bit as deep as the Grand Canyon, but half again as narrow.

It was the steepest descent I'd seen into the Canyon, near vertical down a jumble of angular sandstone blocks. The Hopis used ropes made of braided strands of bighorn sheep hide to negotiate this trail. I couldn't image how they traversed in reverse carrying huge sacks of salt weighing thirty pounds or more. It rained off and on throughout the descent, a mixed blessing, as it kept temperatures uncharacteristically cool, and made it possible to collect rainwater in potholes in the naked rock, but it made for slippery and dangerous going. It also suffused the air with the fragrance of spiced honey, the aroma of cliffrose. It was a thrill to be back hiking through terrain that was once my backyard. I said hello to the whiptails and the brightly colored western collared lizards, felt the familiar touch of the tall spike of the Utah agave, brushed by honey mesquite trees, Mormon tea, and the deadly jimsonweed, and avoided the prickly pear and the Engelmann hedgehog cacti. After three hours I dropped through the Hermit Shale and the Supai Sandstone, and leveled into a sinuous hallway of Redwall Limestone. The limestone sensually

curved and cradled pools of light green water, ideal for
a desert dip. But I pressed on.

After four hard hours of scrambling, eyes stinging
with brow salt, I finally made it to the confluence with
the river known as Paayu, and from there it would be
just two miles downstream to Sipapu.

But something was terribly wrong. Paayu was legendary for its translucent blue-green waters, the results
of a solution of magnesium salts and calcium carbonate, picked up as it scours a passage from northeastern
Arizona's White Mountains down through the Redwall
Limestone. Yet, as I pulled apart the curtain of bright
yellow tamarisk, I saw a river angry-red with the blood
of sediment and silt flushed by the squalls of the past few
days. The river was flowing fast at the edges, while in
the deeper middle it bubbled up like thick porridge. The
normal seethe and suck of a river was an audible roar.

Paayu was in flood . . . it raced by, overflowing its
banks. Too thick to drink; too thick to plow. The wind
began to bluster. Gusts of sand swirled before me, stinging my face. Lightning split the sky. Volleys of thunder
shook the ozone-packed air. This was a problem, as the
trail down to Sipapu was underwater. I could, no doubt,
scratch a way along the canyon walls, or even wait until
the floodwaters subsided. Instead, I stripped naked, as
Hopis were supposed to do when visiting Sipapu, and
jumped into the red water to consider the situation.

Perhaps, I thought, the endless streams of obstacles
thrown in my path were intended as a message. Perhaps
I really was not meant to see Sipapu. Perhaps it would
be for the better.

An hour I soaked in the gritty waters, as a Monarch
butterfly played around my head. I decided to leave

my quest unfulfilled, and head back out. After waiting twenty-five years, and traveling over 1,000 miles, I was going to turn back two miles and two hours short of my goal. It was the right thing to do.

Redressed, I stepped over a canyon tree frog, listened to the happy descending trill of a canyon wren, and started the long slow slog upward. At first it rained, hard, and I knew that somewhere Hopi were dancing. At sunset, I arrived at the rim, and started to drive east across the open desert. A bright double rainbow spilled in front of my hood, a sight so wondrous I had to stop the car. For a few magical moments I didn't harbor Panglossian yearnings for my artificial goal; I didn't begrudge unfulfilled promises or imagined copy. Sipapu, like the double rainbow, was a manifestation of the unattainable, existing as a perpetual destination, or not at all, the ideal form of a sacred place.

As I turned the ignition key, and jounced towards the kaleidoscopic arches, I decided the vision through my windshield was either a grand visual parting gift, offered in gratitude for leaving well enough alone, or a bright beaming path to the next world.

≈ ≈ ≈

Richard Bangs, an international river explorer, led first descents of thirty-five rivers around the globe, including the Yangtze in China and the Zambezi in southern Africa. His books include Riding the Dragon's Back, Rivergods: Rafting the World's Great Rivers, Adventure Without End, Mystery of the Nile, *and* The Lost River: A Memoir of Life, Death, and Transformation on Wild Water, *which won the National Outdoor Book Award in the literature category. His contributions to the world of adventure travel include serving as founder and editor-in-chief of* Mungo Park, *as part of the founding executive team of Expedia.com, as a founding partner of the adventure travel firm Mountain Travel Sobek, as a contributing editor for MSNBC, and as president of Outward Bound. Richard currently runs Richard Bangs Adventures at http://Adventures.yahoo.com.*

꧁ ꧁ ꧁

The Place You Could Be Looking For

They don't make them like this anymore.

IT'S NOT THE ARRIVAL, THEY ALWAYS TELL YOU, IT'S THE journey that matters. But sometimes it's neither. Sometimes it's your hotel.

The taxi from the airport eased off the expressway, U-turned onto an auxiliary road, wound along the sloping driveway of a darkened high-rise, made a sharp right past a lineup of food stalls—a few still lit by bare electric bulbs, though it was well past midnight—and came to a halt at the end of a cul-de-sac in front of a façade of scaffold-like concrete that gave the upper floors a caged look. No sign identified the building; the cabbie seemed as perplexed as I was. Then I noticed the message next to the entrance—"SEX TOUR-

ISTS NOT WELCOME"—and I knew that I had found the right place.

Months earlier I had asked an acquaintance then living in Thailand if he had any hotel suggestions for Bangkok, and he had immediately recommended The Atlanta. The rooms were Spartan, he warned, but the Art Deco lobby hadn't been touched since the opening in 1952, and the restaurant—where Queen Rampaiphanee had regularly dined—was still excellent. Big band music played in both rooms. The owner, Dr. Charles Henn, was a friend to writers, and displayed in the lobby books written by guests. And he had an aversion to shaking hands.

I had then checked the hotel website. A picture of the lobby—staff stationed behind the arched eyebrows of matching reception desks, a bouqueted roundabout centerpieced in a checkerboard sea—levitated above the words, "BANGKOK'S BASTION OF WHOLESOME AND CULTUR-ALLY SENSITIVE TOURISM. *LE PATRON MANGE ICI.*" (The owner eats here.) Not far below ran a line I was soon quoting to friends, neighbors, anyone who asked about my upcoming trip. "The Atlanta is untouched by pop culture and post-modern vulgarity."

The hotel philosophy on global love for sale was stated farther down. "The Atlanta is against sex tourism. Sex tourism is exploitive, socially damaging, and culturally demeaning: those who want to buy sex should do so in their own country." This was followed by a condemnation of all illegal activities on hotel premises, concluding with the recommendation: "Those who cannot go abroad without behaving badly should stay home."

Quietly, I rolled my suitcase into the dimly lit lobby. A thin gray cat lazily licked himself on the round-about. The night receptionist took my name and asked for payment. I had received a long, single-spaced letter from a Roger Le Phoque, "private secretary to Dr. Charles Henn," confirming my reservation and delineating some of The Atlanta's unorthodoxies, including its policy of accepting neither credit cards nor foreign currencies. But there had been nothing about payment on arrival. I had some change from the taxi and three Thai words, *mai pen rai*, meaning, more or less, "not to worry." The reception-ist said I could pay in the morning.

Blurrily, I climbed the wraparound staircase, passing on the landing a sign from which the phrase "catamites or prostitutes" jumped out. I had not come across this term for a particular type of boy since reading the open-ing sentence of Anthony Burgess's 1980 novel *Earthly Powers*: "It was the afternoon of my eighty-first birthday, and I was in bed with my catamite when Ali announced that the archbishop had come to see me." Any hotel that reminds you of literary genius is worth the price.

The price was 500 baht which, with 7 percent tax, came to approximately $13.70 a night.

In the morning I awoke in a room painted pink and yellow. The air-conditioner hummed reassuringly. I took a hot shower with a hand-held nozzle in a curtainless tub and then, when dressed, went down for breakfast.

The restaurant had the same cool, unperturbed look as the lobby. At the far end was a small annex with books, videos, and the *Times Literary Supplement* on wooden sticks. Waitresses shuffled about in loose-fitting blouses and conservative skirts. Small black-and-white photographs of Siam lined the walls, ceiling fans rotated, baroque music played softly.

An expressionless waitress brought me a menu. The cover read: "The Menu of The Atlanta. Please do not

remove. There are only three copies of this menu." The
website, I remembered, had proudly proclaimed this to
be "the world's first menu with serious and learned an-
notations." The first page, however, contained no list of
foods, just another pronouncement against prostitutes.
Please, I thought, not at breakfast. Still, I took out my
notebook. The waitress walked over with a censorious
look on her face. I quickly checked to see if I had un-
thinkingly brought a catamite to dine. Then the waitress
told me I was not allowed to write, and looking down at
the bottom of the cover I read: "Copyright 2003. No part
of this menu may be reproduced."

Properly chastised, I ordered. My pineapple shake
arrived on a coaster of The Atlanta. "zero t ol er ance &
sl eaze f r ee zone," it read. "no sex t our ist s, junkies,
l out s & ot her degener at es."

The reverse side was filled with script:

There are local expats who walk in with what is
obviously a bargirl. They ignore the sign by the
entrance and are oblivious to the ethos of the hotel.
They think they can go anywhere and do what they
like because they are *farangs* [foreigners]—they have
been spoilt by the tolerant and non-confrontational
Thais. Once here, within these walls, they feel
offended if resident guests give them disapproving
looks and when the staff do not make them feel
welcome. They then pompously say the bargirl is
their wife! Courtesy prevents me from asking the
unfortunate bargirl what desperation drove her to
marry that loser.

                    —Dr. Henn in conversation with a writer
                         Number 5 of an indefinite set.

Eating my pork with pickled radish and rice I thought that, to all the other Atlanta superlatives—"the oldest unaltered hotel foyer in Thailand," "the world's largest selection of Thai vegetarian dishes"—could surely be added "the world's most didactic hotel." All hotels have rules; this one had a code of ethics. The trendy ones have attitude; The Atlanta had morality. In some ways it reminded me of an English boarding school—the hushed public spaces, the classical music, the books and journals scattered about, the overriding presence of a stern but wry headmaster—that for some strange reason served gourmet meals. My breakfast was ambrosial.

I walked outside to see "the first hotel swimming pool" and "the first children's swimming pool in Thailand," both set in a tropical garden only slightly disturbed by the roar from the neighboring expressway. The resident terrapins, Archibald and Doris, hunkered chastely by their own watering hole.

Back in the lobby, the gray cat had been replaced on the roundabout by a brown one. The high glass bookcases contained a good month's worth of well-rounded reading: *A Woman of Bangkok* and *Hvor de ti bud ikke gaelder* (*Where the Ten Commandments Don't Matter*) kept company with *The Effect of PGE, Gastrin and CCK-8 on Postirradiation Recovery of Small Intestine Epithelium*. A P. R. Wiles wrote on his copy of *The Homology of Glands and Glandularia in the Water Mites*, "Dear Charles, This is the result of some strange ideas I had at The Atlanta after the Seram expedition." And E. K. Oppenheimer opined from Myconos (sic):

Alas! Alack!
The N.Y. Times is a hack

Writing a tract
On Bangkok's knack
Blowing their stack
Ending in a cul-de-sac
Leaving The Atlanta no slack.

The scientific papers were right at home, for The Atlanta began life as a laboratory run by Dr. Charles Henn's father, Max. A chemical engineer from Berlin, and a world traveler, he came to Bangkok and started The Atlanta Chemical Company, which produced, among other things, dehydrated cobra venom for export to the U.S. (This according to an article from the local English-language paper *The Nation*, now framed in the lobby.) When the business failed, Dr. Henn the senior turned the laboratory and offices into a hotel, the snake pit providing the perfect location for the historic pool.

The hotel enjoyed tremendous success. Royalty came to dine and military brass, such as General Westmoreland, stayed as guests. Meanwhile, the scientist turned hotelier became a sort of founding father of Thailand's tourism industry, establishing the Thai Hotel Association and the Western Union Travel Service.

But a slow decline began in the '70s, and by the mid-'80s it reached a dramatic point. Returning from his studies at Cambridge, the son found the hotel riddled with sex tourists and drug addicts, and set to work on what at any other hostelry would be called renovation but at The Atlanta has to go by the name of reformation. Because not only has the lobby retained its dapper appearance, but the rooms have lingered in the '50s as well (a rude shock to the mini-bar crowd). The alterations were not so much physical (though a good deal of repair work was obviously necessary) and they were certainly not economic (any other hotel would have simply upped the rates to banish the riffraff). Rather, the changes were chiefly behavioral. In what might stand as a unique achievement in the history of hotel management, The Atlanta improved its guest list by preaching decorum.

Framed in the library-museum-lobby was an obituary of Dr. Max Henn, which spoke of his "generosity, old world charm, and incorrigible flirtatiousness—he was a ladies' man through and through (and he always had his way without resistance!); he often admitted that that was his only vice (he had no other; indeed he was never a night-lifer, never went night-clubbing, never went to the bars).

"[He] tirelessly instilled in his nearest and dearest an endless dedication to learning and competence, an impatience with weakness, a loathing for stupidity and for those who would work without engaging their brains."

His portrait hung on one wall; a youthful portrait of his widow, a beautiful Thai, graced another. A footnoted guide to Thai culture and customs, written by the son as a service to guests, sat atop a lectern, while the son's books—*The History of Materialism, L'Idée de l'Etat*—filled the glass bookcase above the two roll-top desks in the small space labeled "Guests' Writing Room." (When not running The Atlanta, Dr. Henn—once again distinguishing himself in the hotel management community—teaches graduate students in the Department of Political Science and International Studies at the University of Birmingham in England. He also serves as an independent adviser on East Asian affairs.) Tucked away in a corner sat a pair of computer terminals.

Heading up to my room, I stopped and read more fully about prostitutes and catamites. (A guest could spend an entire day reading at The Atlanta without ever opening a book.) They were, of course, *persona non grata.* "However," the sign instructed, "a guest who gets desperate and finds it necessary to bring back a bargirl or the like might be tolerated provided no law is broken. Note the word is tolerated, not welcome. Don't expect us or fellow guests to be polite about it. We will not apologize for being unwelcoming, rude, or downright offensive."

After less than a day at The Atlanta I was seized by two conflicting desires: To bring back a bargirl and to meet Dr. Henn.

All hotels are surrogates for home, some of them more luxurious, some of them less. Even the lowly ones we cherish, because in a place where all our senses are stretched—a new city, a foreign land—they make it O.K. to fall unconscious. They conquer the alien with the intimacy of a bed. Staying in a hotel is as close as we get to returning to the womb.

Which is why you often see people deliberating in the lobby, back-slapping in the bar, opening their doors to room-service carts. They're in no hurry to brave the elements. Here is safety and order; out there the big, thrumming unknown.

The Atlanta offered no bar (a magnet for bargirls) or room service, but it had a comfortable, clubby feel that made it an especially difficult place to leave. Stepping out in the morning, even into the gripping maw that is Bangkok, you always had the nagging suspicion that you were going to miss something good. And when you returned in the evening, the people huddled in the restaurant somehow looked more intriguing than the in-house diners at other hotels.

Breakfast was a much-anticipated event. My second morning I studied the menu while listening to madrigals. In addition to footnotes, giving the historical and cultural backgrounds of the various dishes, were literary quotations. "There is no love sincerer than the love of food"—George Bernard Shaw. (One that, banned from writing, I committed to memory.) In the back were specials named for friends of The Atlanta.

When my banana shake arrived, I eagerly picked it up and turned over the coaster.

> There are only two things to do with prospective guests: welcome them if they are decent and clean, or welcome somebody else if they are not. We don't rent rooms to Calibans.
> —Dr. Henn's instruction to reception.
> Number 3 of an indefinite set.

"What does yours say?" I asked the woman at the neighboring table.

"What?"

"What's written on the other side of your coaster?"

"I didn't know anything was."

She was a freelance writer from New York City, traveling around Asia on a quest for self-realization. Which perhaps explained her blissful unawareness of her immediate surroundings. Though she was very conscious of her pocketbook. "You can get better rooms at this price in other parts of the city," she said. "I don't like the Sukhumvit area."

The Atlanta, never at a loss for words, had a sign at the reception desk for people like her. "Complaints are not permitted," it read, "not at the prices we charge."

The hotel sat next to a Baptist church at the end of

Sukhumvit Soi 2, one of the quietest of the numerous dead-end streets that stretch off from Sukhumvit Road like the elongated legs of a centipede. Sukhumvit Soi 4, by contrast, throbbed with bars—musical stockyards—that spilled forth women of wide-ranging affections. It was one of those places in Bangkok where Western men suffering from low self-esteem can receive instant cures.

The night I discovered it, Dr. Henn's exhortations no longer seemed so excessive. Nor did they derive, I realized, from simply a moral position. For over half a century, his family's hotel had graced a neighborhood that he had watched turn from modest to grotesque. The sex industry had become a blight on his home; its hangers-on culture an affront to his sensibilities. In one of the articles displayed in the lobby he was quoted as saying: "I am more in sympathy with the nineteenth century, or pre-war Europe, than I am with post-war Europe, let alone the twenty-first century." And this was reflected in his inheritance. Hotels by their very nature transport you to a different place; The Atlanta deposited you in another time. That it was a little voluble in doing so was understandable; it was a strident fogey because the world outside had become a strident boor. It didn't just provide a wholesome environment for foreign tourists, it carved a preserve of civility out of the encroaching 'tude. It was as advertised—"untouched by pop culture and post-modern vulgarity."

Returning to the hotel that night I noticed a sign (what else?) above the entrance: *This is the place you're looking for—if you know it. If you don't you'll never find it.* And finally I saw the hotel's name, engraved on a small silver plaque by the door.

"I wouldn't think this is the sort of place Americans would like."

My new breakfast neighbors were two cheerful, stereotyping Englishwomen on vacation. (Though perhaps they had met the writer from New York.)

"I rather like that the staff's not friendly," the brunette said, smiling. "We were in the lobby yesterday and a woman came in, without a reservation, and asked if she could see a room. And the receptionist said, 'No.' 'Well, can I have a brochure?' 'No.'" Surely, I thought, a Caliban.

After they had gone, I picked up the list of hotel videos. The introduction, which took up three pages, explained that guests would find no pornography (even though, as was pointedly noted, it is available in some upscale hotels), no gratuitous violence, and no pop music videos because they "are common and can be found elsewhere." Waiting for their viewing pleasure instead were numerous films set in Asia (an aside remarked on the large number of Western movie stars who've appeared in such pictures, and a long list followed with all of their names) as well as great films built around the theme of food, including *Tampopo, Eat Drink Man Woman, Babette's Feast,* and *Big Night. La Grande Bouffe* was not in the collection because, for one thing, its humor was scatological.

My pineapple shake arrived on its aphoristic coaster.

> The staff are nice; I am not—which is why the staff are nice. Anyone who expects me to be an obliging, hand-wringing sort of inn-keeper will be sorely disappointed.
>
> —Dr. Henn in conversation.
> Number 1 of an indefinite set.

On my next-to-last morning at The Atlanta, a young woman sat down at the table next to me and then asked the waitress if she could take breakfast in the garden.

"I could not stand the music," she explained when I found her, a half hour later, sipping tea in the shade.

"You don't like baroque?" I asked.

"I think this morning I could not have stood any music."

Jutta was a scientist from Berlin (like Max Henn) but her specialty was nutrition. She was doing research in Bangkok before heading back to "her" village in Laos to gather more data for her doctoral thesis.

"I brought some food with me," she said. "Monkey meat, insects, snakes. I had to keep it cool so I asked Charles if I could use the refrigerator. It was only for a few days. Then I took it to the university, to be analyzed."

I was impressed, not just by her provisions but by her familiarity with Dr. Henn. She wondered if I had met him. I said I hadn't even seen him, though I felt as if I knew him.

She told me that he was setting up a patronage that would allow people in the arts and sciences to stay at the hotel for extended periods. "He wants to encourage people to meet and talk," she said, "like we're doing here."

All over the world I have visited famous literary hotels—the Ritz in Paris, Raffles in Singapore—that today have rates prohibitive to any author not on the bestseller list. The Atlanta, in yet another cap feather, was a writers' hotel that writers could actually afford.

Jutta said that "Charles" had planted a vine that is reputed to prevent as well as treat malaria, and together we searched the garden for it. *Tinospora crispa* was its

Latin name, she said, *kheua kha hor* in Lao. The Laotian woman from the hotel travel office joined us in the hunt, leading us outside and into the parking lot of the Baptist church. A young man appeared from the parish hall and, speaking with the two women, said that the vine we were interested in was available at the market. He'd bring it to the hotel at six that evening.

"That's what I like here," Jutta said. "You ask for something and one thing leads to another. People help you. They look after you."

At precisely six o'clock the man appeared outside the hotel on his bicycle, a plastic shopping bag of *tinospora crispa* hanging from the handlebars. Jutta was nowhere to be seen. The punctual Thai and the tardy German. I handed him 500 baht (the price of a one-night stay) and carried the knobby vine up to my room.

The next day I gave Jutta her medicine, put in a request at the reception desk to see Dr. Henn, packed my suitcase and then ate lunch—a delicious Vegetarian Mussulman Curry—to the sounds of regal jazz. A sign outside the restaurant carried the schedule: "12 noon to 1 p.m.—Music composed by HM the King of Thailand is played during this time every day. Music from 5 p.m. Mondays & Fridays—Big band, historic recordings. Tuesdays, Thursdays & Saturdays—Classic jazz. Wednesdays & Sundays—Big band, modern recordings. Music selection by Charles Henn. All royalties paid."

After my meal I retired to the garden to pass the time before heading to the station. As I was writing my notes, a man appeared in white slacks (I was sitting down) and a dark green shirt (the button-down collar cavalierly—or professorially—left unbuttoned). He introduced himself as Charles Henn.

This was a surprise. He shied away from publicity, to such an extent that he had acquired a reputation as a mysterious figure. And he didn't look at all as I had pictured him: wizened and sour; instead he was boyish, almost jaunty, with something of a mischievous twinkle in his eyes. A wave of relief washed over me, but I didn't offer my hand.

We moved into the restaurant, where I told him that in three decades of travel I had never come across a hotel like his.

"This is largely because I am not a hotel man," he said. "I am an academic. My intellectual love is political theory." He added, "I don't have the heart to sell it. It is the one concrete thing my parents made. The satisfaction comes from the fact that I've kept it going. And that guests love it so much."

It was not, he said, a profitable venture, and was not meant to be. "I don't even know what the rooms cost. My mother takes care of the financial side."

His concern was its spirit—its appearance and character. He insisted that the décor, at least in the common areas, conform as closely as possible to his father's original design. The plastic chairs by the pool were a constant source of irritation to him, and he planned to replace them very soon. "What you see today is 20 percent of what I want to do with the place. There's still 80 percent more I want to do. Whether I actually do it is another question."

The staff provided a measure of continuity, with families staying on sometimes for generations. "It's almost like a tenured job," he said. "The staff know what to do but, being Thai, they often don't do it. But the loyalty is there. They don't have the superficial manners that you find in some other hotels, but they have a tremendous sense of goodwill toward the guests.

"Security is good here because the staff feel it's home. Nothing ever goes missing; it wouldn't occur to them to take something."

I asked about the signs and messages. They appeared after his father's death in 2002. "Bangkok is viewed as a place where you can do anything," he said with the faint hint of a twinkle, clearly relishing the fact that he had created within it a tasteful space where you can't.

As he talked, it became clear that he was not the puritan the signage might suggest. He had become, he said proudly, the only non-British member of the British Academy of Gastronomes. And he expressed surprising sympathy, considering all his dictums, for older men who come to Bangkok for obvious reasons. "Often they're widowers or divorced. They treat the girls much better than the young ones do. The young ones say, 'We're not sex tourists, not like those guys with their beer guts.' I say, 'You just hope that at that age your gut is not so big and that you still have a libido to want a girl.' I don't condone them. I just prefer them to the young ones."

I complimented him on the music. "Truthfully," he said, "I tolerate jazz. I like opera, and classical music. I don't listen to modern composers."

He was a patron of the traditional performing arts, and was currently working with the Joe Louis Classical Thai Puppet Theater in connection with their upcoming production, a scene from the Ramakian, the Thai version of the Indian epic, Ramayana.

"I'm translating the libretto so that they can have subtitles in English," he explained. "I translate from classical Thai into Shakespearean English." I thought of the father's obituary, and his antipathy "for those who would work without engaging their brains."

A young woman had come in during our conversation and taken a seat at the far end of the restaurant. Dr. Henn now told me that she was from the theater, here for their appointment. I thanked him for his time, and apologized for taking so much of it. Then I walked out to the lobby to collect my bags while the hotelier moved on to his libretto.

❦ ❦ ❦

Thomas Swick is the travel editor of the South Florida Sun-Sentinel. *He is the author of* A Way to See the World: From Texas to Transylvania with a Maverick Traveler *and of the travel memoir,* Unquiet Days: At Home in Poland. *His work has appeared in* The New York Times Book Review, The Washington Post Book World, The American Scholar, Oxford American, North American Review, Ploughshares, Commonweal, *and* National Geographic Traveler. *His essays have been anthologized in* The Best American Travel Writing.

~ぐ ~ぐ ~ぐ

Clutching My Soul in Paradise

A boy learns indelible lessons about time and life.

"'OARS! OARS!' HE INTENSELY WHISPERED, seizing the helm—'grip your oars, and clutch your souls, now! My God, men, stand by!'"

Herman Melville's Ahab had never been to Papua New Guinea, and pursuing a whale was not really akin to investigating a plane wreck, but the words he uttered were dead on. It was May 1986, and I was twelve years old. My introduction to the world outside America had begun.

Papua New Guinea was ten years old and still grappling with what it meant to be a nation in 1986. Its 5 million citizens spoke some 800 languages, and its towns and villages hosted more missionaries than tourists.

Its stamps celebrated traditional skirts, but also Queen Elizabeth's birthday. Its markets were laid out lazily in the shade, swollen with ripe tropical fruit sold by betel-nut-chewing mothers nursing their babies. Tropical, laid back, young—Papua New Guinea was what some called paradise.

But it was another title that I heard more often. "Land of the Unexpected," read the Air Niugini posters, stunningly illustrated with slender palm trees, a thatched-roof hut by the sea, and smiling locals. But they could just have honestly depicted belching volcanoes, earthquake damage, or a gang of unemployed youths sporting machetes and homemade shotguns just before raping someone. Paradise is never postcard-perfect.

From the provincial capital of Madang my father and I flew aboard a single-engine Cessna into the heart of the country. From the grass airstrip we took a motorized canoe several hours up the log-infested Sogeram River, arriving in the village just before sunset, where we were welcomed by an American missionary who called this remote corner of the world home. It was a typical village: kids wearing ragged secondhand shorts or skirts, angled palm trees, huts elevated on posts, topless women cooking sago, insatiable mosquitoes, infected sores, debilitating disease.

A couple days after arriving we received a radio message from Madang: The U.S. Embassy had received a report of a downed aircraft about fifteen miles from our location. Would we be willing to hike to the site and confirm the crash and then, if possible, determine if the plane was American?

When World War II finally ended in 1945, the remains of 78,000 U.S. military personnel had yet to be

either identified or recovered. Sixty years later the search
continues, and each year remains are found and brought
home. The Pentagon estimates that more than two hundred and fifty aircraft are still unaccounted for in Papua
New Guinea alone, where the jungle gives up its war
ghosts reluctantly and will surely never reveal them all.
But when it does the army dispatches a team from the
Central Identification Laboratory in Hawaii. A typical
recovery operation might include medics, forensic an-
thropologists, an explosive ordnance disposal technician,
a photographer, and mortuary affairs specialists. But
first the wreckage needs to be confirmed, and at least on
one occasion it was a twelve-year-old and his dad whom
the government asked to investigate.

When we set off from the Sogeram with a local guide,
the morning fog had yet to give way to the sun, and
smoke from breakfast fires hung low around the houses.
Hoarse roosters were still issuing their cries. Being off
the power grid (as was most of the country), the village
pulsed to a rhythm I had not known in the West—it
woke slowly, almost gently, and in a way that connected
you to thousands of years of human history. It was a culture carefully attuned to the position of the sun instead
of the product of wires strung to poles. Here I tasted a
forgotten simplicity (not to be confused with easiness), a
new intimacy.

I also learned that a remote village can seem like the
center of civilization once you exchange it for the jungle.
It took only a moment for the village to vanish behind
us. Gone was the subtle comfort of numbers, the smoke
which signaled community, the land cleared of trees so
that light could reach earth. The jungle canopy was an
impenetrable shroud, and in its shadow people ventured

but did not dwell. It belonged to the wild pigs and cassowaries, the hornbills and cockatoos, the pythons and legions of insects. It did not belong to people.

The path was littered with leeches. Looking like black inchworms, they stood upright in the wet foliage along the trail, as if eager to praise those who passed by. They latched hungrily onto legs, however, even slipping deep into sneakers, and found their way to other parts of the body as well. We paused often to pluck or burn them off.

We stumbled over roots and waded through shallow swamps, but always we charged forward. I had never walked thirty some miles in a single day, but we had to reach the plane by midday if we were to return to the village by nightfall. About an hour before reaching the site we emerged from the jungle, squinting into an intense sunlight that beat down on thatched roofs, naked children, grunting pigs, and baby cassowaries that ran around looking very confused at our presence. I was the youngest white person many, perhaps all, had ever seen. The village was tiny, home to maybe a dozen families. It was also remote, even more than the one we had slept in last night, which at least had river access to the outside world.

Someone brought us each a stick of sugarcane. The ultra-sweet juice, as well as the act of chewing hard to get at it, refreshed us. We also shared a papaya. The most interesting moment of our short pause in the village, however, was meeting an old man who, with tremendous gesticulation and excited eyes, relived the day he saw two planes fighting in the sky. A red circle was painted on one plane, he said, and in the struggle it exploded not far above the jungle canopy. The entire village was terrified and for a time moved away from the area.

We left the village with a better idea of what to expect at the site. The wreckage would not be intact and it was likely Japanese. Still, I wondered. All morning the image of a weathered skeleton crumbled in a rusted-out cockpit had stayed fast in my boyish mind, and I wasn't yet willing to let it go.

Several weeks earlier I had visited a different village and hiked to another wreck that rested deep in the jungle. It was American and the site had already been excavated and the airmen's remains recovered. The plane was partially intact, indicating that the jungle canopy had broken its fall. A giant propeller lay twisted to one side of the fuselage and was planted in the earth, as if it were standing guard over the rest of the wreckage. But perhaps the most moving sight was the white star that still clung to the fuselage. It had faded, but its shape had not changed at all, nor did the symbolism behind it. This was a piece of America which, like the temples of Angkor in Cambodia, was now forever wed to the jungle.

Village children accompanied us to the site and crawled all over the aluminum hulk with typical agility and balance. Several dug into the soil and pulled out corroded .50-caliber cartridges to offer me as a gift. They were only children, but they knew that once my country had fought here, and they were keen to connect me to the wreck.

This same week, perhaps on a morning I heard Johnny Cash's voice groaning from a villager's short-wave radio, the United States bombed Libya. A few days later, when a twin-engine prop plane circled our village, people ran to us with an urgent question: *Do you know who is in that plane?* No, we said. Moments later many fled deep into the jungle, certain that Libya had come to bomb the village since PNG was a friend of the United States. It happened in the 1940s with Japan, so why not now?

Paradise, I learned, has a history, and in ways one least expects it affects the lives of its people.

"Hap bilong balus!" a guide exclaimed, pointing to a barely discernable scrap of metal that must have belonged to the plane. We had arrived. For half an hour we crisscrossed the area, examining debris. A propeller sat off alone among vines and was the only clue that these hundreds of screws, rings, pipes, and scraps belonged to an aircraft. We confirmed it was not American by locating a mechanical part—the specs were written in Japanese.

It was a long hike back to the Sogeram, made even longer by the several-pound chunk of metal I felt compelled to carry with me. Our guide—cut like a gymnast and physically unfazed by thirty-miles-in-a-day—moved at warp speed. Perhaps convinced that "white skins" couldn't move fast enough to make it back by sunset—and Papua New Guineans are loath to travel by night in the jungle—he had urged us to spend the night in the village near the site. It wasn't a bad idea, but the village on the Sogeram was expecting us and would worry if we didn't show. And so with rubbery legs we emerged from the jungle at dusk. Civilization had seldom looked so attractive—it had a chair for relaxing, a river for bathing, and it was clear of leeches.

Days later, Dad lay sprawled out in the dugout, reading a *National Geographic Traveler* article on some

European city, as we motored back to the airstrip en route to Madang. We rounded a bend and disturbed a crocodile that, like us, was engaged in the prehistoric art of sunbathing. Just as the jungle consumed wrecks, the river consumed entire trees, sweeping them off their banks during rainy season and driving them downstream till they lodged in awkward positions. But in the land of the unexpected, it was not just machine and tree that were consumed. Riding with us in the canoe was a healthy sixteen-year-old boy who had one of the brightest smiles in the village. I would never see that smile again—several weeks later he would die of cerebral malaria.

Late in the afternoon the Cessna touched down in Madang. A picturesque coastal town with a population of 25,000, Madang's significance at the moment rested firmly in the availability of French fries, cold Coke, and electric fans and lights—things you didn't have in the bush. Cars rolled down lazy streets, giant fruit bats screamed from their pine tree perches, and a modest supermarket rented videos. The local theater, a Quonset hut built at the end of World War II, announced the upcoming feature: *To Live and Die in LA*.

But in the end, to be honest, it was the sea that made the town great. The tiny islands dotting the harbor, the vibrant colors of fish and coral below, the towering volcanic island visible far to the north, the silent fisherman in an outrigger canoe, the occasional foreign ship filling its hull with a cargo of copra—it was the sea that contained these things.

And it was the sea, so vast and undefined, that mirrored back to me the depth and mystery of my own spirit. Madang's lighthouse, which rises at the harbor's entrance, was dedicated in 1959 to the Australian men who stayed behind enemy lines during the war to observe Japanese ship and plane movements. I went here to observe as well, but I saw other things on the horizon. I saw my future being shaped by my present—by people and wrecks, rivers and fruit, by things unexpected. I saw that time darts as quickly as a spooked fish, and that sometimes our spirit rumbles with the terrible beauty of a volcano. I saw also that there is such a thing as a human hull, which our years generously, and sometimes painfully, load with experience. And I saw that in moving forward we cut through uncharted waters that will never be explored in full. All this to say, I saw what made Ahab cry, "Grip your oars, and clutch your souls, now! My God, men, stand by!"

I was twelve years old, in a place some called paradise.

❧ ❧ ❧

Joel Carillet has a master's degree in Church History and has spent much of the past six years working overseas. He taught at a college in Ukraine, worked for a study abroad program in Egypt, did human rights work in the West Bank, and spent fourteen months traveling overland from Beijing to Istanbul. Among his memorable experiences traveling was listening to Henry Kissinger talk politics with a White House official as they all stood before their respective urinals in a Washington, D.C. hotel.

~~ ~~ ~~

Bees Born of Tears

To be healed is to take a journey into all of creation.

Sonia shifts her baby to the other hip and tosses me a stick. "Here, Laurita," she says, breathless. "For the dogs."

The main street of Huajolotitlan—"Turkeyland" in the language of the Aztecs—is a 45-degree angle, so steep you want to use your hands to crawl up. Brutal midafternoon sunlight glares off the pavement. Low buildings line the street, cement and adobe shops painted pastels and stained with urine. I catch a whiff of fresh blood from a pink *pollería* with its plastic bowls of goopy, featherless, dead chickens. Other shops sell only a handful of bare necessities—tiny packets of chili peanuts, toilet paper, cooking oil, Coke, warm beer, all neatly lined up on shelves behind the counter. Shop owners peer out of the cool interiors; a man in the shadows hisses at me, *güera, güera*—white girl, white girl. Sonia and I walk in silence, keeping our mouths closed to seal in the moisture.

We are on our way to see María Chiquita—María the Very Little One. All I know about her is this: she is tiny; she is nearly a century old; she is a *curandera*—a traditional healer.

I've been staying in a nearby Mixtec town in Oaxaca, Mexico, where I lived and taught English two years earlier. This summer I'm visiting villages, talking to women and healers for my Master's fieldwork. Sonia, a former student with family in Huajolotitlan, has offered to take me to María Chiquita.

Two years ago I would have been bursting with the anticipation of meeting this *curandera*, but now my forehead is furrowed and my eyes stinging from the dry heat. Despite the constant presence of people, I feel alone, an observer of life more than a participant. I have just turned twenty-seven and nearly every woman my age here has several kids already. During my interviews, women shake their heads and cluck sympathetically when they discover I have no children. Around me, despite poverty, people are having families, living their lives.

On this trip, my former students, who haven't seen me for two years, seem worried about me. "You look different," they say, "pale, thin, sickly." A poet friend said with deep concern, "Laurita, you seem *demacrada*." I'd never heard that word before—it is a poet's word, not something I could pick up on the street. "Something is missing," he explained. "Your *chispa*." Your spark.

I tried to joke about it. "Oh, it's the bad food up North. No fresh mangoes and chilies and tortillas."

He didn't laugh.

I finally said, in a naked, shaky voice, that the two years with my ex-boyfriend, Manuel, were hard, very hard. The half year since the breakup has been just as hard, in a different way. Manuel's words come back like a curse, each syllable punctuated in precise Spanish-accented consonants: "You will never be in love again."

Sonia and I veer onto a dirt path, where turkeys peck at old plastic bottles and silver potato chip packages.

"We're here," she says, motioning to a small reed hut with a woven palm roof. It is a quaint, lopsided structure, suggesting the home of a witch, a fairy, an elf, some other-worldly creature. A horde of dogs guards the dwelling, their skin stretched taut over the ribs, sparse fur standing up angrily. They begin a cacophony of barks and growls, which makes the baby wail.

Sonia quickly pulls the blanket over her daughter's head and whispers, "*Chchch, m'hija,* don't cry." There is urgency in her voice. I wonder if she worries that her daughter could get sick from *espanto*—fright—from the dogs. This belief is so pervasive that even miniskirt-wearing, web-surfing, twenty-one-year-old Sonia probably feels it in her bones. When a person is frightened, her spirit separates from her body; at that moment, the spirit-owner of the land captures her spirit and holds it prisoner. The person grows ill and could even die unless a healer performs a ritual to retrieve the spirit. Most people I know here say they have been afflicted with *espanto* at one time or another, often from encounters with the ubiquitous, vicious dogs in Mixtec communities.

I wave the stick in the air like a sword, and the dogs keep their distance. Sonia and I huddle in a sparse bit of shade under a mesquite tree, waiting for someone to call off the dogs. She murmurs under the blanket all the while, into that intimate space between baby and mother.

After the conversation with my poet friend, I looked up *demacrada* in my dictionary. Emaciated. What he meant was spiritually emaciated. I tell myself that life is a series of little deaths and rebirths—part of yourself dies; a new part is born. But what if some essential part of yourself disappears, and there's nothing to replace it?

Maybe the heat is making me delirious, launching me into the dreamy beginnings of heat exhaustion . . . but something odd is seeping into this scene in María Chiquita's yard . . . the ancient, musty odor of a folk tale. A wanderer approaches a hut, thirsty and exhausted, having climbed a nearly endless hill and confronted savage beasts, hoping to see the mysterious wise woman who will bestow upon her . . . ? For a moment, life takes on the crystalline structure of a myth, the pattern of a snowflake, the spiral of a shell. Everything is part of the movement drawing me closer to the center, closer to some truth.

Two girls appear at the door of the hut—about three and eight years old—and walk toward us. They're wearing jelly shoes and well-worn dresses a few sizes too big. Their brown twig legs are scaly with dust.

Sonia shifts her baby to the other hip. "*Buenas tardes, niñas.* We're looking for Doña María Chiquita."

Whispering together excitedly about *la gringuita,* the girls lead us to the door of the hut, protecting us from the dogs with well-aimed stones, and call out "*¡Tía!*"

A tiny woman appears at the door. She barely reaches my shoulder, which would put her at about four-foot-four.

She wears a pink polyester dress, a blue-checked cotton apron, a red cable knit cardigan, and a heap of tangled necklaces—plastic pearls and gold chains and leather strings, each holding its medley of saints and crucifixes. A round pair of glasses with thick lenses, eighties-style, covers much of her face. Intricate networks of wrinkles spread out from her mouth and eyes, like the dried-up, folded skirts of mountains. Age spots a shade darker than her brown skin speckle her face. Her thick, muscular hands seem out of proportion to her bird-like body.

"*¡María Purísima Santísima!*" She smiles a toothless smile and gives me a tight hug saturated with wood smoke and copal incense.

Sonia glances at me with raised eyebrows and a shrug that says she has no idea what's going on.

It *is* strange. María Chiquita had no way of knowing we were coming, yet she acts as though she's known us all our lives, as though she's been expecting us. She is overflowing with something, exploding with it, even. No doubt about it, this woman has *chispa*.

"*¡Ay, muchachita!*" she says to me. "Come in, come in! Sit down, *m'hija,* my daughter." Her voice is nasal and urgent.

I duck through the doorway and follow her into a dark, windowless room with parallel slivers of sunlight spilling through the walls onto the dirt floor. There's an altar to the right, a wooden table crowded with candles flickering in small glasses, and a multitude of framed saints and Virgins amidst vases of carnations and daisies. A clay incense pot with charred remains of pine and copal holds a lingering smell of smoky resin. A few *petates*—woven palm mats—are rolled up in the corner. Clay pots with their bottoms burned black hang from the wall. The only furniture is a small stool and two wooden chairs. The air smells cool and earthy like a cave.

María Chiquita gestures to the chairs. "Sit down, sit down, *muchachita!*" She is barefoot, her century-old feet caked with dust and dry as leather, rough as paws or hooves.

Here in the Mixteca, people tell a story of a spirit woman called the *bandolera*, a beautiful woman with the feet of an animal—in some versions, turkey claws, in others, *burro* or horse hooves. She lives in a cave full of candles, each representing a life. The short candles are lives about to end, the long ones, newborn babies. In my favorite version, she brings certain people to her cave to teach them the secrets of life and death.

A woman appears at another door that leads to a dirt courtyard where people are milling around, engaged in various tasks. The woman is middle-aged, a bit taller than María Chiquita and much wider. She introduces herself as María Chiquita's daughter, visiting from Mexico City. "Fidelina Lopez Martinez. *Para servirle.*" Light from the doorway illuminates her face, round and damp with sweat from some exertion in the courtyard.

The girls carry in an extra chair—a plastic one with a Sol beer logo—and a bottle of Coke. The older girl pours me a glass and the little one offers it to me with both hands. "Here you are, *gringuita.*" The warm syrup feels sweet on my tongue, the bubbles sharp.

Now Fidelina and María Chiquita let the questions fly. Where are you from!? What are you doing all the way out here? Do you like our food? Do you like our village? Where is your mother? Are you married? Do you have children? Wave after wave of sheer, giddy exhilaration. The air is electric.

Fidelina tells us that her mother doesn't hear well, so I talk loudly, imitating Fidelina's loud, slow voice. "I'm from the United States," I say. "Maryland." I translate the state's name as *"Tierra de María."*

"¡María Santísima Purísima!" María Chiquita shrieks. "You traveled far!"

I answer the rest of the questions, explaining that I haven't lived with my mother for nearly ten years, that I like spicy food, I like Turkey-land, and that I'm an old maid, childless and husbandless.

As we talk, bees spiral and dip around our heads, attracted, I guess, to the Coke. Sonia shoos them away from her baby, who has fallen asleep. I move my head around in a dance to get out of the bees' paths. The last time I was stung, years ago, on my finger, my entire hand ballooned up. María Chiquita and her daughter let the bees land on their shoulders, rest in their hair.

"And what are you doing all the way out here, *m'hija?*" María Chiquita asks.

"Sonia tells me you're a *curandera.* I wanted to meet you."

"Ah! So that's why!" Fidelina shouts. "My *mamacita* is ninety-six years old! Can you believe it? Ninety-six! And look! Still strong, isn't she?!"

María Chiquita nods vigorously.

She does look strong. More than strong. The whirl-wind inside her nearly lifts her small body off the floor. There is something I can learn from this woman, with her candles, with her secrets of life and death.

Fidelina turns to Sonia. "Who is your mother?" she asks, trying to place her in the web of families of Huajolotitlan.

Sonia tells them and adds, "My mother brought me and my sister here when we had *espanto.*"

"Ah, yes, *muchacha!*" María Chiquita says. "I remember you."

"What gave you *espanto?*" I ask Sonia.

"Some dogs." She kisses her baby, who is asleep now. "They scared me, and after that I couldn't sleep. I cried a lot. I didn't feel like eating."

People say that unless the child is cured she might die, or continue to live in a weakened state, missing the essential part of herself. I wonder if you can get used to living without parts of your spirit, like someone who's missing a finger and compensates with others. How many bits of my spirit have I lost over the years? Is my spirit scarred and mutilated, with chunks missing here and there? Or have they grown back, like the arms of a starfish, the tails of lizards?

When I was nine, one day I was rollerskating in the alley near my house, when two Dobermans—trained attack dogs—were let out of a parked car to enter their cage. The dogs bolted toward me and pounced. I clung to a splintery telephone pole as the dogs tore into my upper arm and thigh. The owner retrieved them, and, ignoring the blood and tears, told me to go home. "You're okay," he insisted, probably afraid of being sued. I skated home in shock.

That's when I started acting weird. I was terrified of any door clicking shut, convinced I would get locked in. I refused to be left without an adult for even a minute. I tolerated no dark corners, and frantically turned on all the lights in the house. My weirdness tapered off after a year, replaced by occasional dreams of wandering lost in a labyrinth of alleys. They were eerie dreams, very real, as though some part of myself was stuck amidst the trash cans and wire fences and weeds poking through cracked concrete.

I wonder now if I needed someone to retrieve my spirit and return it to my body. Literally or symbolically, it didn't matter. And now, after this relationship with Manuel has left me *demacrada,* I need a ritual, too. A part of myself got lost, and I need to find it.

María Chiquita must notice that part of my spirit is missing, because she announces, "I'm going to give you a *limpia, m'hija.*"

"Good," I say. "I need one."

Sonia stares at me. "Are you sure?" She lowers her voice. "You know what she's going to do to you?"

"*Más o menos.*" More or less.

"But Laurita, your clothes will get soaked. You don't have to do it."

"I want to. Really." Anyway, Fidelina and the girls are already spreading out the *petate.*

"Take off your clothes, *muchachita,*" María Chiquita orders.

This is an unexpected twist. I hesitate, trying to re-member which underwear I have on.

"Down to your underwear!"

I take off my sandals. At least my clothes won't get wet this way.

Sonia bites her lip and watches, amused.

Voices float in from outside, where men and women are doing chores in the dirt courtyard. Hopefully they can't see me undressing.

I strip. My underwear turns out to be an ancient pair, once white, now grayish, mismatched with a grubby, frayed bra. I sit like a skinny plucked chicken on the *petate,* goose-bumped and shivering. The dried palm itches my thighs. I wonder if tiny bugs live between the fibers.

María Chiquita pulls a bottle of neon green liquid from a crate in the corner. I've seen *limpias* done with clear mezcal—fermented agave nectar—but I don't recognize this stuff. *"Agua de Siete Machos,"* she calls it. Water of the Seven Macho Males? She holds it under my nose. It smells like cheap cologne. I sneeze.

Fidelina hurries out the door and returns moments later with a handful of fresh *sauco* leaves and hands it to her mother.

María Chiquita prays at her altar, then rubs the herbs over me, in my hair, my shoulder, arms, back, legs, the soles of my feet. The *sauco* smells fragrant, potent. She prays to God, the Virgins, the saints, punctuating her chanting with "Laura." My self-consciousness fades, and I focus on her voice, on the leaves' friction over my skin.

Then she murmurs, like a stage direction between prayers, "Take off your glasses, *muchachita*."

The older girl carefully takes them for safe-keeping.

"Close your eyes!" María Chiquita whispers.

I obey. I feel the shock of cool alcohol spit onto my skin. It is a jarring sensation, pulling me out of a certain dullness. I imagine all the *mal aire*—bad air—blown away with these great bursts. I imagine my spirit, something iridescent and alive, something like a blue butterfly, flying through the door and into my open chest, nestling where it belongs.

When the spitting ends, I open my eyes. The girl hands me my glasses. I look down at my ratty underwear, now spotted with lime green. I shiver and smile at María Chiquita, her eyes huge and wild behind her thick lenses.

The bees seem even more attracted to me now that I'm covered in neon green stuff. I'm fully clothed again.

I'd like to stand up to have more space to dodge the bees, but in a gesture of politeness typical in Mixtec villages, Fidelina insists I stay glued to the chair. The bees zoom around my head. I pray they don't sting. Who knows if the local hospital is stocked with epinephrine.

"Don't mind the bees," María Chiquita says. "They are good, these bees!"

The bees are buzzing around our heads like crazy now, two bees in particular, circling each other, spiraling around each other as if dancing. I duck out of their way.

"Don't worry," Fidelina says. "They won't sting you."

"But I'm allergic."

"Look! Look how those two bees are staying near you and my *mamacita*."

Sure enough, the two bees seem to be doing figure eights around María Chiquita's and my heads. Urgent, frenetic spirals.

"The bees are your spirits. See, they have met before, your spirits. They met each other first and they led your bodies together."

María Chiquita nods.

The wings inside my chest move, I can feel them. They move with a thrill, a sense of discovering layers of meaning like ribbons intermingling in the wind. They move with the sudden knowledge that the world is a strange, deep, rich place.

Sonia's baby starts to fuss, and I realize it's nearly dark. "We should go, Laurita," Sonia says.

I hand María Chiquita thirty pesos—about three dollars—her charge for a *limpia*. She hugs me hard and grasps my hand, unwilling to let me go.

"You'll come back tomorrow, right?" Her eyes are full of tears. Her grip is as powerful and genuine as a three-month-old baby's.

"In a few days," I promise.

"Last night," she says, "I was kneeling in front of my altar, crying because of how we suffer. Because we are poor, my family. I asked Nuestro Señor to look after us. '*Señor Jesús, ¡ayúdame!*,' I prayed. 'Help me!' And in my sleep, a baby came to me. A fat white baby in green clothes. Really fat, and really white, like your skin!"

There is a framed picture of a fat white baby in green on the altar, I notice: *El Santo Niño*, the holy baby Jesus.

"And he told me, María, *m'hija*, have faith. Just wait until tomorrow."

She looks at me dramatically. "And today, you come to my door, *muchacha!* He was right, *El Niño Jesús!*"

I think about the three dollars I gave her—possibly enough for a small sack of beans, some eggs, dried corn—enough food for a few days if they really stretched it. Is that what she means? Or is she referring to our new friendship involving bees and spirits, a friendship with its own momentum that won't let a seventy-year age difference and thousands of miles stop it?

A few days later I'm back in the hut, on the plastic Sol chair, with bees once again circling my head, although I don't mind them as much now. Since the *limpia,* I've felt elated. I don't care exactly how the *limpia* worked. I simply enjoy the feeling that my *chispa*—my spark—is returning.

"You remind me of the gypsies!" María Chiquita announces. "They traveled from far away, too." She turns to her daughter for confirmation.

Fidelina nods. "*Muy buena gente,* the gypsies, really good people."

"They don't come anymore!" María Chiquita's eyes fill with tears. "*Ay,* how I miss them!"

"Your skin is white like theirs," Fidelina says.

"And you speak our language in a strange manner, too!" María Chiquita adds, giggling. Her fluidity of emotion amazes me, how she cries at any hint of sadness and laughs heartily at the smallest joke.

"And you're so tall!"

Reminiscing about the gypsies inspires María Chiquita to tell us her story. When she was about six years old, a gypsy woman read her palm and predicted she would live to be a very, very old lady. Soon afterward, María Chiquita came down with a severe and sudden sickness.

Fidelina jumps in. "She died, the poor thing."

"What?" I thought I'd mastered my verb conjugations. "Who died?"

"My poor *mamacita, pobrecita.*"

I turn to María Chiquita. "You died?"

María Chiquita nods solemnly. "I died."

The family mourned her and put white candles all over the room as villagers came to pray and cry over her. In the midst of the darkness and smoke and tears, a drop of candle wax fell onto María Chiquita's arm. She flinched. She woke up. People say that her experience with death gave her the power to heal.

She doesn't remember what happened to her while she was dead, but I wonder if she met the spirit woman of death and life inside her cave of candles. Maybe she taught her how to heal. I imagine each of us with our own cave of candles, parts of ourselves burning down to wax pools, dying, other parts of us just beginning, the candles freshly lit.

It is nearly dark, time for me to leave. I tell María Chiquita and her daughter that I won't see them again for a while. In a few days I'll be heading back to Arizona to finish grad school.

From her altar, María Chiquita takes a photo of a statue of San Sebastián and puts it in my hands. He is dressed royally in a sequined, flowered outfit of turquoise, red, and gold, draped with gold chains and bracelets, flowers and ribbons. His arms are tied to a lopsided cross flanked by two small dark-skinned Jesus crucifixes. Small daggers pierce the man's throat and limbs and his wounds drip blood. Fidelina's reverent look makes me realize this is a very special thing her mother is giving me.

Suffering saints usually frighten me a little, but this one doesn't look in pain so much as wistful. No, this tortured saint is not creepy. It is oddly comforting, actually, to see how he endures his suffering, trusting that his pain will be a flash in eternity, knowing that his wounds will heal, only flowers and sparkles and ribbons remaining.

I think about all the prayers focused on this photo, all the energy directed to it. It is a sacred thing, a thing of power for María Chiquita, and she has given it to me.

We hug. She cries and moans and sobs and chants and prays, making small crosses over me with her hands. "*Que Dios te bendiga, muchacha,* God bless you, girl." Over and over and over again, for a long time.

I'm embarrassed by the attention, unsure how to respond. Not even my own mother has ever given me such a farewell. Then I realize that neither María Chiquita nor her daughter can read or write, so letters won't be possible. She has no phone. She has no money to visit me, no visa. And she is ninety-six years old. Of course she's worried this is the last time we'll see each other.

I am used to traveling, meeting people, saying goodbye. I naïvely believe that we will see each other in a year or two.

Within days, I get an email from Ian, the man I've known for years and will eventually marry. Our relationship is a stream that surfaces, goes underground a bit, and resurfaces. His email now comes after years of little or no communication, since Manuel discouraged our friendship.

Ian's email is three lines. It says he has been remembering the way sunshine smells on my skin. I imagine my spirit, a velvety bee, flying up to Colorado to confer with his spirit. I write back to Ian, and we arrange for him to visit me in Tucson. The following year, we are living together, engaged, in Colorado.

Bees, I discover, are associated with gods of love— Cupid among the Greeks and Kama among Indians. The Welsh believe that bees came from paradise down to earth to give humans gifts of wax and honey—honey to nourish them, and wax to make candles for altars. A bee entering the house is lucky, and one flying around a sleeping child is a sign of a happy life to come. And in Egypt, bees were born of the tears of the Sun-God, Ra, and symbolize the afterlife and rebirth.

A year and a half later, Ian and I walk up the hill in Huajolotitlan, just at dusk, when the air is blue

and magical and tinged with sadness. We have heard
from Sonia that María Chiquita passed away last year,
although Sonia is not completely sure; it could be a
rumor. I remember how María Chiquita defied death
as a six-year-old. I hope it's another mistake.

I pick up a stick to fend off the barking dogs. Someone
is walking toward us, a stout woman. Fidelina.

"*¡Jesús María José!*" She hugs us, moaning and crying,
and then leads us to her siblings, who have come from
other villages. They know my name although we've
never met, and hug us with the same force that Fidelina
does.

"How we prayed you'd come!" she says. "My poor
mamacita always remembered you!"

It turns out we have arrived precisely on the night of
María Chiquita's *cabo de año*—the one-year anniversary
of her death, where family members and friends spend
a week mourning her. I can guess Fidelina's explana-
tion—that the spirit of her *mamacita* buzzed up to the
U.S. to invite my spirit to the *cabo de año*.

Fidelina ushers us into the hut and gives us sweet cin-
namon coffee and sugary pastries.

The altar is overflowing with carnations and roses.
The light from the candles is stronger than that of
the bare bulb dangling overhead. In back of the hut
are shadows of people milling around, talking quietly.
Other relatives wander into the room and greet us. They
have heard of me, María Chiquita's dear friend from
the United States. They have heard how our spirits flew
together as bees.

The sugar, the caffeine, the shadows, the candle-
light—they lend a surreal quality to the night, and I can
almost see, in the midst of so many flames, a tiny body

laid out. I tip over a candle, let a drop of beeswax fall, and wake her up, knowing that resurrections happen all the time.

☙ ☙ ☙

Laura Resau teaches Cultural Anthropology and English as a Second Language at Front Range Community College in Fort Collins, Colorado. Her writing has appeared in magazines including Cicada, Cricket, *and* Brain, Child, *and the anthology* By the Seat of My Pants. *Her young adult novel,* What the Moon Saw, *about an American girl who spends the summer in Oaxaca with her shaman grandmother, will soon be published. Visit Laura at www.lauraresau.com.*

❦ ❦ ❦

Road Roulette

They redefined the meaning of laid-back for him.

BY MY SECOND DAY OF THUMBING RIDES THROUGH Lithuania, I finally feel like I've hit a hitchhiking rhythm, even though my progress (less than one hundred miles) hasn't been particularly impressive. Standing at the edge of a town called Marijampole, thumb aloft, I keep my patience—despite the fact that I'm in my third hour of waiting for a ride. The Polish border, my goal for the day, is still a tantalizing twenty miles away.

Regardless of where you are in the world, hitchhiking comes with its own set of basic procedures: choosing a safe roadside hitching spot where traffic is slow enough to stop; refusing to accept rides from drunk or suspicious or crazy people; staying wary, bringing a map, using common sense. Patience, that mossy old virtue, is central to all of this. With the proper amount of patience, hitching can be a safe and interesting way to see Europe and—most importantly—it can allow you to interact with the kind of people you'd never see on the tourist routes.

The inspiration to hitch first struck me two nights ago, while I was researching my Poland guidebook in a McDonald's near the Vilnius bus station. I'd heard great things about Poland from other travelers, but the more I read about places like Gdansk and Poznan and Czestochowa, the more demoralized I became. From a planning perspective, Poland was just too big and interesting. To tackle the Tatras Mountains in the south might mean missing the Bialowieza Forest in the north; to tour the Renaissance village of Zamosc in the east might mean missing the avant-garde university town of Wroclaw in the west; to experience the cosmopolitan culture of Warsaw or Krakow might mean missing the folk culture of the countryside.

Sometimes, choice presents itself as a glossy act of destruction—of eliminating possibilities in the name of decisiveness. This is why—halfway through a Lithuanian Big Mac—I decided to give Poland up to chance instead of choice: I decided to simply find a highway, stick out my thumb and let fate take me for a ride. Thus, by turning my travels into a kind of road roulette, I could experience each moment of Poland without having to worry about where I stood in relation to point A or B.

Each new ride and random stop-off, I'd hoped, would reveal Poland not as a mere destination—but as a continuously unfolding mystery.

The most immediate challenge upon starting my hitchhiking adventure yesterday came in trying to get out of Vilnius, my starting point. The problem with Vilnius isn't that Lithuanians don't stop for hitchhikers—the problem is that hitching rides in Lithuania is a wildly popular pastime. On a warm Sunday afternoon in Vilnius, the competition for rides can be daunting. When I arrived at the A1 highway ramp at noon, I was greeted by an outright crowd of Lithuanian hitchhikers strung out down the road. Keeping true to etiquette, I took a place twenty yards beyond the last person, stuck out my thumb, and waited.

And waited.

When competing with other hitchers on a balmy Lithuanian day, being male, solo, and six-foot-three is hardly the best marketing formula. After two hours of wagging my thumb at traffic, my arm was sore and my feet were tired. Over a dozen hitchers ahead and behind me had already been picked up, almost all of them females. Male hitchers (myself included) stood forlornly at the front of the queue while female hitchers got whisked off within minutes of arriving.

This ongoing phenomenon was about to drive me into pessimism and despair when a Lithuanian girl stepped off a local bus one block down and walked right up to where I was standing.

"Do you mind if I hitch with you?" she asked. "I have this habit of not hitching by myself."

I looked at the girl and blinked. She had a Betty Boop haircut, a small shoulder bag full of gear, and fantastic green eyes. She'd approached me without a trace of apprehension, and she'd somehow known that I spoke English. Since I'd only seen this kind of luck as a beer commercial plot device, I decided to clarify.

"Why do you want to ride with me?"

"You're American," she said. "Foreign travelers are always a safe bet. Plus you speak English and so do I."

"Yes, but how did you know I spoke English? How could you tell I was American?"

"You look American," she said. "You're wearing white socks."

My new partner introduced herself as Edita ("Just like the boss of a newspaper," she said) and went to work. Standing at the edge of the road, she lay one hand across her heart, raised the other into the air and gave her eyelashes an exaggerated flutter—as if she were portraying a coquettish onstage vixen. Within a minute, a white van pulled over and picked us up.

"You're good," I told her as we climbed into the van.

"I got involved in drama at university," she said. "I used to be shy. I still am shy by nature, but acting has helped me become a stronger person. If I ever get into a situation that seems difficult, I can just 'act' my way through it. I was acting when I met you back there, by the way."

"Bravo," I said.

As luck would have it, both Edita and I were headed to the city of Kaunas, where the A1 highway to the Baltic Sea intersects the A5 route into Poland. Had my beer commercial reveries (which had kicked into high gear by this point) been actualized, Edita would have introduced me to a bikinied gaggle of her actress friends in a Kaunas hot tub. Instead, Edita gave me something much more subtle but just as lovely: She took the evening to personally walk me through her city.

Kaunas is a remarkable old settlement tucked into a small gorge at the confluence of the two widest rivers in Lithuania. Some of the buildings and ruins date back to the days before Lithuania—the last pagan holdout in Europe—was Christianized in the fourteenth century.

Kaunas has been burned to the ground thirteen separate times in its history, and once served as the national capital when Vilnius fell to the Poles. Kaunas has one street (Laisves Avenue) where it hasn't been legal to smoke a cigarette since the twilight of the Soviet occupation, and it is the only city in the world—to my knowledge, at least—with a museum devoted entirely to folk-art devil figurines.

Following a 700-year-old cobblestone street into the Old Town district, Edita shared with me the secrets of Kaunas: how in 1812 Napoleon launched his ill-fated Russia invasion from a nearby hill; how the embalmed bodies of Lithuanian aviation heroes Tesporas Darius and Stasys Girenas were secretly sealed into the walls of a local medical building during Stalin's reign; how Yasser Arafat once had his private helicopter renovated at the local airplane factory.

Our cobblestone walk terminated at Rotuses Square, where we found a pipe organ concert underway in the baroque-styled confines of St. Francis Church. Admittedly, I know more about Moog tunes than fugue tunes, and I wouldn't recognize a diapason if one hit me over the head. But the complex, sonorous hum of the old pipe organ left me enchanted as I stood with Edita in the back of the crowded sanctuary: I felt like I'd come to Kaunas just to hear that strange music with a green-eyed girl.

Thus far, today hasn't been quite so charmed. Two short rides took me out of Kaunas to the A5 ramp at Garliava this morning; then I had to wait three hours before a man in a blue Mazda took me thirty-five miles to the back streets of Marijampole. All three drivers were friendly, but none of them spoke English or interacted much. Now, at the south edge of town—almost within walking distance of the Polish border—my arm is beginning to tire again.

Pessimism creeps in as the traffic whizzes past me. The sun is sinking into its late afternoon groove, and I'm considering my backup plan: to forgo a ride and hike a few hours out of the city limits so I can find a safe place to camp for the night. Since I'm carrying a hammock and a Gore-Tex bivy sack, I figure it will be easy to blend into the forest for an evening's sleep. Then I can walk the rest of the way to the border tomorrow and wait for Poland-bound cars as they pass through the checkpoint.

As I'm pondering this possibility, a white Ford Focus pulls over onto the shoulder and a college-aged girl sticks her head out the passenger window. "Do you speak English?" she asks.

"Sure," I say. "I'm American."

"Good, because my friends and I don't speak much Lithuanian. We're just visiting from Hungary. We're going to Krakow. Where are you going?"

"I just need to get into Poland. Anywhere across the border is fine."

"Well then, please get in. I'm Christina, and this is my boyfriend Ervin and our friend Sepi."

Thanking Christina, I unsling my pack while the Hungarians rearrange things in the car. The Ford Focus is so full of food and gear that it takes them ten minutes before they can shift enough items to clear out a space for me.

"You are very lucky today," Christina says to me as we try to jam my pack into the trunk.

"Why's that?" I ask.

"Because you are the first hitchhiker in Ervin's new car. He used to hitchhike all the time—he even made it to Amsterdam once. Now that he's driving, he finally gets to say thank you for all the people who picked him up. Maybe this will be the best ride of your life!"

Once I wedge myself into the back seat, I have so many sausages and melons and grease-spotted cookie boxes in my lap that I can hardly move. Sepi, a stocky, bearded fellow who shares the back seat with me, assures me that there is one easy way to free up some breathing space. "You look hungry," he says.

Sepi hands out some plastic plates and passes the food around the car as the swampy Lithuanian forest land rolls past. Bit by bit, we eat ourselves some elbow room.

"Why do you have so much food?" I ask, gnawing my chunk of watermelon.

"Our Lithuanian friends were married in Marijampole this weekend," Sepi says, cutting a thick slice of ham sausage onto a piece of bread. "Lithuanians are wonderful. When the family of our married friends found out we'd come all the way from Hungary, they treated us like brothers. When it was over, they gave us all this food."

"There was no room to sleep at our friends' house," Christina adds, "so we just slept in the wedding hall. The next morning, all the guests came back and we started eating and drinking and dancing again. So much happiness."

"Too much happiness," Ervin says. "If I didn't have this car to get us home, they would have made us stay there forever."

As we slow to pass through customs, I tell my new Hungarian friends my hitchhiking strategy. "I want to see Poland by thumb," I say. "I was thinking you could just take me to the first Polish city after the border station. The map says it's a town called Suwalki."

"Why do you want to stop there?" Ervin asks.

"Well, I want to discover things as they come in Poland, and that's a good place to start. I just want to keep a laid-back attitude and go where fate and chance take me. That's the best way to discover things, I think. Road roulette."

"Roulette, yes, like gambling," Sepi says. "I think that sounds romantic. But what is 'laid-back'?"

"Relaxed, casual," I say. "Not worrying about goals."

Ervin looks back at me from the driver's seat, a fire of mischief in his eyes. "But how can you be laid back," he says, "if you want to get out of the car at Suwalki and wait for a different ride? That's a goal, yes? We are already going to Krakow. If you are laid back, you will come with us."

Sepi nods seriously. "You must come to Krakow."

"But Krakow is all the way at the other end of the country. If I go there now, I'll miss most of Poland."

"Krakow is not the end of Poland," Ervin says. "Krakow is just the south of Poland. If you want to see more of Poland after Krakow, just hitch north."

"I know roulette," Sepi adds, "and I think you can't change your number now. If Ervin picked you up, then you have to go where Ervin is going."

The Hungarians have me checkmated: To argue otherwise at this point would be to contradict the impulse that led me to hitch in the first place. "Krakow it is, then," I shrug.

A few dozen miles into Poland, the day fades out; we speed south on the darkened road. The Hungarians

seem as inspired by my presence as I do by their hospitality, and I soon get a Hungarian-slanted crash course in
Eastern European history and politics. Christina, Ervin,
and Sepi all attend the elite University of Economic
Sciences in Budapest, and I am amazed not just by their
socio-political knowledge—but by their nonchalant skill
at discussing and debating these issues in English.

The most entertaining aspect of this free-wheeling
culture lesson is that Christina, Ervin, and Sepi can't
bring themselves to agree on any one interpretation of
the world. When Sepi tries to teach me the details of
the 1956 Budapest Revolution, Ervin and Christina get
into an argument over Imre Nagy's tactical wisdom
in standing up to the Soviets. When Christina tries to
educate me regarding Hungary's progressive new Gypsy
policies, Sepi and Ervin bicker over whether Gypsy social shortcomings are the result of culture or prejudice.
When Ervin describes how recent economic growth and
reforms have brought Hungary into a new golden age,
Christina and Sepi debate whether the last great age in
Hungary was the nineteenth century monarchical alliance with Austria or the fifteenth century empire under
King Matthias Corvinus. Whenever such debates get
too heated, everyone switches over to Hungarian, and I
have to wait several minutes before they translate their
conclusions into English. I sit spellbound in the back seat
under my pile of half-eaten Lithuanian sausages.

Well into the night, about forty-five minutes south of
Warsaw, Sepi is talking about the fate of the three million ethnic Hungarians living in Transylvanian Romania
when Ervin coasts the car to the side of the road. He says
something in Hungarian, and Sepi hands him a big plastic cup from the back seat. Very businesslike, Ervin takes

the cup, opens his door, and hops outside. I peer out the back window as he takes off running back up the highway like some kind of lunatic superhero.

"What's going on?" I ask.

"We ran out of fuel," Sepi says. "Ervin always forgets to check the gauge on his new car. He says he saw a petrol station a few kilometers back."

While we wait for Ervin to complete his mission, Christina spreads a blanket onto the grass at the side of the road and we snack on some more of the Lithuanian wedding delicacies. Sepi fishes a couple of bottles of red wine from the trunk and mixes the vintage with some Coca-Cola.

"Why are you mixing wine and Coke?" I ask him.

"This is red wine," he says. "It goes best with Coke. Sprite is best for white wine."

"Is this normal—mixing wine and soft drinks?"

Sepi shrugs. "Hungary is famous for wine, and we begin to drink it when we are very young. For kids, it tastes better with Coke. So maybe right now we're just drinking like children."

Sitting at the side of the road, I have my first ever wine-cola cocktail while Sepi and Christina discuss sustainable growth, dismantling state sectors, and the best ways to attract foreign investment.

It occurs to me at this moment that I am sitting on a Polish roadside with Hungary's future leaders: that Sepi and Christina (and Ervin) will one day be part of the brain trust that helps make their country a vibrant part of the European Union. And the fact that they are so down to earth and alive—the fact that they would road-trip across four countries to see their Lithuanian friends get married, or teach a hitchhiker about their economy (or, for that matter, sweeten their wine with Coke because it tastes better—an honest populist gesture if I've ever seen one)—makes me suspect that Hungarian democracy is going to do just fine in the twenty-first century.

Thirty minutes into our picnic, Ervin returns with a full cup of gasoline. He carefully empties the cup into the tank, and we sputter back up the road to the petrol station. As Christina squeegees the windshield and Ervin turns on the gas-pump, I realize that a full day of hitching topped off with wine-cola cocktails has made me sleepy.

By the time Sepi wakes me up, the car is parked on a narrow city street and it is daylight. Though I've been semi-awake all night, I'm still not sure what has just happened.

"We are here," Sepi says as he shakes me awake. "Ervin and Christina have already gone to sleep in their apartment. I'll show you to the dormitory on Horansky, and you can stay in one of the empty rooms there."

Something about this makes no sense at all. "Christina and Ervin have an apartment in Krakow?" I ask.

Sepi laughs. "You have been asleep a long time, I think. This is not Krakow. This is Budapest."

I try to draw a map in my mind—to figure out how Krakow can turn into Budapest without me knowing—but it's too early in the morning for this. "I thought we were going to stop in Krakow," I say.

"We did stop in Krakow, but it was too late to call our friends there, and Ervin felt like driving some more. So we went to Slovakia."

My mental map still isn't materializing. "What happened in Slovakia?" I ask.

"I don't know; I fell asleep before we got there. Slovakia isn't very big, so I guess Ervin felt like driving all the way home. He loves his new car, you know." Sepi pauses for a moment and shoots me a rather apologetic grin. "Who knows? He might even drive you back to Poland, if that's what you want."

I sit for a moment to mull over this unexpected shift in geography. By giving Poland up to chance—by attempting to unravel the mystery of Poland on a thumb and a prayer—it seems as though I have discovered something entirely unexpected: Hungary.

Figuring it's always better to assume you've hit the jackpot than to obsess over what might have been, I yank my pack from the crammed trunk of the Ford. As I follow Sepi to my Budapest crash-pad, I feel a small, indescribable welling of joy at the odds that brought me here.

Road roulette, indeed.

꿋 꿋 꿋

Rolf Potts is the author of Vagabonding: An Uncommon Guide to the Art of Long-Term World Travel. *The former Salon.com columnist is best known for promoting the ethic of vagabonding—a way of living that makes extended, personally meaningful travel possible. His work has appeared in* National Geographic Adventure, National Geographic Traveler, The Best American Travel Writing, *and on National Public Radio. Visit his website at www.rolfpotts.com.*

⫷ ⫷ ⫷

Dying with Custer

They meet at the crossroads of pain and healing.

"WHO WANTS TO SEE CUSTER GET KILLED?" the emcee cheerily asked the thousand-strong crowd gathered on a dusty plain just outside Hardin, Montana.

"Y-e-e-e-s!" went up the roar from the bleachers, as a string of bluecoat cavalrymen rode out waving from a reconstructed wooden fort, behind the Stars and Stripes. Out in the wings, a string of Indians in war paint were impatiently waiting on horseback, ready to recreate the Battle of Little Bighorn—especially its cinematic climax, Custer's Last Stand, an event that had occurred 128 years earlier, to the day. On that suffocatingly hot June 25th, 1876, the "boy general" George Armstrong Custer led his 209 men to attack an Indian camp by the Little Bighorn River, only to discover that he had charged the

149

biggest concentration of Sioux, Cheyenne, and Arapaho in Western history; the Indians overwhelmed the cavalrymen "like a river flowing around a stone" (as one chief poetically remembered), with every last man of Custer's command wiped out. It was the biggest victory of Indian forces in the entire history of the Old West—and a stunning shock for the United States, the 9/11 of America's Gilded Age.

Today, for Indians and whites alike, the emotional focus for all these memories has become the June 25th anniversary, when for three days this serene countryside erupts into a Western extravaganza of celebrations, religious services, academic symposia, and general whooping it up. It's a sprawling, raucous event, which combines "Little Bighorn Days," put on by primarily white-owned businesses in Hardin, with "Crow Native Days," a rodeo and fair held on the Crow reservation (upon whose land the battlefield lies), and the participation of four other Indian nations, involving a powwow, buffalo feasts, and a Northern Cheyenne peace pipe ceremony. And there is not one but two historical reenactments of the battle, held by rival groups—which means you can meet two Custers, two Crazy Horses, and two Sitting Bulls walking about the vicinity. The result is a unique mix of the light-hearted and the deadly serious, the tragic and the kitsch.

Now, as my first show for the weekend geared up on a steaming hot afternoon—the parades of bluecoats and Indians evoking the inevitable echoes of Buffalo Bill's Wild West show—I found myself sitting next to Joy Austin, wife of Custer #1, Tony Austin. I asked how she felt about watching her husband die three times a day. "It's O.K.," she sighed, fanning herself with a program.

"The only place I get choked up is when he says goodbye to his wife Libby and rides off. You know she'll never see him again."

When I first arrived in Hardin, a lonely-looking, hard-bitten prairie town with a string of boarded-up bars, the town was gearing up for the anniversary that keeps its economy alive. Every hotel was sold out and reennactors wearing uniforms and war paint thronged the streets, chowing down on Indian tacos (fried bread, spiced meat, tomato, lettuce, and cheese). The next morning was the day of the anniversary, so I got to the battlefield before sunrise. The Little Bighorn National Monument is a genuinely moving place: All across the bare Montana hills lie bone-white markers, each one showing where a soldier of the U.S. Seventh Cavalry is thought to have fallen. The densest cluster is at Last Stand Hill, where forty-two bluecoats held out—and at their center, next to a small American flag, lies the memorial of their flamboyant, controversial leader.

But the main activity that morning was occurring about fifty yards beyond this Anglo-American sacred site, at a new Indian Memorial, dedicated to the five Native American groups involved in the battle (the Sioux, Cheyenne, and Arapahoe on Sitting Bull's side, plus the Crow and Arikara, who fought as guides for the U.S. Cavalry). Unveiled in 2003, the memorial is a circular earth and stonework balustrade, with a weeping wall, interpretive panels, and an elegant wire sculpture of Spirit Warriors riding out to defend the Indian village from attack in 1876. In a spot thick with symbols, the memorial has been credited with making Native American groups feel welcome at the battlefield, which for many years had been run as a shrine to Manifest Destiny. Now, as the sun rose, seven Cheyenne elders in cowboy hats and dark glasses conducted a peace ceremony before a crowd of about fifty people. Donlin Many Bad Horses lit a wooden pipe and said: "When things were bad for us, we could not do this. There were times when we could not come in here to the battlefield. But now a door has opened to us. We can come in and worship and pray. I hope this opening will continue to grow."

By noon, Little Bighorn was thronging with visitors, all passionate about 1876. The event was nothing if not gregarious. One minute I was talking to Ernie Lapointe, a great-grandson of Sitting Bull who wore a baseball cap identifying him as a Vietnam veteran. He told me that Sitting Bull had had a vision before the battle that "told him our warriors shouldn't take the spoils of war, or injure the dead—but they did. That's why we're oppressed to this day—by the losers in the battle!" The next, I was being introduced to Lance Custer, the twenty-eight-year-old, sixth-generation family heir, descended from one of George's brothers. Lance was visiting the site from his home in Kansas for the first time, and was a little surprised by his instant celebrity status amongst "Custer buffs." Even while we were chatting on Last Stand Hill, an elderly man interrupted for an autograph, adding in awe: "He looks very much like the young Custer's brother Tom, don't you think? It's uncanny ... " (Lance smiled at him politely. Only a few feet away in the grass was Tom Custer's headstone. He had been so badly mutilated after the battle that he could only be recognized by a tattoo on his arm.)

And every day I went to one of the reenactments, for a dose of blood and gunpowder.

One reenactment has been held on and off since the 1960s in the predominantly white town of Hardin, while the other is on the Crow Indian reservation—but it's not a simple Anglo versus Indian version of events. The script for the "white" Hardin pageant was actually written by a Crow Indian, Joe Medicine Crow; although it was based on discussions with a Cheyenne veteran named Brave Bear, it has echoes of the 1940 Errol Flynn film classic *They Died With Their Boots On*, and is filled with messages of reconciliation. ("In this battle of the Little Bighorn, there were no victors . . . we red men and white men live in a united fortress of democracy, the United States of America.")

The "Indian" reenactment, put on by the Real Bird family on the Crow reservation, also contains little that would offend an old school Custerphile, except for a caustic reference to the deaths of numerous Cheyenne women and children at the so-called "battle" of the Washita in 1868. When it was first staged in the early 1990s, the Real Bird script delved into fantasy, with Custer being killed by Jesse James or surviving the battle to marry an Indian girl. But these days, the show sticks close to the historical record—and has proven a huge hit with serious white re-enactors, who travel from all over America for the chance to participate, at their own expense, on the battlefield itself. What's more, the Real Birds lure a large number of Indian horsemen to the event, creating a scene that is both spectacular and dangerous.

"I'm going to fight here every year until I'm too old to do it," said one cavalryman, Jason Heitland, as we wandered amongst replica military canvass tents by a shady creek. "You're fighting on the *actual* battlefield! You sleep where the *actual* Indian camp was, where the Cheyenne dog soldiers slept. And the battle itself is totally un-scripted. You've got whooping Indians coming from all directions. It's quite a thrill."

"And the horses don't know it's fake," added Niccolo Sgro, a coffee salesman from Michigan in his mid-thirties. "That's why it's so dangerous!"

Since Niccolo is Italian-born, he was playing the part of First Lieutenant Carol Camillo DeRudio. Forty-two percent of the Seventh Cavalry was actually foreign-born. ("Even then, the US army was the prototype for America's multicultural society," said the park historian, John Doerner.) Curiously, Hardin's Custer re-enactor, Tony Austin, was actually born in Brighton in the U.K., although he became obsessed with Custer even before he emigrated to Canada at age thirteen; today, he lives in British Columbia, where he works as a postman, but still has his English accent. A fixture at the Hardin event, Tony also has an Old World sense of historical irony, musing at times on what the real George Custer would have made of today's anniversary celebrations. But the Real Bird's Custer, Steve Alexander, stays firmly in character. He is addressed as "the general" by his troops, as well as his co-workers in the land-surveying office back home in Monroe, Michigan—where he and his wife have actually bought the Custer's home from the 1860s, and are renovating it to its original period look. As one of his men respectfully put it, Alexander virtually "channels Custer." "My bed is just like General Custer's," Steve told me. "So when I wake up, I *am* General Custer."

Like the original Seventh Cavalry, many re-enactors had signed up for adventure. I met Angus McCrudden, a feisty English tourist from Portsmouth. Since one of the re-enactors had dropped out after being kicked by a horse, Angus was fulfilling his lifetime dream by stepping into the wounded man's shoes, inheriting his uniform and sleeping in a teepee. Now he was going out for his first battle. "I'm chuffed to bits!" he declared.

The recruits were given a safety brief, and reminded to fire their guns upwards, since blanks could still blow a man's fingers off at short range.

"O.K.!" said the Italian. "So now we go to give hell to those savages!"

Nightlife at this time was predictably bizarre. That Saturday, I joined the crowds at the Four Aces in Hardin. A hardscrabble bar that's seen its fair share of cowboy brawls, it was as crowded as a New York nightclub. Still in their uniforms—but now splattered with fake blood—re-enactors rubbed shoulders with ranch hands from the Northern Cheyenne reservation, documentary TV producers, and the odd college professor doing a semiotic study on the festivities.

Angus from Portsmouth, who had carried the *guidon*, or company flag, that day, was delirious. "It was brilliant!" he raved, about the experience of being killed with Custer. "This Indian bloke came up behind me, and said real polite: 'Is it all right if I take the flag?' And I said, *'Orright.'* And then he shot me and I lay down dead!"

"Tomorrow I'm getting a gun. I'm getting all tooled up!"

By Sunday night, after the last shot had been fired and the last memorial wreath laid, Hardin was a ghost town. In the Four Aces, a couple of ranch hands nursed their beers in silence, beside a silent jukebox. Everyone had packed up their 4WDs and hit the highway, leaving "Custer country" to its memories for another year.

By now, it was a relief to see the battlefield return to its eerie serenity the next morning—just me, a couple of goats, and the ghosts. My mind was still crowded with blood-soaked images from the last few days, so the bare white markers scattered across the hillside now told a poignant story. Strolling across the sagebrush, you can follow exactly how the Seventh Cavalry fell apart, when "tactical disintegration" had set in. I was left with a sense of tragedy for those on both sides—the cavalrymen, who were paid fifteen cents a day to risk their scalps in an alien land, and the Indian warriors, who were desperately trying to preserve their nomadic way of life, having refused to be herded onto a rump reservation by the U.S. government. The park historian John Doerner had summed it up pithily: "This was Custer's last stand, but it was also the last stand of the Indians. Within a year after the Little Bighorn, there wasn't a truly free Indian left on the plains."

≈ ≈ ≈

Tony Perrottet, an Australian author based in New York, is the author of Pagan Holiday: On the Trail of Ancient Roman Tourists. *He is currently working on a book about travel in the old American West. Visit Tony at www.route66ad.com.*

❧ ❧ ❧

A Million Years of Memory

It's all there, in your own cells.

W E PUT ASHORE AT TAGUS COVE IN THE BRONZE
light of late afternoon, scraping the bow of our
Zodiac onto the hard black sand beach. A few yards inland, a mountain rises up from the sand, buttressed with
thick ridges. It looks raw, freshly created from the earth.

I have studied local maps and know I will need a
steady uphill climb to give me a perspective on the landscape that I couldn't realize at sea level. The spine of one
ridge is fluted, and there is a narrow trail hidden inside
it. I follow it up atop a thin patina of red soil, iron and
magnesium and sulfur once spit out of the volcano as
ash and smoke and fire, now finely ground to dust. The
path, which is at first a steep heart-pumping natural
stairway of small boulders, becomes more of a gentle
incline as it goes higher.

It leads me above a thousand feet, up to where finely woven nests of ground finches hang from the bare limbs of the ghostly *palo santo* trees. Looking down, I see that the cove, in the shape of a perfect half moon, is what remains of a volcanic crater. Time and tide collapsed the seaward wall of its caldera long ago, and now the ocean fills the geological bowl where magma once roiled. I have walked up the rim of the other half of the crater that still remains.

I'm in the Galapagos, 600 miles off the coast of South America in the Pacific, the lone writer aboard a research ship full of marine scientists. These islands straddle the equator, and common sense would have them tropical and warm. But they are also washed with bewildering crosscurrents, like the Humboldt, which transports ice-cold water up from the Antarctic. Wayward penguins once rode this current northward, and today they have become part of a menagerie of animals and plants, which after drifting, flying, or swimming here, have been singularly molded by the isolation of the place. They include giant land tortoises with shells shaped by how they feed on the individual islands where they live; iguanas that have learned to swim underwater and graze algae from boulders; a finch that hunts insects like a woodpecker, except that it holds a twig in its beak and uses it as a tool. Entire families and classes seem to have changed anatomically, just by the act of being in a place my shipmates call the "cradle of evolution." The scientists are here hoping for new discoveries, ways of describing a genus or a species that has never been examined before. I am here for discovery, too, except my logic is more inexact, a childlike sense of anticipation rooted somewhere deeply in my gut.

In some vague way, this place is a reflection of how
we are all fashioned by our own realities. Here in the
Galapagos, without the nonsense of civilization to mud-
dle up the point, it is just more evident.

This is an odd piece of geography, where cold water
meets warm sky and mist sometimes rises up unexpectedly, clouding everything in a pale blur. I have been on
the deck of our research ship at dawn by myself, and
could not see more than a few yards in any direction.
Once, a whale surfaced and splashed, maybe fifty feet
away, fully hidden in a vacuum that was white, cool. As
I stood there alone on the stern, I heard it release the air
from its massive lungs in one extended monstrous breath.
It sounded as if the entire sea itself was exhaling, expelling a million years' worth of memory in a single giant
burst of spray and power and light. The mist gradually
parted, perhaps from the force of the whale's exhalation,
and I could see a portion of its immense body, dark and
barnacled like the bottom of a ship, moving deliberately
through the water. The moment seemed vaguely hal-
lucinogenic, and I felt as if I were there but also somewhere else, my lonely soul like the disembodied spindrift
of the whale's breath. And then as suddenly as it had
surfaced, the great cetacean had vanished, dissolving
back into the water without a sound. I was still alone on
the deck, and with me in the white were only the sounds
of the gulls, shrieking at each other, and then, even that
too was gone. No wonder the early Spanish, not sure if
these islands were real or imagined, first mapped them
as "*Encantada*," enchanted.

And now, up here on the edge of this collapsed volcano, I realize the ridge I've been hiking has taken me to
the top of the rim shared by Tagus and the wholly intact

bowl of an adjacent caldera, one that sprawls out for a few hundred yards inland. A young naturalist named Charles Darwin made this same hike after arriving here at Isla Isabella aboard HMS *Beagle* in 1835. For Darwin, these islands offered a rare glimpse into the beginning of the world itself. The experience was so powerful that it changed him from a creationist; but the dissonance was palatable—it took him the rest of his life to work up the courage to finally admit that animals and plants alter to adapt to their place on earth.

The inland volcano cradles a small, sullen lake at the bottom of its bowl. It is a steep walk-crawl down the sides, and I have no reason to go there. But Darwin was here in the heat of the midday sun and, without a canteen, hoped the lake might quench his thirst. He scrambled down to the bottom of the caldera with no hesitation. But when he cupped his hands to drink, he was startled to find the water was saltier than the ocean itself. All was not lost: Mapmakers named the crater "Volcán Darwin" in his honor.

Seaward, I look down on the broken and submerged crater of Tagus through my binoculars and see a half dozen green turtles mounting the shells of each other, frothing the turquoise sea in their passion. As I watch, each raises its ancient, armored head up out of the water, gulping air in sheer turtle bliss. I have seen other sea turtles underwater during my month here in this isolated archipelago. And each time I have been struck by their primitive grace, the way they glide like huge stout hawks through the water, the glint of another millennium shining in their eyes.

I start to hike back down to the craggy shore of Tagus just as the sun dips below the volcanic peak of nearby

Isla Fernandina. The air out here, free from mainland
dust, is remarkably clear, unencumbered with the resi-
due of human conceits. On the horizon, the curvature
of the earth falls away on both sides, and guilelessly, I
catch myself wondering why the ocean itself doesn't
simply drain away. In the cusp of the bright scarlet light
between late afternoon and evening, I see Jupiter and
Venus burning atop each other next to a crescent moon,
watch the brightest meteor I have ever seen streak a long
white trail past them all. It seems to be checking off one
more day of life, Darwin's creationist God still at work,
busy with timekeeping, dutiful and sure.

After dark, back on the ship that brought me here, I
put on scuba gear and with ichthyologist John McCosker,
slip under the black water at the edge of the cove. Here,
with our dive lights turned off, we settle slowly to the
bottom at eighty feet, flashes of bioluminescence spar-
kling in front of my mask like the fireflies I used to see
as a kid in country fields. We are here in these islands
to capture new specimens of fish, and with nearly 40
percent of marine life found nowhere else on earth, our
chances are always good. Fish sleep too, and they hide
very well, so it helps to look deep and at night.

I look for McCosker, but he seems to have been swallowed up by the ebony sea. Finally, he exhales, and the
upwelling of his air exhaust tears through the plankton
over his head, outlining each tiny bubble in a rim of blue-
green. It is cold down here, and even in a thick wetsuit,
subtle waves of chill move through my body and my teeth
chatter inside my regulator. Briefly, we turn on our lights
and shine them under the rocky ledges, down into places
where the molten lava flow from the craters ran so long
ago. The sea has done a magnificent job of colonizing

itself over the eons, upholstering the old lava with a thick fabric of coral and worms, sponges and tiny invertebrates, all united here in their isolation from the mainland. From under the ledge, a Port Jackson shark swims excitedly out, a slender and spotted dwarf-like creature no bigger than my arm. As it does, it swiftly pinballs off a rock, and my light and my attention ricochet with it. I hesitate, look down and see a nudibranch the size of my little finger in a crevice just below. Striped and iridescent, this marine slug is speciated, custom-designed for tasks we humans can barely imagine. Local Ecuadorian fisherman, in awe of its vivid stripes, call it *El Tigre*.

We flick our lights off again, plunging back into primal darkness. I watch as a large discus-shaped form moves easily away from us in the water, its shell and flippers clearly outlined by the broken bioluminescence, a sizzle of muted cobalt. It is a sea turtle, perhaps one of those I saw earlier on the surface. It disappears and the field in front of me is filled again with flashes of bio-energy, random synapses firing in the salty wet pulp of unconsciousness.

They tell me reptiles don't dream, having evolved long before the rest of us earned the genetic right to that sweet luxury. But I wonder: Do they even need to, out here in an enchanted place that is still part dream itself?

Isn't it enough to fly underwater like colossal thick-bodied birds, tiny wings of scales moving them as fast as they ever need to go? Isn't it enough to thread their blue-green trail through the eye of the cosmos until it is hemmed shut, and the world becomes still again, volcanoes and tortoises, finches and humans, all waiting patiently to be finally born from the liquid wakefulness of the earth, of its God, of memory itself?

I blink, shaking my head, heavy now with nitrogen and visions too powerful to fully absorb. My intellect stirs, and I find it astounding that my regulator is still in my mouth, and that I have remembered to breath. Time has shifted somehow, and I inhale slowly, ever slowly, not wanting to disturb the water with my exhalations. Around me, fish I cannot see softly moan, and shrimp click their tails, sounding like the muffled hum of cicadas.

I am waiting for the whale now. I think I hear her sweet night voice, calling from somewhere deep inside the black sea.

⤢ ⤢ ⤢

Bill Belleville is a Florida-based magazine writer, author, and documentary filmmaker specializing in environmental issues. His books include River of Lakes, Deep Cuba, *and* Sunken Cities, Sacred Cenotes and Golden Sharks: Travels of a Water-Bound Adventurer. *His work has also appeared in* Sierra, Islands, Newsweek, Salon, *and* The Washington Post.

~∻ ~∻ ~∻

A Time to Kill

The author absorbs the lesson and spectacle
of a Spanish tradition.

W E HADN'T BEEN IN THE ANDALUCIAN MOUNTAIN
village very long. We had moved into a house,
Barbara and I, made friends as much as possible, given
our deficiencies of language and the huge gulf in culture.
We had wanted to spend a year in total immersion in the
Alpujarras valley while we tried to write and paint. We
had hunted wild *setas* in autumn and danced at the fiesta,
gotten drunk on the crude wine of the Contraviesa. But
there was another small bridge to cross in our relationship with our neighbors.

For weeks we had feared its coming. Now, as the days
turned colder, and the stands of poplars burned like yellow flame in the folds of the Sierra, it had nearly arrived.
It was almost time for the *matanza*.

When it is time for the annual slaughter in Cantilla, this is how it happens. It is a Saturday, and the men have stayed home. All day long they have been at it, gathering expectantly in mute clusters at corners and wide places in the village streets. Kids are not going so far from home, and the dogs, whose duties often carry them miles away, are snuffling humbly around the legs of the women. These women have been here since early morning. They have built great olive wood fires under huge vats of water. Steam rises white into the blue margins of the sky. For once the men are not grumbling about the lack of rain. It is a cold, clear Saturday in December, and they are going to kill the pigs.

Perhaps it is the season that gives this sense of expectation. The air bites a little in the mornings. The people haven't bothered much with fresh litter for the pigs under the houses recently, and there is a harsh putridity at certain doorways. There have been last efforts to add fat to the *marrano*, the pig, at this late hour. People have been liberal with the unshelled maize that has been drying in the open attics.

The architecture has changed. Thick poles have emerged from the lofts and been placed, attic to attic, across the streets. The strands of drying red peppers which have been here all autumn are retired, but the racks made of cane still remain like flag standards across the house front, waiting for the gleaming lengths of *morcilla*, blood sausage.

At about four o'clock, men—specialists—can be seen entering the village from the highway. They are in-laws and cousins and friends whose skill is killing the pigs. They wear green rubber boots and blue boiler suits. From their belts hang a hook with a handle, and they carry long grooved knives. Their coming is greeted excitedly, but they remain aloof, as if to invest their tasks with solemnity.

At the killing places tables have appeared. These measure exactly 105 centimetres in length and 75 in width and are 70 centimetres above the ground. They are made of mulberry wood, olive and *almes*. They have probably always been the same. They are very strong, as they need to be. Some foreigners buy them for charming kitchen tables when they can find a carpenter willing to make them one, but the villagers use them just once a year, for the *matanza*.

Kids alert the clusters that the butcher has arrived, moving in telepathic sympathy with the other clusters up the streets, sensing everything an instant before the adults. Dogs are banished with a few well-timed kicks. The women, wearing their worst old clothes and head rags, move back. The men go forward to meet the butcher.

Things move quickly. A delegation, including the householder, vanishes into the corral. A rope is tied to the foreleg of the pig, and he is coerced and dragged into the street, letting out the first of an accelerating series of disconcertingly human-like squeals. The excitement rises; dogs whimper in greed and sympathy from their places of banishment. The pig, blinking, sees the sky for the first time since last April, when he was an infant. He grows calmer again as the expectant circle readies itself. As the men move forward, the pig senses exactly what is about to happen, with that prescience that you can almost always see on the faces of prisoners.

The knot of men closes on the pig, surprisingly long and pink under its sparse hair. He turns into the rope and fouls his foreleg. The butcher steps forward, concealing the hook behind his thigh like a matador (for that is what he is) and suddenly catches the pig underneath his jaw with its sharp point. The squeal rises in volume. The pig resists. Its human eyes sweep the crowd as it is hauled like a fish off its front feet. The other men close in, fumbling for a handhold on the 200-pound bulk. Seizing hair, tail, knee, they drag it on its side onto the table. The wails are now continuous. The butcher spits instructions, but the men can hardly hear them. A leg is bound and tied to the table. Two men lean their full weight upon the hams; another pair hang from a rope hastily pulled across the pig's belly. There is something almost furtive about their movements. It is easy to imagine guilt beneath their tight faces.

Once the pig is firmly tied, it is allowed to grow calm. Only its eyes show its terror, darting back and forth across the crowd, searching for the source of danger. This is now in the deft hand of the butcher, who turns his back and gives the blade a few ceremonial swipes across a whetstone. On this cue, the woman of the house comes forward with a metal basin. It is placed on the road downward and to the left of the pig's frantic eye.

The matador cuts slowly, inserting the knife with the finesse of a surgeon looking for a vein in a patient. This is exactly what he is doing. Once sure he has found the jugular, he presses the haft of the knife with the heel of his hand. It slides inward easily. All at once, the pig knows. Its great bulk surges against the weight of the men and undulates like a wave. A scream begins; the butcher leans back against the pull of the hook and stretches the jaw forward. A jet of bright blood spurts out, overshoots the basin, which is hurriedly adjusted. The force of the blood makes a metallic drone as it flows.

The pig's cries are now rhythmic, and the rate ebbs and flows with its movements. The pan fills rapidly.

The pig, it is clear, feels no special pain. Its dismay is cosmic, and something of its despair is communicated to everyone. There is no talking except for the rushed instructions of the butcher. I have seen slaughters in other places where the animal has been mocked, and a carnival air prevailed as in a witches' sabbath. Here there is no frivolity. Even the dogs and children are subdued. They are in the presence of something profound. What is before them is a paradox that only ends, but is never resolved.

The flow weakens. There is a glaze on the pig's visible eye. As the last of his blood flows out, all can see him die. It happens quite suddenly, and always the same thing happens. The body, abandoned, exerts its earthly force in a single long spasm. The men half climb onto the pig to constrain it as it nearly jackknifes, gives a long rippling shudder, and is still. A boy actually is heard to say, "*Adios, Marranico.*"

The mood shifts. They are one fewer now. The pig has been transformed into meat, a huge and worrying quantity of meat. Hurry rules the crowd. The women join the men, pouring boiling water onto the flesh, scraping with the sharpened edge of a tablespoon. The scraping noises intersperse with excited conversation. Soon the pig is bare. Except for one single act, the dividing of the carcass into sections, the women now take over. They move forward eagerly. You can feel the sexual power shift as the carcass is hauled into the air and left swinging from the poplar poles. The entrails spill out into a plastic tub. The women will heal this pig now, deliver it from its condition of alienation into *morcilla*, *chorizo*, ham and bacon. It is almost part of their children and men already; you can see it in their eyes.

They will not sleep tonight. There are onions to peel, great sacks of them, spices to express, blood to boil, links to tie. Tomorrow you will see them, crusty with meat, hoarse and sweaty and strong, in the plaza, laughing from their state of sleepless intoxication and joy. They are so powerful that the men, slow with a night's feasting, avoid them. This could be a day to redress old wrongs.

When the day came at last, Barbara balked. We had seen the preparations underway from our kitchen window. I resigned myself. I looked at her questioningly when the knock came on the door. I knew that I would have to help the neighbors. Not because I was wise or clever, but because I was heavier than the sturdy but diminutive men of these mountains, and someone had to lie across the hams of the pig to keep him from thrashing. I looked at her beseechingly.

"You do eat pork, you know," I said.

"My chops come in little white packages from the supermarket. Not from the murder of innocents at four in the afternoon."

"Hypocrite."

"That's what you can tell them. 'Barbara can't come, because she is indisposed with hypocrisy.'"

The pig departed without undue trauma. At the crucial moment, I heard Barbara playing "Nimrod" by Elgar on the stereo to cover the squeals. When I came home, weary but satisfied, she met me at the door. I thought she would have something sympathetic to say to me, but after ten years I should have known better.

"Take that shirt off down here," she said. "You're not bringing pig shit into my kitchen."

≫ℰ ≫ℰ ≫ℰ

Art Lester was born in the USA, but has spent much of the last twenty-five years working as a teacher and development trainer in Botswana, Kenya, and the Dominican Republic. A freelance journalist since his first job on a North Carolina weekly paper at the age of nineteen, for the last twenty years he has owned a home in a remote village in the Sierra Nevada range of southern Spain. He has published many stories and articles, and in 2005 his book Seeing with Your Ears *won first prize in the Writer's Digest International Self-published Book Competition. His new book, from which this story was excerpted and adapted, is* Almost Home: Lost and Found in a Spanish Mountain Village, *currently under representation by Natasha Kern Literary Agency.*

PETER HELLER

⚜ ⚜ ⚜

Riding with the King

Water is the best teacher of all.

"ALMOST READY?" ASKS LEONEL PEREZ, THE National Masters Surf champion of Mexico. He asks me that every morning. Since I'm standing beside his two-door Chevy completely transfixed by the waves, and haven't taken off my shirt or waxed my board—and since it's still dark, and we haven't had breakfast or coffee—I take it as a metaphysical question, like, *Are you ready to believe in a force much bigger than you?*

As I watch the tiers of surf near the Pacific resort town of Ixtapa, I realize that there are three things I appreciate about surfing as a near beginner: the raw beauty of waves; the anticipation of getting repeatedly thrashed; the possibility of one good ride, a kind of fleeting touch of grace. Also, my coach. I can't believe he's even standing up after last night's party.

Leon rubs wax briskly over the deck of a board propped against his thigh. He is in training for the Nationals in Baja's Ensenada in two months, and he can't bear to miss a wave. He is honing himself like a weapon. He doesn't wear a rash guard or sunscreen. His baggy shorts come below his knees. He is forty-six years old, short (about five-foot-six), broad-shouldered, and wiry. His ears are small. His nose, broken years ago, is slightly flattened. Even his buzzed hair is thinning, as if obliging a lifelong imperative toward sleekness. It occurs to me, watching him, that he is a man completely shaped by the sea.

Only four hours ago, Leon was working on his second bottle of tequila *blanco*. Café tables had been shoved together outside his surf shop, Catcha L'Ola ("Catch the Wave"), behind the row of tall hotels lining Ixtapa's shore. A bunch of local surfers, four Texas longboarders, a pair of tourist police with shotguns, brothers and sisters of Leon, and two young women on holiday from Brooklyn were annihilating cases of Corona. The mother of Leon's two-year-old daughter was warily grilling redfish. Leon worships his daughter, whom he named Auramar—"Aura of the Sea"—but only tolerates the mother, who, he says, tricked him into having a child and once threw stones at his girlfriend. The fiesta was in honor of his forty-sixth birthday. Today would be another party. Three days ago was yet another bash, but nobody can remember what for.

"The waves look bigger today," I suggest.

"There is a swell coming. You are ready?"

"I guess I am."

Today I'm going to try a six-foot-six-inch shortboard for the first time, a personal threshold. I'm Leon's age, and most guys who start surfing late stick with the more stable, less responsive longboards. To hell with that: I'm having a midlife crisis. This is my party and I can cry if I want to.

"You don't even look hungover," I say to Leon.

Now he looks up. He smiles—I can tell because the left side of his mouth lifts just a little.

"Practice," he says. He tosses the wax to me over the hood of the car and nods at the local kids carrying boards who are beginning to trickle in from the road. They have walked the last mile from the end of the bus route from Zihuatanejo, eight miles down the coast. They regard Leon with specific awe: He will catch many more waves than any of them today, and have better rides, which is unnatural, since some of the younger boys have grandfathers Leon's age. Leon is nonchalant about his status as the old master. "I just surf every day," he says simply.

I look behind us. Out of the mountains, unbending slowly from dense groves of coconut palms, pushes the sweet water of the Rio La Laja. The sun has not yet risen over the Sierra Madre del Sur, so the dark water reflects only a rose wash of dawn and the light of a single fisherman's fire burning on the sand. The river cuts the beach and empties into the sea where the surf breaks over the sandbar. Even in the half-light I can see that the sets are easily head-high.

Leon straightens and turns toward the beach. And then, since he teaches with the minimalism of a Zen master, he gives me the lesson of the morning.

"Paddle toward the peaks. On that board, you have to be at the peak."

"O.K."

"Lock the car door."

"O.K."

Then he jogs toward the water.

I have come to Ixtapa for three weeks to train with Leon. I started surfing six months ago, while visiting a friend in Huntington Beach, California, and got hooked. After twenty-five years of kayaking whitewater, it seemed a natural progression to begin again where the rivers end. I went back to California two more times last spring and now have a total of thirty-five days on a board. I wonder if, on day 365, I'll be able to ride a North Shore Hawaiian tow-in wave like the ones you see on TV. I'll need constant instruction to keep the learning curve steep. So when I met Leon while on a family vacation in Ixtapa last summer—I'd already heard about him in California—I asked him if he'd coach me.

It's not surprising that Leon doesn't believe in holding a student's hand: All his life, his only teacher has been the thumping waves. As a small boy, living in a tiny village called Chutla, up the rugged Guerrero coast, he saw a neighbor who had been to California as a migrant worker wearing a t-shirt with a picture of a surfer shooting a tube. Six-year-old Leon kept thinking about that barrel. A few years later he began to see vans of American hippies with boards on the roof passing on the narrow, potholed coastal road. "I was thinking," Leon says, pointing to his sun-burnished head, "I want to do that."

When his father, a traveling electric-appliance salesman, moved the family to Zihuatanejo—then a small beach town with one dirt road out to the highway— Leon stole a scrap of plywood from a wood shop and began boogie-boarding. When he was twelve, he heard that an American friend of Jacques Cousteau's who lived across the bay had a longboard. Leon and a dozen other local kids asked to borrow it and took turns, and a local surf culture was born.

The same phenomenon of scrappy local kids hitting the waves any way they could was occurring up and down Mexico's Pacific coast. Unlike California surfing, born in the early 1900s, the sport in Mexico didn't have a direct pollination from Hawaii, with its centuries-old surf culture. There was no Duke Kahanamoku bringing showy exhibitions and aloha spirit; there were only way-ward gringos. American legends Bud Browne and Greg Noll took some trips to Acapulco and Mazatlán in the late fifties, but, according to Nathan Myers, a historical-minded editor at *Surfing Magazine*, Californians didn't start poking down the coast of mainland Mexico in sig-nificant numbers until the 1960s, after the Gidget movies and the Beach Boys craze had ignited the American surf-ing boom that suddenly crowded California's beaches. The majority of the first Mexican surfers were the sons of poor fishermen and hotel workers. I asked Arturo Astudillo, now fifty-two, one of the early Mexican pio-neers around Acapulco, how he and his friends got their first boards. "We stole them," he said. He hung his head. "I am sorry. It was the only way."

By the late seventies, Leon, then a teenager, was shredding. He bargained with gringos for beat-up boards. He dripped candle wax on the deck for traction and made his own leashes out of surgical tubing. He began working in the booming new tourist center of Ixtapa. One morning, he and a friend named Antonio Ochoa paddled out into a wickedly fast hollow break beside Ixtapa's recently built breakwater. No one had attempted it before. They dropped in on an overhead, right-breaking barrel that blasted them through a tube like buckshot. The wind at their backs almost flattened them. They came back the next morning, and the next, and named it Las Escolleras, "the Jetties." Then they began exploring northward, finding the Rio La Laja break on the other side of a crocodile swamp.

They heard about a legendary Mexican surfer from Acapulco named Evencio Garcia Bibiano, who everybody said was like a demon on the waves. In 1978, they went to watch him compete at the first Mexican national competition on the mainland, at a break in Guerrero called Petacalco, a fifteen-foot barrel that broke dependably twice a day. Garcia, despite long nights spent partying, was beautiful, almost frightening, to watch.

Leon never missed a day on the waves. When he was twenty-four, he became a waiter at the club Carlos 'n' Charlie's, right on the beach in Ixtapa, a five-minute walk from the Jetties. At Carlos 'n' Charlie's, every night is spring break, and Leon quickly became chief partymaker. He wore his shirt unbuttoned to his waist, danced on the tables, judged bikini contests, administered a devastating sangria from a spouting pitcher. He knocked back tequila every night and was such a ladies' man that he is still called El Tigre. He dated models and TV stars, often didn't sleep, and, when the sun came up, grabbed his board and went surfing. When the onshore winds blew out the waves in the late morning, he'd nap for a couple of hours, then come back to the bar and load up the donkey with buckets of ice and beer.

"The donkey's name was Lorenzo," Leon said. "We shared free beers on the beach, for advertising. As soon as he saw me open the first beer, he chased me down. I taught him to drink. By the time we came back, he was drunk.

"Too much party," Leon admits. After fifteen years in the fastest lane, he downshifted to a slower one, surfing with single-minded devotion and opening his shop. He, a sister, and two younger brothers started renting boards, giving lessons, and taking customers on day trips to nearby breaks. And once Leon got serious about competing, he won the nationals in his age class—over-forty in 2002 and over-thirty-five in 2004. There are few men alive who know the Pacific coast of Mexico as well as Leon.

At a tangled pile of drift logs, I unwind the leash from the board and secure the Velcro strap at my ankle. Then I wait for a little shore wave to break, jog into the water, jump onto the board, and start to paddle. The strong tug of the rip current pulls northward. I make it over a few steep swells and hit a low ridge of whitewater, paddling hard. It floods over me, stops my progress. I bob up paddling like a possessed turtle, shoulders burning, and when I shake my eyes clear, the only thing in front of me is a pelican and a head-high wall already breaking. Oh, shit. Duck-dive! Wait until the white pile is almost on top of you. Big breath. Rock the nose down hard with both hands, press the tail down with one foot…Yes! When I buoy to the top, the wave is past. Dang. "Paddle again even before you can see," Leon said. I do and make it over the next wave just as it peaks. And then there's only open, rolling water. Phew. For me, there is always this race to get past the break, always a little desperate.

I catch my breath and look left in time to see Leon hunting the next set. While the other three surfers are just sitting on their boards, he is already moving, paddling smooth and fast, angling both toward deeper water and down the beach. Abruptly, he spins. He is just in front of a perfect peak, the rounded top of a glassy, inexorably forming mountain. No one else has seen it coming. And then he is an explosion of motion. "Everything moves," a local told me with a grin, describing Leon catching a wave: His arms windmill, his feet kick in a violent flurry. But what you remember most is his expression: He looks like a gunfighter in the middle of a fast draw against five men. When the wave is steepest, hanging for a split second at its own angle of repose, with just the top beginning to fold, Leon is up, rocketing left down the wall with the speed of a diving tern. He is crouched, perfectly balanced, the wave ripping white down the line, unpeeling behind him and trying to devour him like a jaw. He stands upright and pumps, bouncing the front of his board for more speed, swings up to the stiff lip, and caroms down off it in another crouching swoop. I laugh out loud.

I am thinking, like the six-year-old Leon, I want to do that.

Ten Mexican states now hold circuits of *torneos* to select teams to go to the annual nationals. Each will send as many as thirty competitors in all categories. Serious surf competition in Mexico is booming, the result of a maturing homegrown scene fueled by access to global culture via the Internet, movies, and television. While there are no Mexicans on the World Pro Tour, and their best surfers need more pro experience to be truly competitive, the nation has fielded surf teams to the World Games in Brazil, Ecuador, and South Africa in the past five years. Two contenders of note: Raul Noyola became the first Mexican surfer to win a World Qualifying Series pro-tour competition in 2001 and, in 2004, he won the Mexpipe Open, in Puerto Escondido; and one of the country's best female surfers, twenty-year-old Sofia Melgoza, of Guadalajara, has had promising results in international events. Meanwhile, surf clothing and gear companies—like Mexpipe, Olea, and Squalo, the biggest, which operates fifty clothing retail stores in Mexico—are springing up and providing sponsorship for competitions and individuals. Mexican shapers are producing beautiful boards in Cabo and Puerto Escondido.

On my fifth day in Mexico, Leon and I drove the five hours down the coast to Acapulco for the Torneo Evencio Garcia Bibiano, a Guerrero State selection qualifier that Leon would have to win in order to go to Ensenada. Garcia, for whom the competition was named, was the legend Leon had first seen compete in '78. He was from Acapulco, and at a 1985 championship here at Playa Bonfil, south of town, he used the home-field advantage and devastated the competition. He was a quintessential fearless big-wave rider and the first native to do aerials and floaters and 360s. On his last heat, he already had more than enough points to take first place, but he had a few minutes left before the horn, so he paddled back out for one more ride—just for show. Before a crowd of a thousand spectators, he took off on a steep left, and it closed out and collapsed. He seemed to kick out over the back side. His board flew into the air, then...nothing. The board washed onto the beach, and no one ever saw him again.

In a superstitious culture, Garcia has become the resident spirit of Mexico's waves. Surfers will tell you with a straight face he was transformed instantly into a dolphin who still patrols and protects surfers. He was El Campeón, "the Champion," claimed by heaven, and every time a wall of green water rises out of the sea, a surfer may sense Garcia's ghost gliding like a dolphin down the line. I met a twenty-five-year-old top surfer named Julio Cesar La Palma, whom everyone calls La Pulga—"the Flea"—and when I asked him if he has a hero, he blinked and put his hand on his chest. "Sometimes when I dream," he said, "I dream that Evencio Garcia is surfing in my body."

If Garcia were there on that Sunday in November, he would certainly have heard "Guantanamera" booming out of the giant speakers next to the judges' platform—not the old song but the hip-hop version by Wyclef Jean, Celia Cruz, and Lauryn Hill. Leon was out in the surf loosening up. I recognized him right away even from a distance—his bullet head, his constant roving back and forth, hunting. In surf, he rarely stops paddling, even between sets, his eyes on the horizon.

"*Guantanameeera—*"

According to the big posted roster, Leon's finals heat was coming up. At the top of some crumbling steps off the sand, wedged between a palm tree and a shaded slab of concrete covered with plastic chairs, where surfers were eating *sopa de mariscos* (seafood soup), was a beat-up white Chevy van with PRENSA painted in block letters across the front. It didn't look like any press van I'd ever seen. A wooden skeleton in sunglasses was chained to the grille. A faded photocopy of a dog was taped to a window, with the words cuidado! peligroso! I could see why: Chained underneath were two tawny pit bulls.

A short, thin-faced young man with a sparse mustache hustled around from the back of the van. His loose hair hung down his shirtless back. He had skull tattoos and a skull pendant, and his official government press card hung on a necklace of shells and claws of black coral, along with a fancy Nikon. I introduced myself, and he ducked his head agreeably. "*Andale*," he said, and pushed aside a bamboo curtain across the van's open side door. He sat against a bag of dog food, under a poster of Bob Marley.

Oscar Diego Morales, a.k.a. "Fly," is a roving reporter for *Planeta Surf La Revista*, a magazine by, for, and about Mexican surfers. It's slick and fun, splashed with Aztec design motifs, crisp action photos, and ads for Mexican beachwear. The second issue had just hit the stands. Oscar told me that surfing in Mexico was at a tipping point. It was growing more popular by the month. "Every time a good swell is forecast, more and more people come out," he said. Then suddenly, hearing a particularly irresistible riff from the speakers on the beach, Oscar leaped out of his seat and, bent over, began to do a crazy little dance to the music. He sat back down. I asked him how many dedicated surfers he thought there were now in the country, and he began, remarkably, to tick off each major break.

"Puerto Escondido, 60 . . . Acapulco, 25 . . . Ensenada, 50 . . . Mazatlán, 15 . . . San Blas, 15. Nobody knows," he concluded. (Matt Warshaw, who wrote the seminal *Encyclopedia of Surfing*, estimates there are 30,000 native surfers in the country, though Mexicans say there are far fewer.)

"What's with the skulls everywhere?" I asked.

"Skulls? Oh. No matter if you have green eyes, blue eyes, white skin—in the end everybody is going to be the skull. It's the true face at the end of our life."

As I left the van, a small pickup skidded to a stop at the end of the sand street, and ten shirtless teens with boogie boards and shortboards jumped out. Some had fade haircuts with long, red-streaked tops. Earrings, eyebrow piercings, blond-streaked ponytails.

"Hey," I called, "where are you guys from?"

Playa Princesa, a break a few miles up the coast.

"Are you students?"

Most of them work as lifeguards and in restaurants for a few dollars a day. Another generation.

Back down on the beach, I found Leon. His final master's heat was about to start. He was with some other surfers in the shade of a *palapa*, stretched out in a plastic chair, drinking from a water bottle. He looked much too relaxed.

"Isn't your heat coming up?"

"In a few minutes. I am ready." I was more nervous than he was. I felt like a soccer dad.

We heard the blast of a horn announcing five minutes to go. Leon stood, stretched his arms back like a man waking up, grabbed his tiny board. How long can a warrior keep going to war? He reminded me of the graying soldier in *The Seven Samurai*, the one who would always survive on seasoned judgment, discipline, and patience. Then it occurred to me that I was Leon's age and I was just starting. What would I survive on?

Twenty minutes later, Leon won his final heat handily. He was now a Guerrero State champion, heading to the nationals. He also won the open longboard class. He shrugged it off. That night, after four days in Acapulco, we drove back up the coast to Ixtapa in the dark. We arrived too late to find a room for me, so I slept on the floor of his apartment, in a concrete block at the edge of the tourist zone, crowded by jungle. I slept under a shelf of trophies, a rack of six bagged boards, and a photo collage of Leon's younger brother Alejandro, who died in a motorcycle wreck fourteen years ago. The young man held a surfboard in half the pictures, was as handsome as Leon, and looked very happy. "His nickname was Karma," Leon said before he turned in. "Everybody loved him. He was a very good surfer. That is why we name the annual tournament in Ixtapa 'the Karma.'" I saw a flicker of emotion cross Leon's usually inscrutable face. Then he said, "You have been working hard. You can do it, the big wave. Practice more. Tomorrow I will take you north." Then he flicked off the light. I went to sleep listening to the calls of a loud night bird and thinking how everything is connected: Evencio and La Pulga; Leon and his brother Alejandro; Antonio Ochoa and Oscar and me. And the waves out of the Pacific, which were now pounding the long, empty coast in the dark.

The next morning, Leon jostled me awake in pitch blackness.

"Almost ready?"

"Are you crazy?" I could see his white teeth floating like a canted moon. First we surfed Rio La Laja, and then we started driving north. We passed through the industrial town of Lázaro Cárdenas, where the legendary tube of Petacalco used to break, before they built a dam on the Rio Balsas. We drove into the desolate, lovely country of Michoacán. Tall saguaro cactuses came down to the beaches. The road snaked over high bluffs and around rock coves that cradled blue water. We drove in third gear. The foothills were covered with white-flowering *bogote* trees, and rioting bougainvillea edged the dooryards of the sparse villages. It was like a more tortured Highway 1, but empty, with the Pacific crashing on the rocky points and fringing the long beaches with peeling waves. Mainland Mexico has 2,500 miles of Pacific coastline—enough surf for a millennium.

Leon and I spent three days at Rio Nexpa, where there is no phone or running freshwater, just a point break and a beach break going off all at once and a long, cupped strand with a few dozen thatch-roofed cabins built for surfers, each with a balcony and a hammock. On the second evening, Leon sat on the porch rail, drinking a beer, looking out at the ocean. I swung in the hammock, replaying in my head a long ride I'd had that afternoon. A surprising set had loomed, and I found myself in position, suddenly taking off on a fast overhead left and looking down at the pod of other surfers, who seemed far below. Some cheered. I popped up and crouched, and when I'd gotten ahead of the crashing white, I roller-coastered to the top of the lip and shot back down. I did it again and again. The sensation was one of the finest I'd ever had. In my life.

"Look at the moon," Leon said. It was nearly full, rising out of the palms past the point. The sun was still a few degrees off the water, burnishing the tiers of breaking waves. A faint onshore breeze brought in the sound, a rhythmic thresh almost like breath. I didn't think he was waxing poetic—I knew what he was thinking: After the sun went down, there would always be the moon. He was already taking off his shirt.

"Aren't you tired?" I said. I think we'd surfed five hours already.

"A little. Almost ready?"

I stared at him. I burst out laughing. "What's my lesson for the day? You forgot to give it to me."

The left side of his mouth lifted just a little. "Surf whenever you can."

≈≈ ≈≈ ≈≈

Peter Heller is a contributing editor at Outside Magazine *and a winner of two Lowell Thomas awards for adventure writing. He is the author of* Hell or High Water: Surviving Tibet's Tsangpo River *and a collection of travel essays,* Set Free in China: Sojourns on the Edge. *His work has appeared in* National Geographic Adventure, Harper's, Men's Journal, *and on National Public Radio's "All Things Considered." He lives in Colorado.*

※ ※ ※

The Book

The author goes in search of the "Talmud of travel."

THE PAGES IN THE BOOK ARE YELLOW NOW — NOT FROM time (what's sixteen years?) but from the careless caresses of too many readers. Thousands of grubby hands have pressed their oily fingers on these pages. The drunk, bored, pissed-off, and horny of many nations have pawed through them, used them as drink coasters, and dribbled falafel crumbs into their folds. The corners are curled up, and the cover was long ago wrapped in butcher paper, as if it were porn.

This Book—this one volume in an uncountable chain— began the 7th of October, 1989, in a restaurant in La Paz, Bolivia, when somebody with time to kill inscribed the first tip. Written in English, with a slightly unsteady hand, the author recommended the Hotel Torino as "probably one of the cheapest hotels in central La Paz," despite a few drawbacks ("rooms don't have windows...dark and dingy...smelly and dirty"). Here in the very first entry were the muses that have dominated the Book before and since: Thrift and her handmaid, Squalor. There was one more piece of advice on that first page. Somebody had scrawled right over the earlier text: "The night porter ripped me off ASSHOLE!!!"

There are other strange, obscure, and clandestine guidebooks and traveler's compendiums out there—the Appalachian Trail is dotted with eccentric registers, the Web bursts with blogs and tip sheets on every kind of travel. But none can claim the same global reach or high standards of gripe, rant, and insight as the Book, the best unknown guidebook in the world.

The Book has no one author, editor, or publisher. Defined physically, it is merely a set of loosely connected, handmade, decentralized notebooks cached throughout the vagabond meccas of Latin America and Asia—a collective, disorganized stash of travel tips, phone numbers, discount deals, crazed illustrations, conspiracy theories, backbiting marginalia, and boozy reminiscence, penned by and for the deeply broke backpackers of the world. It is known sometimes as the Traveler's Book, or the Memory Book, or the Israeli Book, because it depends mostly on Israelis—that new diaspora of young travelers who, with a mean age of twenty-two and some hard, mandatory military service under their belts, have given rise in the past dozen years to a global sub-tribe of poncho-wearing, sandal-sporting nomads. For the Israelis, the Book is a fluid concept, a kind of viral hypertext flitting from cork bulletin board to pocket notebook, as much an oral tradition as a written one.

Although the Book is scarcely known outside the world-within-a-world of the Israeli travel scene, it is

hidden in plain sight. Four volumes are available in a
certain laundromat in San José, Costa Rica. Four at an
unheralded youth hostel in Bogotá, Colombia, called
Platypus. In Peru, the Book is variously located in a
travel agency, an upstairs watering hole in Huaraz fa-
vored by gringo trekkers, and the House of Fun, a Lima
hostel that isn't even listed in Lonely Planet. If you know
where to look, the Book is everywhere. Otherwise it is
nowhere.

I first heard it mentioned in the early 1990s, by an
Israeli paratrooper who'd just arrived in Puerto Montt, in
southern Chile. "So where's the book?" he asked another
Israeli. The answer, given in Hebrew, was: in a butcher
shop run by a Chilean Jew. It took me a decade to understand what he had really said—not "Where is our book?"
but "Where is our knowledge? Our community?"

I began to ask for the Book wherever I went, figuring that if anyone would know the best spots—or the
least bad spots—it would be the Israelis. More than any
other nationality, they have absorbed the ethic of global
tramping with ferocity: go far, stay long, see deep.

Sooner or later every Israeli in Latin America drops
a rucksack at least once at a restaurant, hostel, and social club called El Lobo, "the Wolf," located 11,220 feet
above sea level, plus one last, cruelly steep flight of stairs
up into the thin night air above La Paz. El Lobo's walls
are lined with photographs sent by grateful members of
the backpacker nation, travel snaps of themselves taken
all over South America, often engaged in stunts, especially when naked.

Owner Dorit Moralli's family emigrated from Israel
to Bolivia after the Six-Day War, the 1967 victory over

Syria, Jordan, and Egypt that bestowed on Israel the dubious prize of the West Bank, Gaza Strip, and other soon-to-be occupied territories, with their Palestinian populations. As far back as the 1930s, Bolivia welcomed Jewish immigrants (the country welcomed some ex-Nazis, like Klaus Barbie, too), but the Jewish community never really took root. Today Bolivia has only around 500 Jewish citizens—as compared with Argentina, which has over 200,000, more than half the Jews in South America. Buenos Aires remains the one big city on the continent defined by a large Jewish presence, but Dorit did her part for La Paz by opening El Lobo with her Israeli-born husband in 1986, offering the best—well, the only—Israeli food in town.

The Book appeared "one month after we opened," Dorit said as she settled into one of the restaurant's picnic tables with a plate of meatballs and rice. Back in '86, four Israeli backpackers came in, ate a meal, and asked for "the Book." Dorit had no idea what they were talking about. Elsewhere in South America, they explained, there were blank books where Israelis were writing down travel tips; they'd been in Rurrenebaque, a jungle town that they thought other people would like. "They actually bought a book, and brought it here for us," she marveled.

That original 1986 Book, entirely in Hebrew, is now safely tucked away in storage. El Lobo's second volume, a mix of English and other languages that began in 1989, remains the oldest still-circulating example that I could find.

The Book got its start back in Israel in the early 1970s, and by the early 1980s it was spreading around the world. Over the years El Lobo's version grew to become a kind of master edition, with up to sixteen regional volumes describing most of South America. Dorit—warm, zaftig, practical—became a den mother to the Israelis and other backpackers. El Lobo expanded in the 1990s, adding twenty rooms and a sort of clubhouse, which used to be entered through an unmarked door in the kitchen. Today a thoroughly global crew of Israelis, Austrians, French, and even the occasional American can be found sitting back there on ratty sofas, playing board games, drinking $2 shots of Johnnie Walker, and watching Israeli comedians on the VCR. Lonely Planet finally discovered this back room, advising travelers in the 2001 fourth edition of its Bolivia guide to visit El Lobo and "take a look at their books of travelers' recommendations in both English and Hebrew." That single sentence is the only published reference to the Book I've ever seen.

To get to El Lobo's Book, a dark-haired Israeli staffer named Yiar led me past a pile of used camping stoves for sale and over to a chaotic shelf. With a grunt, he extracted a heavy notebook. Then another, and another—six in all, each carefully preserved under hard binders and butcher paper. Five covered, respectively, Bolivia, Brazil, Chile, Argentina, and Peru and northern South America. The oldest of the six was the crumbling, venerable 1989 volume.

The title page read:

> livre international pour les voyageurs
> international travel book
> internationell resehandbook
> libro internacional.

And so on, through Portuguese, Japanese, and what looked like Welsh, down to the last line, where someone had added, book of the smarmy, conceited been-there-done-that-so-i'm-groovy wankers.

The polyglot entries were random, frustrating, and beautiful, a carnival of ideas, pleas, boasts, and obsolete phone numbers. One page recommended the "beautikul girls" (sic) in a certain disco; the next tipped a particular ice cave as "a must" (at least until someone else scrawled a huge "NO!" over that entry). This was followed by a half-page in Japanese and a dense passage in German, with bar charts of altitude and diagrams of various plants; then there was an outpouring of druggie philosophy, which was daubed with retaliatory graffiti (sad hippy wanker).

After that there was a full-page scrawl devoted to buying a canoe in the rainforests of Peru's Manu National Park, with seven parentheticals and a postscript that wrapped around the margins sideways; a warning against so-and-so's couscous; and an ornate four-color drawing of a toucan named Felipe.

What differentiates the Book from other travelers' message boards from Kathmandu to Chiang Mai is what Yiar called "the warnings," special alerts about anti-Semitism. In an overwhelmingly Christian continent, the young *israelitos* are a welcome curiosity from the land of the Bible, but, as anywhere, small skinhead groups do exist in Argentina, Chile, and Brazil. The El Lobo Book sounded an alarm about a hotel in Peru run by admirers of the Third Reich. Another entry cautioned anyone with "a shred of conscience" to avoid a hotel in Sorata, Bolivia, run by an alleged arms dealer, a man linked in police reports to, as the scribbler put it, "the shadowy rule of that great philanthropist Klaus Barbie."

A special CUIDADA page ("BEWARE") covered regular crimes and cons, citing rip-offs in Rio, bogus policemen in Bogotá, and grifters in La Paz. One sponger was always just a few dollars short of lifesaving surgery. ("Careful," someone added two years later, "he is still around.")

That touching up of a two-year-old tip reminded me why reading the Book is an experience fundamentally different from surfing message boards online. Israelis themselves do use websites like www.lametayel.com ("For the Traveler"), the portal of a popular REI-style super-store, to post some of the tips they used to carve in the Book. But anyone who has ever bogged down in Lonely Planet's Thorn Tree site knows that the Net's strengths are its weaknesses: The Web can be too broad, too accessible. Plucking wisdom from its infinite bramble of white noise can take all night. For the young Israelis, raised almost from the cradle with cell phones and computers, all that technology is just one more thing to escape when they hit the road. They search out online information until the day of departure but turn to the Book—in all its handmade glory—once their travels begin.

A journey of a thousand miles often begins by shift-ing your ass five feet. Mine had started by popping over to another of El Lobo's picnic tables, and now, three days later, I'd found myself out on Bolivia's southern altiplano, stuck in the rainy mining town of Oruru, my backpack and my Israeli companions missing in action.

It was a simple question that got me in this trouble: "So where's the Book?" I'd asked around at El Lobo. The answer from two Israelis named Avi and Elad was equally simple: "Follow us."

Avi was twenty-two, with long hair and a poncho. Elad, twenty-four, was unshaven, with untamed dark curls. Both had just finished their military service. At eighteen, virtually all Israelis are drafted into the Israeli Defense Forces (IDF); men serve three years, women two. Fresh from the tense duties of checkpoints and patrols, their fondest goal is to live normally for a while. The IDF was "great," Elad said, but "there's a lot of pressure. Everyone runs away after that."

These veterans travel for a year or more, hitting the beach, climbing mountains, dropping out, hooking up, and blowing their minds—and then repeat chorus, month after month, all over the world. Places like Bolivia are perfect for this: exotic, dirt cheap, and full of people who've never heard of Ariel Sharon.

Elad was three months into his trip, with nine to go, which he hoped to divide between Asia and Latin America. He'd read the Book even before his trip, starting with a volume kept in a bookstore in Tel Aviv. Since it was summer, he and Avi told me, many Israelis were heading south to the cooler climes of Patagonia, and they invited me to come along. When I asked where we were going, Avi pulled a crumpled scrap of paper from his jeans, smoothed it on the table, and slid it across. It was their list of Israeli places between here and Tierra del Fuego. The spots weren't just for Israelis, of course: the same network attracted a random assortment of Canadian climbers, German ethnospelunkers, and Swedes who'd worked on kibbutzim. For all of them, the route ran south to a hostel called Marith, on the outskirts of Uyuni, near the end of Bolivia's southern rail line. From there, the Book recommended crossing into Chile with Cristal, a tour agency that specializes in the Bolivian salt flats. In Chile, the main stops were the Hotel Indiana, a flophouse somewhere in Santiago, and

Pucón, the adventure-sports capital of southern Chile, where there was a hostel previously owned by two Israeli expats named Edi and Shay, and therefore called "the place that used to be Edi and Shay's." In Argentina, we could find a place in the swish alpine town of Bariloche called Room 1040. Or was it Apartment 4010?

Though we knew where we wanted to go, getting there was something else. The trip south from La Paz was a disaster. I loaded my backpack on the wrong bus, and while I waited two days in Oruru for it to arrive (it did), Avi caught the train south to Uyuni, in the desert. Elad, meanwhile, abruptly changed course—he'd met these five sisters in La Paz, he explained. By the time I reached the Marith guesthouse, Avi had departed, leaving me a note on the bulletin board urging me to catch up. For four days I bumped south and west over Bolivia's vast salt flats, climbing toward Chile in a jeep that seemed to collide with Israelis in the wilderness. At a wind-formed rock outcrop, I met Hanit ("It means 'Spear'"), a skinny Sephardic woman who'd just finished her service in the IDF ("of course") and had just come from El Lobo ("of course"). The next day, atop a cactus-covered island in the vast salt pans, at something like 13,000 feet, I stumbled on a couple of guys from Haifa tricked out in ten-gallon Stetsons. They'd bought the hats while passing through Boulder, Colorado, a few months before. We'd been talking for two minutes when one of them said, "You mean Avi with the long hair? Sure, we know him." Avi was up ahead, "somewhere out there," they said, pointing toward the snowcapped 20,000-foot Andean peaks along the Chilean border. On my last night in Bolivia, in the guest register of a tiny village museum, I saw that Avi had signed out that morning.

After crossing the border and dropping down into the desert oasis of San Pedro de Atacama, I promptly ran into Hanit again. But this was a tourist town—too expensive for Israelis, she said. The bus station was crowded with her sticker-shocked countrymen, including a dreadlocked couple with a baby, five years into their global ramble. Hanit and I took different buses south—I paid the extra $11 for a sleeper—to Santiago. Twenty-four hours of rumbling down Chile's desert highways dropped me in the gritty capital.

It was easy enough to follow the Israeli trail, even without Avi and Elad. One Jewish person on his own is lonely, "like a candle in the dark," Elad had told me. They gravitate together, adding "another candle over here, and another candle over there," until the world grows less cold.

"You put them all together," he'd said, cupping his hands, "and you have a warm fire."

Exile is the Jewish condition, so perhaps it is no surprise that travel away from Israel has become central to the Israeli identity. The origins of this itch, as well as the origins of the Book itself, go back to the aftermath of the Yom Kippur War, in 1973, when the country defeated the combined armies of Egypt and Syria. For the first time, Israelis could venture abroad knowing their country would still exist when they returned. "You didn't have the Rough Guides translated into Hebrew," notes Tal Muscal, the former tourism correspondent for the *Jerusalem Post*. "People were xeroxing their notes from trips, and you could find them in cafés in Tel Aviv or on university bulletin boards."

Thirty years later, Israelis can buy Lonely Planet and other guidebooks in Hebrew, but the Book is still widespread, a grassroots Talmud of travel, a commentary without beginning or end. If it has a home in Israel, it's Lametayel, the chain of gear stores, which offers lectures and detailed notebooks filled with trip reports from returnees.

For Israelis, travel is therapy. "There is a sense of a mental prison living here, surrounded by enemies," explains Yair Qedar, editor of the Tel Aviv–based travel magazine *Masa Acher*. Every moment is pregnant with menace. A trip to the pizzeria can end in the flash of a bomb. And there is the claustrophobia of tight-knit families in a miniature country hemmed in by ancient social traditions. "Suffocation is a constant feeling," Qedar says. "When the sky opens, you get out."

In the early 1990s, the sky opened. Israeli and Palestinian leaders signed the Oslo Accord, the economy boomed, and airfares dropped. *Masa Acher* grew from a minor rag into Israel's largest monthly magazine. A tiny nation—now almost 7 million people—churned out enormous numbers of travelers.

The backpackers call this mass movement *gal*, or "the wave." "Everyone goes the same route," explains Darya Maoz, who teaches a class at Jerusalem's Hebrew University called Sociological and Anthropological Aspects of Tourism and Backpacking. "Depending on the seasons, it's Ecuador, Peru, Bolivia, and certain places within each country," she says. "So if they start in February, they start at Carnival in Brazil."

Maoz backpacked all over the world, off and on, for eight years, interviewing Israelis for her Ph.D. thesis ("Aspects of Life Cycle in the Journey of Israelis to India"). Many societies, she notes, encourage their youth to drop out for a period of self-discovery. (This is called a "gap year" in Britain, "walkabout" in Australia, and "wasting your life" in America.)

No nation can flee its stereotypes—think of Japanese shutterbugs, Germans in socks and sandals, and solipsistic Americans searching for someplace exotic with all the conveniences of home. Israelis are criticized for...well, maybe Maoz should say it: "They tend to be rude, to curse the locals, to ruin things if they are not satisfied," she sighs. Living on a shoestring budget, they will argue over the price of anything—even, she recalls, a cup of tea costing five rupees. After venting for several minutes on the flawed character of her compatriots, she concludes with the indictment that "they don't respect local people, they party all night, they take a lot of drugs, and if people say something, some Israelis call them Nazis."

This can deepen grudges and feed the very stereotypes Israelis are hoping to escape. "Personally," one scowling hotelkeeper told me in Chile, "I would not deal with the Israelis." I asked why. "They are not reliable," she said. "Not trustworthy. They will always try to get the best bargain from you. They are not all the same, but still, I don't recommend you go with them."

"We are not so nice," concedes Kobi Tzvieli, a manager at the Tel Aviv branch of Lametayel, who himself relied on the Book in Colombia and Thailand. Lametayel has started a program called Good Will Ambassadors to teach Israelis to be polite while abroad.

This can be hard when you're traveling in a pack. Military life and thousands of years of anti-Semitism have taught Israelis to rely on tight, strong units, and they tend to create their own ecosystems wherever they go. El Lobo, for example, is now surrounded by shops, travel agencies, and even juice carts equipped with

Hebrew signage. In India, a whole village called Kasol is wall-to-wall restaurants serving hummus and matzo.

There's a popular joke in Israel that Maoz was the fourth person to tell me. It always begins with an Israeli backpacker walking into what he thinks is a remote village (in India, Thailand, Chile, or Guatemala, depending on the narrator). He puts his passport on the counter and the hotelkeeper asks, "How many are you?"

"Seven million," the Israeli replies. The owner nods and says, "And how many back in Israel?"

The wave was in the house at the Hotel Indiana. The place was a peerless, spectacular dump. The rooms were airless cells. The foul mattresses were lit by bare bulbs swinging from wires. The shower gave me an electric shock. It cost 4,000 pesos, or about $7, a night.

Hanit arrived shortly after me, the Jewish cowboys the next day. A dozen Israelis were usually in the front room, watching TV, with another dozen in the courtyard. A muscled kid, released from IDF service days before, ripped out twenty pull-ups as beardless boys and blooming girls compared notes on Gaza and Jenin, suicide bombers and outpost sieges. Most of them had been drafted in 2001 and sent into the maw of the latest intifada. Kids shot at them and they shot back. Several confessed to having done things in battle that they were ashamed of, or to having strong sympathy for Palestinian nationalism, yet they were universally proud of having served. "When I was a child someone protected me," the pull-up champion told me, with fatalism. "Now it is my turn."

There was a shadow in the courtyard for each of them, the Palestinian in every traveler's memory. No wonder they loved travel. On the road you could wake up every morning with the one thing you never got in the Middle East: a fresh start.

The Indiana's version of the Book consisted of dozens of notes in Hebrew and English, covering the walls. They offered discounts at a certain laundromat (I got a dollar off), requested travel partners, and inquired after members of the opposite sex. Mating rituals like this were once a staple of the Book, but here, alas, the tracking abilities of Hotmail were proving far superior to bulletin-board flirtations.

At sunset, I climbed one of the small peaks that loom over downtown Santiago. On top, an Israeli tapped me on the shoulder. His name was Yaniv, he said, and he recognized me from the Indiana. Like a lot of young Israelis, Yaniv had overcompensated for years of military haircuts by sprouting everything he could: His chin was a wispy scruff and his sun-bleached hair had twirled into a mix of short dreads and Orthodox earlocks, all swept up into a kind of werewolf 'do. "The hair is because of the army," Yaniv admitted. "First the hair, then the travel."

Yaniv had been in the infantry, making incursions into Palestinian areas. "I actually looked at it as travel," he explained, with a wry smile. "I couldn't go to these places—to Nablus or Ramallah—as a traveler. But with a gun in my hand, I could. It's nice there in Nablus. You should go."

I'd been, I told him.

"Yes," he said, with sudden sadness. "You can go there."

IDF soldiers are paid a bonus at demobilization, and Yaniv, as a combat veteran, got close to the maximum: about $3,000. That was his budget for an entire year. In seven months he'd visited France, Colombia, Ecuador, Bolivia, Peru, and Chile. The trip was healing him, he said, closing wounds he'd never acknowledged even to himself.

"One thing I can say," he told me, "is that I am more *tranquilo* here than in Israel. I don't know if it is the war, or just a tense society, but being here has changed me."

To save one of his combat-pay dollars, Yaniv and I walked to the Indiana, halfway across the city. He used the time to coach me on blending in with the dewy Israelis—a tall order for a Scotch-Irish forty-year-old. First, Yaniv said, I should hide my guidebook. He relied on the Book where he could—the one at the Platypus Hostel, in Bogotá, was the best he'd seen, and there was a good one in Quito, Ecuador. Cuzco, however, was a nightmare. "Too many Israelis," he said. "If you are going to Cuzco, practice your Hebrew. Even the drug dealers speak it."

Second, I had to bargain hard. This was a stereotype but a true one, he insisted. "It is part of our culture to bargain, a Middle East thing," he said. "Don't come out *frayer*."

Pardon? "Don't come out *frayer*" is a crucial expression in Israel, translating as "Don't be a sucker." As an example, Yaniv cited the Indiana. "They told me the room was 4,000 pesos. Now, I thought, I can get a better price. So I argued, and now I am paying 3,500 pesos. That's O.K. But I think that maybe some of the other Israelis are paying only 2,500 or 3,000 pesos. So if they find out what I'm paying, then I'm *frayer*."

I, of course, was paying the full 4,000 pesos. The Indiana was such a dive that it hadn't even occurred to me to bargain.

Yaniv stopped walking when I told him this. "My friend," he said with pity, "you are *frayer* already."

I rolled south on an overnight bus, passing through an increasingly green and rugged landscape. In Pucón, I bunked at "the place that used to be Edi and Shay's." It was yet another dump: beds piled into rooms, gear everywhere, a cybercafé with Hebrew keyboards. Israelis on paragliding outings were landing in the pasture out back. Edi and Shay had recently decamped to the Holy Land, but there was a new Book at the tourism office, with the usual temperate observations in many languages.

I took the next bus out, motoring up curvy roads to the Argentinian border. Watching as the passports were checked, I realized that I was the only American. There were several Latin Americans, a couple of Canadians, even a few Koreans. There were nine Israelis.

"That's because there are 500 million of us," the guy behind me said, exaggerating by a factor of 71. His name was Amatsia. Next to him sat Ayala, a dark-haired physics-and-math double major who'd delayed her military service until after university. They both got out to join a cluster of Israelis standing in the road. They opened their little notebooks and swapped hotel names and addresses, everyone writing quickly.

Back on the bus, Ayala shared her list of the spots ahead of us. "Apartment 1004," she said, reading the Hebrew glyphs. Aha. So that was the real name of what Elad called "Room 1040." She gave me the address. "In San Martín," she continued, "it's Naum's."

San Martín was our next stop, a resort town surrounded by forests and lakes, just a few hours into

Argentina. We piled off the bus at dusk, just as a hefty man on a scooter pulled up: the owner of Naum's himself, Jorge Candel. The ten of us donned our packs and shuffled across town as Jorge puttered ahead. Naum's was easy to spot—it had a menorah in the yard and an electric Star of David hanging over the street.

Jorge had neglected to mention that the hotel was full. There was now a polite discussion, Israeli style: eight people crammed into the office, shouting demands at one another, waving their arms, marching back and forth, and emitting vehement displays of disgust. Apparently several alliances were built only to crumble, and ground was taken, lost, and then regained. After ten minutes there was a sudden eruption of amity, and handshakes all around.

Ayala emerged from the scrum looking stunned. "I had no idea I was going to meet so many Israelis," she said. "I just ran into a guy from high school."

As usual, the deal was cheap and lousy. We paid $5 each to sleep on mattresses in a hallway, between the bathroom and a heater. In the morning we packed into a van to Bariloche. As we pulled away, Jorge reached through the door with a Swiss Army knife.

"Patrick," he said, "if you are really ready to be a Jew, then we have a certain operation for you."

I rolled the van door over his toes.

That night in Bariloche, the address Ayala had given me looked dubious. The building was a half-abandoned office block. The lobby was deserted. The elevator shuddered and then stopped between floors four and five, where some plumber-commandos out of the movie *Brazil* crawled aboard. On ten, the highest floor, I found myself in a dank, silent hallway, following numbers beneath burned-out bulbs. At the end of the hall, at the last door, there it was: 1004.

Inside was a funny, five-dollar paradise. Hostel 1004, as I finally learned it was called, was beautiful, with wraparound views of Lake Nahuel Huapi and the Andes from a carpeted lounge. There were two big fireplaces. The rooms were nice, with good bunk beds, and the bathrooms were clean. At a sun-drenched picnic table on the terrace, two Israelis were quizzing a Frenchman about the skiing in Bariloche. It was the best crash pad I'd ever seen.

Here was a reason to follow the Book. The Book knew. Though Hostel 1004 does appear in guidebooks, you would never have picked this one dive from the foolscap wilderness of low-rent listings. But as they had throughout history, the Israelis passed knowledge along, mouth to mouth, ear to ear. The Book learned what they learned.

"So where's the Book?" I asked. The manager, a rocker-tressed Argentinian named Juan, sucked in his breath. "We don't know," he confessed. They'd had a good volume, five years of entries kept up by Israelis and everybody else. But in October, when they were repainting the place, the Book had been shoved into storage, casually, only to disappear. (Indeed, on the message board, a huge note read "EL LIBRO?")

"A lost treasure," Juan said. But he didn't doubt that eventually the guests at 1004 would start a fresh one.

I couldn't doubt it. People would make the Book anew, somewhere, somehow, because they needed it. The Book was an analog artifact in a digital age, diminished by Web updates and nomadic e-mail, but never obsolete. Back at El Lobo, Dorit had suggested that the Book's golden age might be over. "Before," she said, "the Book was like the Bible. Now, almost nobody asks for it." She had opened a cybercafé and encouraged her guests to post their entries on El Lobo's Web site, www.lobo.co.il. "This is history," she'd said, slapping the soft brown paper.

If so, then it is history that's still being written. The Book shouldn't exist, yet it does, a counterintuitive survivor like the underground postal system in Thomas Pynchon's *The Crying of Lot 49*. And if it shrank in one place, like El Lobo, that was only because the wave had moved on. It flourished in four volumes at a laundromat in Costa Rica; it was on the rise at the House of Fun in Lima; it was blossoming anew in some cheap hostel you and I have never heard of.

A few days later I set out, south as always, but alone this time. I never saw Avi or Elad again, not in Patagonia or anywhere else. Elad would write from various ports of call: Boulder, Israel, Manhattan. South America had been great, he reminisced, calling the experience "the first time I was really free."

With the clarity of distance and time, the Israeli-Palestinian conflict suddenly seemed "silly, unnecessary," he wrote. Although Israelis had every material advantage, they were still "blind," trapped in a narrow view of the conflict, unable to imagine a way out. "If that is the situation in Israel," he said, "just imagine what is going on in Gaza and the West Bank," where Palestinians lived in an even narrower bubble. Elad suggested sending leaders from both sides on a six-month world tour, just to open their minds.

The last time I heard from Elad, he was on his way to India. Maybe he'd see me, here, or there, or somewhere.

The trip wasn't over yet. There were always more pages
in the Book to fill.

≈≈≈

Patrick Symmes is a contributing editor at Harper's *and* Outside
magazines and also writes for GQ *and* Condé Nast Traveler. *He
has traveled with Maoist insurgents in Nepal, visited both main
guerrilla groups in Colombia, and profiled drug gangs in Brazil. He
is the author of* Chasing Che: A Motorcycle Journey in Search
of the Guevara Legend *and* Ten Thousand Revolutions.

❧ ❧ ❧

Cutouts

The night once had a thousand eyes.

ON NIGHTS WHEN THERE WAS A MOON, ALDO AND I would leave Poggio al Grillo without a lamp. It wasn't hard to pick our way down the dirt road, and anyway Aldo knew its twists and turns by heart.

Some nights we walked as far as Vito Lippini's. There we might see, through a door cut into the stucco walls of an outbuilding, the family's *nonna* sitting on a stool in a golden rectangle of light, wearing a black dress and headscarf, as silent as Whistler's mother, staring down the vat of red wine. Some nights we would run into Ernst, the Swiss farmer, on his bicycle, hurrying home to his wife and children from a tryst with the Englishman's wife. Other nights we stopped in on Nino, who came from Milan only on weekends and brought his mistress with him.

Only a month earlier, it was me whom Aldo had stopped in on. I had just finished dinner and was cleaning up when I heard a deep voice outside. "*Cosa succede qui? Chi abita in questa casa scura?*" (What's happening here? Who has turned on the lights in the dark house?) I opened the door to find a tall, fit man with gray hair, black eyebrows, and a neat, gray beard, accompanied by a silent German shepherd.

(Upon hearing that I would be traveling in Italy, a Milanese couple—friends from a theater class in Berkeley—had given me their country place in Tuscany for the fall. They hadn't warned me of this ad hoc night patrol.)

"*Sono amica degli Riccardi*," I heard myself blurt out. "*Non parlo italiano.*"

"*Benissimo!*" the man replied. "I leeved two years in Feelahdellfeeah."

And so we became friends: the twenty-six-year-old American girl, feeling very alone in a sprawling house in the Tuscan hills, and the fifty-six-year-old painter from Milan with his dog Doc. It didn't take long before we were eating dinner together every night.

After dinner we would walk, leaving the red traces of our wineglasses to seep into the new beech table ("It is too new, too perfect," Aldo complained) and leaving dishes to soak in the sink ("*l'acqua calda soltanto nella mattina*"; no hot water till morning.) Often we didn't stop in on anyone. We just wandered.

On a night when there was just a sliver of a moon, I was taught an Italian children's rhyme:

Gobba a ponente,
Luna crescente;
Gobba a levante,
Luna calante.

In Tuscany, apparently, the man in the moon was a hunchback. If his *gobba* protruded to west, the moon was swelling; if his *gobba* protruded to the east, the moon was diminishing.

On another night, I fantasized about the people of the town, Castagneto Carducci, imagining them as giant blue nudes. Aldo was going on and on about how they were "cut out," their isolation leading not just to poverty but also to provincial pettiness. Only later did I realize that he was translating *tagliati fuori* a bit too literally: he meant "cut off," not "cut out." His mistranslation took me to Matisse and the cutouts that the aging artist made in his last years in Provence. It didn't matter to me that these hills were a palette of ochre, umber, sage, and sienna; that night I imagined the townspeople as cobalt cutouts against an all-white background.

On another night, I learned that those same townspeople had taken to calling me *la ragazza molto in gamba*. "What did they mean," I asked, "that I had big thighs?" Aldo laughed. To be very much "in one's legs," he explained, was to show pluck.

This had come in one of our conversations about my writing. At the time, I dreamed of becoming a writer; I scribbled in a journal and suffered from dark self-doubt. I didn't have a clue as to how to "become" an artist. I had not so much as tasted the kind of success he took for granted. He, after all, was a renowned painter. His studio at Poggio al Grillo (Cricket Knoll) included not just his own landscapes and nudes, but also a Warhol lithograph of Marisa Berenson, a Magritte, and a Picasso—all acquired in trades with other Italian artists. Aldo even prided himself on having once wittily put de Chirico in his place.

"What could you understand," I jabbed defensively, "about my predicament?"

"Ah," he consoled. "I know too tenderly the swing of the pendulum. One day: I am a genius! The next: I am a nothing."

I never called him my lover. It's not that we didn't share a bed—in this case, a modernish wood frame of his design that firmly held two independent twin mattresses together. It's just that that term failed to describe what I found in Aldo. It was as though I had met the person I would have been if I had been born exactly one generation earlier, and in Italy, and a man.

Aldo had the nerve to live ideas I was only beginning to flirt with.

He had never doubted that he was an artist. Not that he didn't take risks: He had grown up in a bourgeois Milanese family and had forsaken the family legacy for a deeply nonconformist life. He was still a Communist, long after that party had gone out of favor. He had never married. As a young man, he had fled to Philadelphia when he found himself hopelessly in love with his brother Cesare's wife. The exile didn't work; Aldo returned to Italy and helped his sister-in-law raise his niece and nephew. The relationship with his sister-in-law eventually foundered, but he stayed close to his brother's children: during the fall I was with him, he was fretting over the niece's husband, a heroin addict, and giving the nephew his half of La Gallinella, a stone house he owned with Cesare. (In the kind of symmetrical justice only possible in Italy, by this time the cuckholded Cesare was living in town with a former consort of Aldo's.)

The subject of freedom—creative, sexual, political—dominated many of our walks. Aldo was militantly opposed to many things. Like monogamy. Like complacency. Like violence. In the bedroom, a small ragged window was set into the wall beside the bed. Aldo had built the stone house by hand, and during a hiatus in the building project, a spider had spun a web in the valley between two stones. Aldo couldn't bear to destroy the web, so he placed a glass behind the spider and kept building. From the bed, you could stare through the web window, over several ridges covered with olive trees, to the Mediterranean beyond.

One day over lunch, I noticed a very thin steel wire that extended horizontally over my head, from one wall of Aldo's house to the other. Thinking it might be for hanging underwear on a rainy day, I asked about it. "After I built the house," he explained, ever the *maestro*, "I realized that there should be a beam there, for aesthetic reasons. The wire represents the beam."

Despite the aesthetic attractions of his house, I maintained my own quarters at the Riccardis'. I would go there during the day to write, and to play with arrangements of the paintings Aldo kept bequeathing me. They were all watercolors featuring the hills and the sea, or lithographs of black-ink nudes on bright white paper. As I moved them from bedroom to living room, from the seats of chairs to ledges built into the walls, I examined them for flaws. For imperfection, Aldo insisted, was the soul of art. To him, a perfect painting was merely decorative. A bit of watercolor out of control—or the self-doubt I couldn't escape—suggested Truth, Life, the Human Condition.

On nights when there was no moon, not even a *gobba*, Aldo would grab the huge Panasonic lantern that stood sentry next to the front door. We would follow the beam of the massive flashlight down the gravel drive, watch as it animated the pocks in the dirt road, feel ourselves cradled in a roofless room as the light picked up dusty banks cut into certain curves. I'd be transported to the dark courtyard of an ancient villa, or to the eerie majesty of San Galgano—the ruin of a Cistercian abbey in the Val di Merse whose ceiling and windows had long ago been carried off by the wind, whose walls enclosed a grand abbey now consecrated only to Space.

On one particularly dark night, shortly before I was to leave Aldo, in search of my own truths, the beam stretched indefinitely ahead as we fell uncharacteristically quiet, each lost in thought. Suddenly, in that tenantless night, there rose a porcelain-like tinkle. Aldo jerked the lamp ninety degrees, into the black emptiness. There to our right, frozen in the beam and almost near enough to touch, was a flock of sheep. Hundreds of pairs of eyes glazed red-gold. All of us—the flock, the painter, the lamb of a writer—all of us stood frozen for a few eternal seconds. The wonder! Then one sheep turned its head, sharp hooves made the bone-dry grass rustle, and, in a symphony of bells, they were gone.

≈ ≈ ≈

Constance Hale is the author of Wired Style *and* Sin and Syntax. *She has written not just about Latin plurals and internet clichés, but also about national politics, Hawai'ian paniolos, and her family of military men. She lives in Oakland, California, and Hale'iwa, Hawai'i.*

❦ ❦ ❦

Fiji Time

It waits for no man.

"BULA!"

Among native Fijians, *"Bula!"* is the one-word welcome, delivered with enthusiasm and grace, to all who visit the Islands. It's a reception not only to their country, but also to their culture—celebrated for its joyous and leisurely embrace of life.

Travel industry professionals quickly recognized the marketing potential, christening this indigenous attitude: "Fiji time." Brochures designed to lure tourists to these islands glow with glossy four-color photos of white-sand beaches flanked by lofty green-leafed palms on one side, gentle gin-clear seas on the other. The images are of place, but the implication is tranquility. The text invariably describes time. Fiji Time. "Visit the islands time forgot." "Put a foot in Fiji, and step back a hundred years." "Come to Fiji where your only rigor is relaxation."

For many visitors the transition from Western precision to Fiji time is a skill that must be learned. Some never do. A digital watch can be stopped, but it can never ever run slow. For others, it's precisely this lackadaisical tempo of life in the tropics that forms the template of "holiday." For them, Fiji time offers a refreshing intermission, an escape from the tightly-scheduled daily routines of home.

But for native islanders, there is little alternative. Fiji time is standard issue—pervasive and inescapable. It's genetic, borne of climate and culture. Like threads that collectively make cloth, Fiji time is integrally woven into the fabric of this tropical lifestyle.

I chose to cultivate my indoctrination to Fiji time underwater. The apparent daytime rhythm of the reef runs roughly parallel to the land it surrounds. In this endeavor, I was not alone. After completing a medical degree, my friend Chris abandoned ship to indulge his passion for coral reefs. On the outskirts of the small town of Savu Savu, he commissioned an open wooden boat and rented a modest house on an idyllic shore worthy of the travel brochures. The front porch overlooked a sheltered bay whose waters sparkled in the sun, and whose beaches were lined by lanky palms gently waving in the breeze. We had breakfast on this porch. And as we sipped from tall glasses of freshly squeezed fruit juices, discussion eventually turned to our options for the day.

These were pretty much the same as yesterday, and the day before, and the day before that. In fact for nearly a month, we had started our days sipping a glass of juice, companion to the same dialog, while admiring the vista off the porch. Then we had gathered our dive gear, boarded Chris's little boat, and somewhere in the bay, slipped quietly into the clear, tepid water, and immersed ourselves in Fiji time.

Life on the reef is rich and diverse. Finely branching corals—pink, green, blue, and yellow—stretch calcium limbs towards the sky. Massive colonies of green corals have slowly grown over the centuries, like sequoias of the sea, forming living mounds nearly the size of our humble house. Collectively, the corals create majestic pinnacles, whose origins rest on the sandy bottom sometimes forty or fifty feet below, and whose sun driven summits often caress the underside of the sea's surface. Interspersed in crevices, and undulating near the coral's shallow crown, large schools of diminutive fish—orange, lavender, and pink—wiggle their little tails and wave their heads in unison, uniformly choreographed by the current.

Like the festive sulus worn by Fijian men and women, other fish are clad in spots and stripes of radiant colors, as though on daytime loan from the multihued sunsets that punctuate the soft transition into night.

Over the weeks, during our daily indulgence of the reef and Fiji time, the fish, the coral, and their braided routines, became familiar. In these aquatic communities, as with those on land, existence hinges on an elegant equilibrium—a delicately balanced blend of collaboration and competition.

As our familiarity with the dynamics of reef populations increased, so did our appreciation for the intricacy of Fijian village life.

One day early in our stay, the fuel line of our boat's outboard engine became fouled, perhaps with water. We never resolved exactly how or why, and as with so many of life's enigmas, this remained a mystery. But the symptoms were clear. With the boat hauled up on the beach, we pulled off the glistening white plastic cover. As we began to excavate the engine's inner workings, a group of local fisherman gathered to "assist."

In a Fijian village, anyone's affairs are everyone's affairs. This included our engine. Amused, intrigued, and attentive, the group's individual opinions, vociferously expressed in long strings of mostly vowels interspersed with laughter, eventually evolved to consensus. Our investigations were either politely condemned or condoned by the throng. Although boat engines were nothing new to this crowd, we readily observed that interpersonal relations were often just as temperamental as the motors themselves.

After the surgery was complete, and the cover replaced, Chris pulled the starter cord. The engine sputtered momentarily, and with a unanimous and exuberant *Bula!,* was coaxed back to life. We invited the team back to the porch, where we exchanged introductions and congratulations, followed by a few celebratory rounds of Fiji Bitters.

As with our engine, and the colorful scales of reef fish, a simple cover often cloaks complexity. *Bula!,* we discovered, was equally endowed.

Hospitality is as innate to Fijian culture as the people are indigenous to these islands. Soon after the great motor revival, Chris and I accepted unending invitations into the homes of our hosts and gradually, the complexion of "Fiji time" was unveiled.

Village life is both individual and collective. Tools, talents, chores, and children are all shared. Older kids

attend the needs of younger ones, and often they all ca-
rouse the neighborhood, like a playful pack of dolphins.
Whichever children end up in the yard at meal time are
fed. Often the entire gang sleeps at one home, and the
following morning, dressed in fresh clothes to start the
day. The soiled garments, independent of ownership,
are washed and hung on the line, awaiting their occu-
pants' next arrival.

Personal property is communal property. The phrase
"*keri, keri*" is a traditional request that is rarely refused.
"*Keri, keri,* your frying pan," for example, means "please
lend me your pan." Possessions are shared by obligation.
What's mine is yours—by cultural edict. Through this,
and other customs, a village takes care of itself, and all
its members.

What Fijian life lacks in physical complexity it compensates for in social and political doctrine. Personal issues are community issues, often resolved by the chief, or
elders of the village. And while survival is rarely an issue,
personal industry is the foundation of Fiji time. Women,
in addition to all the household tasks, labor in the fields
growing dalo, taro, cassava, and other food crops. Men
typically are entrusted with construction, maintenance,
and at least in this village, fishing. Interwoven with the
work, and in fact supported by it, is the buoyant tem-
perament at whose apex resides the ubiquitous *Bula!*

So it was with some surprise, that as Chris and I
completed a delightful day of diving and saw our village
fishermen gathered beneath the palms of the shore, not
a single *Bula!* was bestowed.

Chris switched off the boat engine, and we quietly
glided closer to beach. The late afternoon sun bathed
the trees and the men in a warm yellow light, casting

long dark shadows on the sand. Equally dark were the expressions of our friends. Soon we saw why.

I remember the sound of our keel softly grating against the sand as our craft came to rest alongside Tui's small white skiff. It's floorboards were afloat in a sea of blood. Chris and I quickly jumped to the beach, and in an instant that slowed to an eternity, we were among the men.

Words were not needed. Beneath a small blanket of green palm fronds lay Evuloni, curled up on his left side, as though taking a nap in the shade. A bloodstained towel was draped across his right thigh. Lemeki pulled back the shroud, exposing the wound. A semi-circular section of flesh, the size of a young coconut, had been excised, neatly and nearly to the bone.

He and Tui had been spearfishing across the bay. As always, the fish were tied to a line around his waist. This time, however, a small but aggressive shark had swallowed the entire catch, and with it, part of Evuloni's leg.

Kneeling down to check his pulse, Chris desperately asked if someone had called the town's only ambulance. The men solemnly replied yes, but now they were waiting for it to come. I looked at our friend on the ground. He was unconscious, in shock, and quivering like a speared fish. This was no time to wait.

I ran down the unpaved road to a small resort, quickly commandeered a pickup truck, and we all carefully placed Evuloni in the back. Lemecki drove, the others crouched in the rear, cradling their comrade as best they could. The truck was soon only an echo of dust left suspended in the twilight air. The ambulance never did arrive.

That was the last time Chris or I saw Evuloni. He died on the way to the hospital, we were told. Lemecki later speculated that Evoluni had baited the shark deliberately—he was having problems with his wife. The village will look after his wife and two children so young they may not remember their father as they grow.

Later that night, Chris and I sat on the porch where just weeks before we'd hoisted beers with the boys. Moonlight shimmered off the glassy ripples of the bay. Beneath the iridescent surface, reef fish peacefully slept, awaiting the dawn. The palms were now silhouettes against a black sky. Over a soft chorus of crickets and geckos, we quietly talked about the incident. The wound was serious but not in itself fatal. Why didn't Tui stop the bleeding? Why didn't the ambulance come? Why didn't Tui just drive the boat to the clinic near the shore where they were fishing? The questions were for our ears alone. There were no answers.

I had never seen a man die. Nor have I since. And over the course of thirty years of diving the tropics, and numerous visits to Fiji, this remains the single shark attack in my experience. Yes, Evoluni died. But it wasn't the shark that killed him. It was Fiji time.

❧ ❧ ❧

Joel Simon is a freelance travel writer and photographer. His photo assignments have taken him to the North Pole, the Antarctic, and over one hundred countries in between. When not traveling, he's at home in Menlo Park, California, with his wife, Kim, their three daughters, and an itinerant possum named Rover.

❧ ❧ ❧

Mirage

Didn't the Buddha say that all is illusion?

I T TOOK EXACTLY TWENTY-TWO MINUTES FOR ME, A mother, a daughter, and a dead chicken to board a bus in the Calabrian village of San Procopio. The driver, a slight man with narrow sideburns who was sitting on a bench near the parked bus, appeared to move at a pace that habit had timed for him rather than a schedule. He pulled up his pants, tightened his long belt a notch, and opened the door for me by bumping it a few times with his hip. I handed him money for the ticket, which he accepted graciously as if it were a tip rather than the fare. He bunched it in his shirt pocket with his cigarettes and pointed to all the vacant seats before walking toward the *tabaccaio*. I quickly asked if the bus was going to the *passeggiata* along the water in Reggio di Calabria and if it would leave on time. He stared at my money belt before signaling me to board, no doubt thinking I was another tourist in search of the miracle of the Fata Morgana along the Strait of Messina, which meant he knew that I knew that unless he got the bus moving, we'd probably get there too late to witness a fantastic city rising from the sea.

It was a foggy and humid morning, and the odds were as good as they were going to get for the Sicilian town of Messina across the strait to be reflected in the water and air, creating the mirage's rare occurrence. The weather in the afternoon, however, was forecasted to turn sunny as was the remainder of my trip. As much as I enjoyed cooling off in the water, sipping fresh-squeezed lemonade made with the region's Bergamot lemons, and snapping shots of the village with my family's *cugini* under red-tile roofs and blue skies, I came for my mother's Fata Morgana and nothing else.

I made sure the driver saw me tapping on my watch before stepping onto the bus. The rows of empty brown vinyl seats were at perfect right angles, which led me to believe this was once a school bus. The seat cushions were so worn, it felt as though I were sitting in a dried-up mud puddle.

After a few minutes passed and there was still no driver, I waved at him out of my window. He nodded and smiled at me from the *tabaccaio* doorway as he ducked inside the beaded curtain. I sat back down, looked at my watch and worried that my one chance to catch a meteorological freak of nature was ticking away.

I gave him thirty more seconds and then I would get off the bus and fetch him. I'd offer to buy him a gelato and he could lick it while he drove. If he were like other drivers in San Procopio, he'd probably use one hand to

steer anyway. Even to navigate the hairpin turns along
the steep cliffside to the water.

Just as I was about to hop off the bus, he poked his
head outside the curtain of beads at the doorway and
shouted, "*Un momentino, signore, per favore.*"

The driver and I obviously had the same difference
of opinion over the likelihood of the Fata Morgana that
my mother and father had. I remember as a little girl
how they would argue. He pulled out the encyclopedia
and read what he called scientific fact: "A Fata Morgana
mirage is when a layer of hot air traps rays of light coming from distant objects such as rocks, which appear to
be towers of a fairy-tale castle. The light rays bend as
they pass from the cool, heavy air near the surface to the
warm, light air above it."

He slammed the book shut and said that if the Fata
Morgana were to occur, which it wouldn't, it was no
miracle that it would be in Calabria. "It's got hot air, all
right. Not just from the sirocco current from Africa but
from all the people down there who have nothing better
to do than listen to themselves talk about the Red years
and revolution! And there's enough rock in the boot of
Italy for a million optical illusions! Ask the *contadini*
who work the land. I don't want to hear no more about
castles in the sky."

When he walked off, my mother opened the encyclopedia to the page my father read from, his sweaty
thumbprint still visible on the corner. She inserted a
small piece of onionskin paper with a few sentences
handwritten so lightly the Italian words were barely visible. When I asked my mother to read it to me, she said
it was the testimony of a priest who, hundreds of years

ago, witnessed the Fata Morgana miracle over the Strait
of Messina. "The sea, washing up the coast of Sicily, rose
up like a dark mountain range. In front of the mountain, a series of white-gray pilasters appeared. Then they
shrank to half their height and built arches like those of
Roman aqueducts. Castles appeared above the arches,
each with towers and windows before it all vanished."

She tucked the thin piece of paper into the encyclopedia as if it were a holy card marking a page in the Bible.
In a cadence of prayer, I often heard her reciting it out
loud. Her eyes slowly closing, her lips moving ever so
slightly, whispering the words so only she could hear
them.

One day, thinking the Fata Morgana was visible from
the rivers in Pittsburgh because my father was always
talking about the confluence at the Point, I asked her if
she would take me there to see the miracle.

"Never in Pittsburgh," she insisted—not only be-
cause the meteorological conditions weren't right, but
Pittsburgh would never take the place of her San
Procopio.

My father was just the opposite. Pittsburgh was where
he came as a Calabrian orphan and made a life for himself. The city could do no wrong—never mind that he
was laid off two years short of collecting a full pension
when the steel mills started closing down. Or the bill
collectors, the bankruptcies, the loss of a way of life for
a class of people. He'd rather be in Pittsburgh over San
Procopio. When I'd remind him of the facts, he'd tell
me to just go to the Point and look at how the two rivers
merge to form a new one. They don't go their separate
ways. They come together. That's a miracle every minute of the day.

He hadn't gone back to San Procopio since his uncle brought him to Pittsburgh when his parents died suddenly. When I asked him about it, all he said was that it was an accident. I could tell there was more to it than that, but he didn't want to tell me. No surprise, he thought I was wasting my money by going to San Procopio to look for the Fata Morgana, but before my mother died, she asked me to do one last thing for her, and that was to come here and look for it. Just look for it. It was as if she didn't care if I saw it or not, but that I believed in its possibility. How could I not go and look for it when what I loved most about my mother was how she kept her faith in something despite the improbability? Not just in miracles like the Fata Morgana but in me.

If my father had his way, my best odds for happiness would have been to go to college to be an accountant or a nurse or any occupation that's recession proof, marry a native Pittsburgher—preferably from a river town—and raise a family there. Take the kids to the Tour-Ed Mine or the Cathedral of Learning for field trips. Pray on Saturdays. Root for the Steelers on Sundays and if there isn't a game, take out-of-town company downtown to ride the incline and view the Point from Mount Washington. But I went to school out of state, got a degree in sociology, live with a man in Queens where the nearest body of water is my neighbor's backed up rain gutter, and am a self-employed critter sitter who specializes in lucrative play groups for four-legged creatures, and I don't mean a crawling baby. I do pray on Saturdays that I get through another week of auditions and at least get a call back for any part where I have a line.

My mother had no objections to my acting aspirations as long as I could afford to live this way. It was no different than having the money to go to bingo or play the lottery. You have to play to win. She'd pull out her bingo purse filled with dabbers and a magnetic wand to gather her chips every Monday—the only day of the week she was as much of a Pittsburgher as my father.

I hopped off the bus and walked toward the smoke shop. The driver emerged with an elderly woman who had to be twice his weight. She held onto the excess strip of his buckled belt as if it were a leash. Despite walking with a stiff knee, she appeared to be leading him and not vice versa. When they got to the bus, he offered to help her up. She took one step forward as he took two steps back for more leverage to give her a boost from behind. I offered to help, but he assured me in between labored breaths, "Please. No problem."

They finally made it to the first row, but she pitched her purse into the seat behind it. The driver held onto her with one hand and removed the front seat cushion with his other, kicking it to the side. I couldn't imagine why until she sat down and he propped her stiff leg through the metal frame in front of her so she could rest it on the springs.

"*Va bene?*" he asked her.

"*Buono,*" she smiled.

"*Miracolo,*" he said, winking at me as if to say getting her in her seat was more of a spectacle than what I'd see at the Strait of Messina.

I smiled and asked, "*Andiamo, si?*"

The elderly woman moved in her seat to reach for her pocketbook. She handed the man a few coins along with a couple of almonds, then muttered something about waiting for her daughter, although her voice was lost in the swishing sound from all the air trapped inside her seat. He asked if she would need help, too. She shook her head and insisted he sit down.

"*Presto. Presto,*" I pleaded.

He opened his leather pouch and recorded a couple of Roman numerals with a felt-tip pen, making each one slowly and deliberately in calligraphy as if the log were going to be hung on a museum wall next to the *Mona Lisa*. I was ready to ask him if he wanted to borrow the pastel chalks I had in my backpack for drawing but was afraid he'd take me up on it. Already he had to fudge numbers on his schedule because we were more than ten minutes late and the daughter still hadn't boarded the bus. Finally, she arrived, wearing a print skirt that matched her mother's top.

"*Permiso?*" she asked, carrying a live chicken pressed onto her pregnant belly. She got as far as the first step before the driver shook his head, pointing to the chicken.

She stroked the bird and said, "*Per favore, signore.*"

"*No, accommodi,*" he said with a tone of regret.

The bird's yellow eyes began to water. Its feathers lifted with anticipation. Its tail twitched with unease.

When she didn't move, he asked her to leave the chicken outside and reached for the rope to pull the door shut. When she didn't budge, he stepped down to help her decide if she wanted to come in or go out.

He shook his head and turned to her mother. She dropped her stiff leg to the ground and hobbled up the aisle, plopping herself down in the driver's seat. The three of them began clucking louder than the chicken.

I couldn't believe what I saw. There the driver was standing on the bus step: the mother above him, the daughter below, and he in purgatory. I took my watch off and put it in my backpack because I didn't want to know how late we were anymore.

The driver began to shut the door on the daughter, who put the chicken's plumed head between the doors so the driver would stop. He turned to the mother and pleaded with her to help her daughter and the chicken safely off the bus.

"*Aspet*," the mother ordered. She grabbed onto the rearview mirror and pulled herself up from the driver's seat. She asked her daughter for the chicken. The daughter handed it to the bus driver, who held the bird for a few seconds before insisting that the daughter take the chicken back and leave it behind or she could not get on the bus.

I offered to take the chicken and put it in my backpack so we could go but nobody listened. I poured my things out and handed the driver the empty backpack.

"*No e' necessario*," he said, asking me to please sit back down.

"*Aspet*," the mother said again. This time, she asked the bus driver to hand her the chicken. She would take care of it. He hesitated but before he could give it back to the daughter, the mother snatched the chicken out of his hands, wrapped her chunky fingers around the bird's neck and snapped it like a wishbone.

"*E' morto*," she pronounced as she signaled for the driver to sit in his seat and let her daughter on the bus. The old woman made her way back to her seat, handing me the dead chicken to hold while she sat herself down. She proceeded to prop her leg up on the springs and ask me to give it to her daughter who adjusted her skirt before reaching for the bird. It rested on her belly once again.

The driver was so stunned that he was gripping the wheel but didn't think to start the engine.

The mother looked at her daughter and asked if she was ready. She nodded. Then she looked at me. I nodded. "We go!" she yelled up to the driver and chuckled as I stood and yelled, "*Brava.*"

Relieved that everyone was settled and somehow a live animal had not been brought on board, the driver started the bus, letting it drift several yards before he stepped on the gas.

I gathered my things back into my backpack and sat down, eager to enjoy the feeling of motion.

The ride to Reggio was a series of windy, pockmarked roads. The floor of the bus vibrated, and I frequently popped out of my seat like a piece of toast. The women, on the other hand, didn't budge. Even the vineyards on the cliff we drove by somehow defied gravity by rooting themselves in the severe angle of the slope. I couldn't imagine harvesting the grapes there. One false move and it was a long tumble to the sea.

Perhaps I couldn't deny that I had this notion of San Procopio as an isolated corner that couldn't be awakened from its dormancy. That while the rest of the world tossed and turned with restless modernity, this little village slept most of the day.

Not long after we began our journey, the mother pulled out a loaf of bread from her pocketbook. She broke it in half and then half again. She reached inside her purse and put a plump fig on each hunk. She handed one to her daughter and gave me two, signaling for me to take one up to the driver. The bread was so crusty and the fig oozed with sweetness. I wondered how he would manage eating it while he drove, but it seemed to fuel him. After every bite, he hummed and stepped on the gas. As much as I wanted to eat it, I gave him mine.

The bus followed the fishy smell of the sea to the promenade. Even from a distance, I could tell the water was so clear that I imagined dropping a penny and being able to watch it land on the bottom. There were sandy beaches, gritty cement buildings, and eroding castle fortresses. It seemed one wave could wash the city away as though it never existed. I supposed that's what the 1783 and 1908 earthquakes really did. Only the debris wasn't cleared. Instead it mounted, and the city was laid to rest, married to the stone that buried it.

Because natural disasters leveled everything, I hadn't expected Reggio to have old-world charm or even a flavor of each of the rulers who conquered this region, a succession of foreign invasions and feudal order. Greeks. Romans. Normans. French. Spaniards. Arabs. Perhaps I'd see a ruin here or there. Some small fragment but never the whole.

No ivory cupolas rose above the fortress. The skyline was so uniform, not one building could reach upwards from the massive concrete heap weighted down with the rubble of history. The buildings were not what I'd call architecture but rather pale gray shells filled out of necessity. This was my father's Italy. Yet my mother believed this land had something that no earthquake could crumble, no drought could evaporate, no famine could starve and no plague could wipe out: the hope of seeing the Fata Morgana.

I looked out my window as we approached the promenade to look for believers like my mother. Surely they, too, could feel the cool air near their feet clashing with the warmer air against their faces. I had this idea that there would be rows of occupied benches, all facing the sea. No newspapers. No chatting with friends. No food in their laps. They'd just sit there for hours with their hands folded, watching the sky as if it were an altar.

Instead, it was still quiet from the mid-afternoon siesta. One man, apparently homeless, was using a store window to give himself a mirror for a quick shave. A few people were sitting on the benches but their backs were to the sea. Their expressionless faces reflected the city's mass of petrified stone as though its citizens slept and watched with both eyes closed. Was the Fata Morgana just one more thing from above that would never lower itself to the depths of this city or was the city refusing to lift itself off the ground to rise to the heights of illusion?

I turned to see if the women were looking out their window. The daughter was repositioning the chicken so her mother could feel the kicks in her belly. I smiled and asked if it were a boy or a girl? She laughed and said twins—maybe one of each.

We were approaching my stop. I wanted to ask them if they came to look for the Fata Morgana, but the mother was now examining the chicken, feeling under its feathers and showing the daughter how she would prepare it for dinner that evening.

Before I got off the bus, I took one last look at the lifeless bird resting on a growing belly, its broken neck draped over the daughter's arm. I couldn't help but think of my mother's and father's San Procopio, and wonder if their two worlds would ever meet, if I was waiting for the impossible. But as I glanced out the window at the grit of rubbled buildings and water softened by a light mist, it didn't seem strange at all.

❦ ❦ ❦

Paola Corso's writing has appeared in The Christian Science
Monitor, USA Today, The Progressive, *and* Women's Review
of Books. *She is the recipient of the 2000 Sherwood Anderson
Fiction Prize. Her story collection,* Giovanna's 86 Circles, *was
nominated for a Pushcart Press Editors' Book Award. She is a
New York Foundation for the Arts poetry fellow and author of a
book of poems,* Death by Renaissance. *She lives in Brooklyn and
teaches fiction writing at Fordham University in New York City.*

PAUL HARPER

The Messiah

The deity had come to rural Ghana,
disguised as a bicycle mechanic.

I SAW HIM COMING FROM FAR AWAY. HE CAME OUT OF
the haze of afternoon heat when the market women
shelter under massive woven raffia hats or simply go
home. When stray dogs find cool respite under long-idle
cars and the schoolchildren over the road seem to somehow shift up a gear to make it all the more unbearable. He
came with bad tidings.

There was something unusual about the way he moved, as
if he was carrying something. In a moment of dustless respite
the image resolved: he had a bicycle. What he was doing
with this bicycle could not be accurately described as riding or wheeling. What he was doing with this bicycle was
dragging and, as a feeling of dark foreboding descended, I
realized that he was dragging this bicycle toward me.

We recorded many slow days in Teshie during the bicycle project's infancy—days when we tallied more animal visitations (goats and chickens) than human. Bicycles did come though, and through the agency of Barnett's repair manual for mechanics, I had made progress in demystifying the art. Without this mighty tome my impersonation of a bicycle mechanic would have been far less convincing, though it must be added that common sense, a topic conspicuously absent from Barnett's index, continued to elude me.

I was most at home with the Chinese imitation mountain bikes that had become all the rage in Accra. Identifiable by a proliferation of bells, giant mirrors, reflectors, and plastic flowers on every available vantage point and bearing memorable names such as Rambo, Flying Pigeon, and the fatefully dubbed Titanic, they fell apart quickly and were a dependable source of income for the workshop.

More problematic were the ancient iron donkeys I had to wrestle with. Chinese- and Indian-made creaking leviathans on which technologies as alien as cottered cranks, internal three-speed hubs, caliper brakes, and Dunlop valves gave rise to dull headaches during the day and long sessions in the company of Barnett at night.

At some point a new breed started arriving, bicycles that fell into a category of their own simply because they were almost unidentifiable beneath their fossilized decrepitude. They started as a trickle, but soon they became legion, an invading force—invading space, invading time, and even invading my sleep with their ghastly forms. The owners, too, were of a different breed. They did not ask for specific jobs—for cables to be replaced or brakes to be repaired—their only instructions were "fix it."

When he finally reached the workshop and the dragging mercifully ended I saw the full horror of it all. I didn't know who had told him about me or from how far he had come but I knew why he was there—this wave of forgotten bicycles being dug from garage graveyards was not happening without reason. Without hesitation the words I feared most issued from his mouth. "Fix it."

"It" was a collection of rusty, rounded-out nuts, broken spokes, crumbling mud guards, and tires hairy with decay all connected to a frame of porous tubing looking less than confident about its future. The wheels had either gone into retirement or, in aged dementia, forgotten altogether that they were wheels and that going around in circles was what they were supposed to do.

In the field of human thought, the twin mysteries of life and death have spawned sufficient quantities of beard-stroking, head-scratching, and brow-knitting to in some way mark the visage of all the descendants of Adam. Questions over resurrection, reincarnation, the point at which life flees the body and death enters with an indefinite lease, and the nature of the afterlife itself have occupied meek and mighty minds for millennia, apparently still with no final solution or formula agreed upon. It was not, however, until after this man had deposited his machine at my workshop that I found myself pondering such imponderables in relation to the humble bicycle.

Can a bicycle join the choir invisible? I can only say that I was sorely tempted to pronounce this specimen dead on arrival. The owner was probably in complete agreement with me, though this was not a deterrent. In fact, it was the very reason he had brought it to me and not another mechanic. He was one of them, a believer, another disciple; he had come expecting miracles. Circumstances had conspired to give me a wildly inflated reputation as a bicycle mechanic.

Months of barberly neglect had rendered me sufficiently endowed with hair to prompt whispers of "Jesus" from young passersby on the street. When whispers turned to shouts and adults as well as children fell prey to this illusion it was usually a good sign for me to get a haircut and a shave. The problem was that this exaggerated opinion of my abilities extended also into the realm of the workshop. As a white man in an unfamiliar position (i.e. not behind a desk) in Christian Ghana I was considered by many as a man in possession of powers well beyond the grasp of any earthly creature. I was, in the eyes of believers, Jesus Christ bicycle mechanic, able to perform miraculous velocipedal resurrections in the blink of an eye.

Unfortunately reacquainting myself with razor and scissors did little to remedy the situation—I couldn't stem the flow. The word had got out—Jesus was fixing bikes in Teshie and all I could do was attempt to keep my head above water as waves of two-wheeled archaeological specimens crashed upon the shores of the workshop. The beard was later allowed to return. It was, in fact, an asset—retaining my messianic air not only inflated expectations but also served as a pair of rose lenses through which my work was appraised.

The disciple was eventually sent away and told not to return for at least a week. I wondered if ever again those slow days of odd jobs in the workshop would return. With Lazarus before me, I picked up a wrench, groaned audibly as the magnitude of the task ahead became apparent, and prepared to work a miracle. Can a bicycle be resurrected? I had Barnett's, I had a beard, I had a Jesus haircut, and with all of that, perhaps there was hope.

Paul Harper is an ex-bicycle mechanic. He currently resides in Perth, Australia where, with pen in hand, he awaits errant muses and Hollywood biopic proposals. His story "Waiting to Arrive" appeared in The Best Travel Writing 2005.

DEAN CYCON

≈ ≈ ≈

The Isle of the
Mushroom King

Parallel worlds unite on an unusual holiday.

BEFORE HEADING OUT TO SUMATRA, I THOUGHT I'D
better do some serious cultural research. I picked
up the phone and called John at Royal Coffee.

"So, John, anything particularly cool I should do while
I'm in Sumatra?" I knew I could trust John, my California
evil twin coffee broker buddy, to give me a good recommendation. John is a long-time java trekker, combining
the search for the perfect bean with a good heart and a
nose for adventure. Plus, being a good California trans-
plant, John knows that life is an ever-shifting boundary
between the good, the bad, and the nutty. Originally from
North Dakota, John is the best thing to come out of that
withered little state since *Fargo*.

So when John said, "Go to Samosir Island. It's on Lake Toba, the biggest lake in Asia, and it's where the Batak people live. Oh, by the way, I think they use magic mushrooms,"—I had to go. Not only do I trust John's personal taste in these things, but he also knew that Samosir held three of the many keys to my soul—indigenous peoples, the sea, and altered realities.

The road from Medan to Prapat, the ferry point for Samosir, was a typical Asian thoroughfare. Dani, my driver, spoke less English than I did Bahasa Indonesian, but we each pretended to know what the other was talking about. (Sort of like my first marriage.) We passed trucks on the left, cars on the right; thank God there were no stoplights or we would have gone through them. Dani seemed to be in a hurry to get to Samosir.

We raced through a dozen nameless towns with loudspeakers blaring out of the mosques. Although I knew they were prayers, they sounded more like an Arabic version of "They're off! Dani rounds the far turn. . . ." We drove through long expanses of rubber trees being tapped to make the condoms of the world and the medical gloves for when those condoms failed.

We got to Prapat in time for the afternoon ferry. This was a very big lake. Samosir Island was not visible from the dock, and it was a really clear day. It was a six-car ferry, so of course there were nine cars and a truck crammed in. As we loaded, I wandered over to the rail to join the other passengers, who were tossing coins into the lake. Dani told me this was a traditional ceremony for good luck on the crossing. Below us, a pod of naked ten-year-old boys dived for the coins. Their little brown butts smiled up at us like dolphins before they arced down to capture the sinking loot. I hoped it didn't screw up the good luck ceremony.

The bow of the ferry was wide open to the sea, the landing ramp long ago removed or rotted off. I pulled up a hunk of plank to join a group of kids dangling their legs over the side. The kids seemed blissfully unaware that if they fell off, they would be sucked under the keel and into the props, providing a different offering to the sea gods. I mentioned my fear to Dani. He nodded knowingly without having a clue as to what I was talking about, and offered me some peanuts.

Two hours later the ferry lumbered into Samosir. As we approached the dock the traditional Batak houses came into view. These houses are built on stilts, with three levels representing the Batak cosmology. The open ground floor is the Kingdom of the Beasts, where the family's animals are penned or tethered. Above the beasts is the Middle Kingdom, the realm of daily existence. The floor is wooden and the walls are wooden slats or woven mats. The family lives here, gathering, sleeping, and cooking in different corners of the large room. Structural crossbeams jut out from the tops of the walls in each corner of the house. Carved into each beam end is an animal guardian, a *gorga*, who keeps the house free of negative forces. The roofs have soaring peaks at each end, representing our yearning for the Realm of the Spirits.

We drove about a mile from the docks, along a beautiful sunset shore cluttered with dugouts, fish traps, nets, and small sandy beaches. We passed a dozen small houses offering "Special Massages." I had heard that the Batak were a very sensual people, but also incredibly aggressive. (Maybe this could be called

Tantric Rolfing?) We also passed several restaurants with English signs announcing "Famous Mushroom Pizza." After dropping our bags off at the curiously named Hotel California Guest House overlooking the lake, we hit Rosie's, the most welcoming of the pizza places. Dani begged off, but I devoured a small mushroom pie and washed it down with a cold Bintang beer. I waited. No hallucinations, only mild heartburn from the greasy cheese. I did the only logical thing—I had a few more beers.

In the back room, some young Batak men lounged on old couches, strummed a guitar, and sang quietly. They caught me peeking in and invited us to sit with them (and buy their beers). They launched into some phonetic Bob Marley:

> Rosie would let a firefly
> Like it was some folks burning in the light.
> No imam no cry

They didn't speak the King's English, let alone the West Indian variety. Now and then another twenty-something man or woman strolled in. More free beers for them—thank God for a good exchange rate, I thought. Rosie, the owner, spoke enough English to keep the conversation fluid and the group invited us to join them in a late-night trip to the hot springs in the hills above Lake Sidohoni. We hopped on motorbikes and sped along the black, sinewy roads up into the hills. Along the way we whacked a dog. We stopped. I wanted to find the dog and see if it was all right. My hosts thought I was kidding, as they were only concerned for the fender of the bike. For the rest of the ride, I kept yelling "Slow down!" which the group found funny enough to repeat as if it were a late-night English lesson.

The hot springs were a series of shallow pools, each one reflecting the moon. While we soaked in the hot, sulfurous waters, one of the young women told me in halting English that the next night was the full moon. She said that the Samosir Batak celebrated every full moon with bonfires and fish fries on the beach. They would sing traditional canoe songs and basically party until dawn. Dani had already connected with one of the women. So, being a culturally sensitive kind of guy, I said, "We're in!"

The next day we spent touring Samosir, visiting the traditional villages on the other side of the island, away from the more frequented ferry port. Along the shore the fishermen cast nets from small dugout canoes. Acres of rice paddies reached to the base of the green hills. In small settlements women wove traditional fabric patterns on hand-carved looms. As we walked through one village, we could hear the distant cacophony of drums, flutes, and some sort of clacky percussion. We followed the sound deep into the woods and came upon what looked like a coming-of-age ceremony. There were six young women in traditional dress swaying in unison while an elderly *datu*, the village priest, chanted. Four musicians beat an increasingly furious rhythm—the gathering storm of womanhood. The *datu* nodded awareness of our presence and gestured for us to sit on a log off to one side. He carried a long wooden staff, the *malehat*, with a small metal figure on top. Dani told me that the *datu* pours a special potion, *pupuk*, on the figure before a ceremony, to awaken its power and connect the worlds.

After about fifteen hypnotic minutes a water buffalo was led out of a shed and tied to a pole in the village square. The pace of the music quickened as a line of men appeared from somewhere and sprinkled the water buffalo with scented water and rice. I got the message. I told Dani that I didn't think I could handle what was coming, and for once we were completely in tune. We got up and nodded appreciatively to the *datu* and the women. None of them seemed to notice our leave-taking as the music pounded and cut the air in frenzied patterns and octaves I could no longer differentiate. We retreated through the woods, the sounds clawing at our backs. Before we got to the road the music and incantations stopped abruptly on the shout of "*Hoy!*"

We drove back to the hotel in a pensive, broody silence, and took an hour's break from each other. Maybe I'm a good Jewish Buddhist. Maybe I watched too much Disney as a kid (and later as a dad), but I just can't get used to animal sacrifice, whether by ceremony or motorbike. We walked down to Rosie's. I told her about the village ceremony and she stated sympathetically that some of the older ceremonies were hard for non-Bataks to watch. How about a nice mushroom pizza and a beer to break the mood and get us up for the evening's festivities? I told her that the pizza was very tasty, but that the 'shrooms didn't really affect me.

Rosie smiled. "Oh, last night I used tourist mushrooms, but since you are going to be a part of the ceremony tonight I will use a more traditional variety."

Well, I thought, when in Rome . . .

The pie that arrived at my table was double cheese, pepperoni, and double mushroom. A Sicilian on steroids.

Great taste, felt like a regular pie to me. Couple of beers, of course, to wash it down.

The gang reassembled in the back room. All were dressed in Western clothing and obviously in party mode. The young women were made up and sweet perfumes laced the cool dusk air. Out behind the restaurant, the lake lapped genially against clean white sand. Some of the guys were building up a roaring bonfire. This close to the equator, day and night are almost equal in length. Dusk is short, so it wasn't long before the sky was absolutely black and more stars than I had ever seen were splattered across the night. Usually, no matter where I travel, I can trust the Hunter Orion to be with me. I always get a sense of security seeing him up there, his shield and club ready to fend off Taurus, the Great Bull. But there were so many stars that Orion's belt was completely lost to me. I must have searched the sky for my traveling companion forever, lying back in that soft sand. Yet the fixed points of light in the sky began to shimmer. Then they elongated and began to dance. Shimmy shimmy Hale Bopp, shimmy shimmy Bopp. Hey, there's Orion. Yep, he's fighting with Taurus. Wow, they're really going at it. Watch out for those long horns!

I heard the guitar and percussion again and shook my fuzzy head. I wasn't lying in the sand looking at the sky at all. Rather, I was sitting up looking at the lake. The shimmering lights were the stars reflecting on the black lake. *Whoa, Dean*, I said to myself, *hold on*. I turned and realized that I was sitting in a circle of people around the fire on the beach. I recognized most of the faces from the pizza joint, including Rosie, whose hard, shining eyes were boring into me. Her very white teeth were outlined by bright red lipstick, and I had the distinct impression that she was a tiger ready to pounce—on me! Next to Rosie sat Nuli, a very pretty twenty-year-old with a much softer demeanor. They were talking to each other in what to my mushroom mind were conspiratorial tones, both staring at me and smiling. I remembered what the famous British Governor Raffles said about the Batak after a visit in 1820: "The Batak are not a bad people, notwithstanding they eat one another." Were Rosie and Nuli checking out the menu?

Suddenly, a tsunami of nausea welled up from somewhere a mile below my navel. I leapt up and staggered toward the lake, landing on my hands and knees near the shoreline. I wretched and wretched until I felt my eyes bursting. *Man*, I thought, *that was awful, but at least I got rid of those mushrooms*. I crawled into the lake and sat down, consciousness returning with each gentle wave pulse against my waist. O.K., thank God that's over. I splashed my face, straightened up and returned to the fire. The music had turned to a traditional canoe song, a sonorous, repetitive chant that was at once soothing and meditative. I looked around the fire. Same dozen or so young people, same Rosie and Nuli. Same white-haired ancient native couple in traditional dress. Huh? Wait a minute. Who the heck were they? The elders sat perfectly motionless, staring at me without any expression that I could translate. I felt very self-conscious. It hit me like a freight train that my mushroom trip was not over at all—it had just begun.

I felt myself on that long canoe ride across the lake. The people in the circle began swaying left, then right, in cadence to the chant. My body was pushed to one side then the other, the nausea returning from that unknowably deep place. Behind the old couple an enormous orange ball began to rise, outlining them in liquid fire. *Hold on, Dean, it's only the full moon coming up*. Back to the lake, this time pressing my hands against my eyes to prevent them from popping out. I felt hands on my shoulders. Rosie and Nuli were helping me up, bringing me back to the circle. The ancient ones were no longer there.

"You need fresh air," said Rosie. "Let me take you for a motorcycle ride up into the mountains."

"Are you nuts? I'd fall off and die!"

She thought about it. "Well, let's go to a dance club by the ferry. You can take some Ecstacy and drink some Jack Daniels. That will balance the mushrooms." Rosie and Nuli still held me. The others chanted or chatted.

"I'm O.K., really. I think it was the pepperoni. It was pretty spicy."

Rosie smiled. "Well, you need the spices to give the dog some flavor."

Oh no, I thought. Dog meat. Rosie's Roadkill Pizza. From Your Grill to Ours. The last time I thought I was eating dog meat was on the Cheyenne River Indian Reservation. My hosts would always joke and tell me that the stew was dog, then crack up when I would barely choke it down. But they were only kidding. Here, I had seen the mangy little fella cut down in the prime rib of his life by our motorbike

"You know, Rosie, I think I'd better just go back to the hotel. I think I want to be alone."

"No, no!" the whole gang erupted. Nuli sounded very worried. "That's the worst thing you can do. It would be dangerous to be alone."

"Why?"

"You would meet the Mushroom King and you are not prepared for such a thing. You better stay with us." Several of the young men also mumbled their concern. The music stopped as my welfare became the focus of attention. Meet the Mushroom King? It was more likely that I'd meet Ralph, the Ceramic Bowl King.

"Seriously, guys, I just want to be alone. I took mushrooms a couple of times in college. I know what the cycle is. I know these mushrooms were very strong"—in fact, I thought they might have been peyote or something undiscovered by modern medicine—"but I want to go explore this trip alone. I can handle this."

Murmurs of disapproval. Rosie spoke sharply to me. "You don't understand. You are being invited to meet the Mushroom King. You are lucky. Be respectful and he will let you approach. You got sick because you are being foolish and disrespectful."

"Please," I pleaded, "I'll just go back and lie down"—and hang on for dear life! But at least I won't be on the tail end of a motorcycle with Rosie and Jack Daniels, whipping over unpaved mountain roads at night and finding items for tomorrow's menu. "I'll think about my behavior and prepare myself better."

Finally, the group assented. We trudged back to the hotel, Rosie and Nuli gripping my arms as if I would fly away to the Rapture. I knew that I had spoiled the party, but I had to take care of myself. I relaxed onto the bed, the whole gang camped on the floor and chairs around me. I felt like the axis of a merry-go-round, as all of the faces spun and bobbed up and down around me. Rosie spoke in Batak and all but she and Nuli filed out and sat on the veranda. In the dark and sticky night I felt the women sit on each side of me on the bed. A soothing hand on my forehead, another on my belly. Ahh, that's nice. A third on my thigh . . . I jerked involuntarily.

"Relax, Dean, we are going to give you a special massage that will help you." It was Nuli. When did her English get so good? I could see their eyes shining in the refracted moonlight that spilled across the room. "We are going to please you very much." The hands began to move. They felt like four hot irons on a damp shirt. The air seemed to sizzle and pulse. I got the massage message.

"Wait a minute. I'm sorry, I can't do this. In my culture this is not right. I have made a vow to my wife."

"But you are not in your culture," Rosie said gently but firmly, "you are in ours. And here this is what we do. You should respect our ways when you visit us."

Good argument. Whose culture trumps? This is every man's fantasy. If only they were twins . . . no no no! That way danger lies. But no one would ever know and, after all, this is a cultural thing. I am really struggling to resist this. Help me! I once taught myself a trick on how to deal with situations like this. Of course, it was always a theory until now. Imagine a little Annette sitting on my left shoulder, watching this. What would she say? How would I act if she were here? I felt the ring on my left hand. The Ring of Power. O.K., Dean, cut the Lord of the Rings stuff and concentrate! Annette is here. In my heart, in this ring, in the strength of my commitment and integrity, she is here. O.K. sweetheart, thanks. I get it.

"No. I really appreciate this, but I must uphold my vow."

"Ahhh," Rosie scoffed, "what happens here has nothing to do with what happens there. Those vows are just in your mind. That's just Jewish Christian talk, it's not real. They are the rules your people made up long ago. We are Batak, we have our own rules."

Oh-oh. Relativism. How many times did I try that out on girls in college? What irony that my philosophical hedonism then is coming back to haunt me now.

"No, Rosie. It may be all in my mind, but I have given my word and made a vow. I have to live by my word. Especially when no one is looking, I have to have my integrity."

Will against will. This is one powerful woman! Eyeball to bleary eyeball.

Rosie blinked at last. The hands slipped begrudgingly from my body. "O.K., but we're gonna be outside in case you get into trouble." She said something in Batak to Nuli, who groaned as they left the room. The sizzle fizzled.

O.K., I thought, *get back to work*. I closed my eyes and began to breathe deeply. O.K., Mr. Big Shot-dipping-into-their-culture guy, here goes. I am not afraid to meet the Mushroom King. I can come out of this whenever I want to. I am not afraid, says I.

An ethereal hole of electric green, blue, and red beckoned me forward. Breathe deeply, hold on. A passageway. I moved into what was becoming a cavern of pullulating light. My hair is tingling. Electricity or fear? Move forward. The cavern seems to be going down now, but I know that I am lying on my back. Hang on, but let go. Funny. Intensity growing. Not funny. Keep moving forward. More intense. My whole body is tingling, pressure all over. Getting too intense. Gotta get out of here! Get out of here! POP!

I opened my eyes. Wow! I'm still on the bed. Haven't moved physically. I'm O.K. Take some deep breaths.

I'm soaking wet. I hear the voices speaking softly on the veranda. Did they hear the POP? A quick trip to the bathroom, as what I pray are the last vestiges of puppy and pizza return to the source.

Close my eyes. I'm going back in. I think I'm ready. The halo is forming again. The cavern of light appears. I stop. Oh, I get it. I can't approach the Mushroom King so casually. I took those mushrooms for the joy ride, not respecting the cultural context. Man, a peoples' thought and beliefs can become as solid as a sledgehammer, can't they? Or are they more than solidified beliefs, are they a different reality? Hey, Dean, don't stray off into mushroom brain. Stay focused on this trek. I am about to visit their Mushroom King, and whether he is real or *volksgeist* or collective subconscious-cum-manifestation, I have to be focused. This is heavy stuff and I am out of my comfort zone.

Sorry I was so disrespectful when I came into your realm. The lights seem to brighten, more intense but somehow more welcoming. Keep talking, it helps focus my intention. Down, down—or is it up? Deep nausea again. Keep breathing.

The cavern seems to end. The wall is pure electricity. I can't focus, can't really tell what color it is. It's a full spectrum. Too bright. Close my eyes. Still there.

Why are you here?

I don't know. All of my adult life I have traveled the world, working with indigenous peoples. I have tried to help them assert more control over their lives in the face of massive cultural, economic, and ecological pressures.

You are a seeker.

No, not me. I'm a giver, not a taker. I do this for ethical and political reasons, not spiritual ones. I don't bop around from sweat lodge to temple, looking for Mr. Righteous.

Not consciously.

No, not consciously.

What is the pattern?

I go, I help, I respect, and I learn.

And then?

I get invited into a deeper level of place each time.

As above, so below.

But that's not why I do it. I have an earthly mission.

Parallel planes of existence.

So, while I am traveling to different places to do my work my soul is trekking, too?

Pilgrimage. What is a holy place but a place where you are made whole?

But what is at the end of the trek? What happens when my soul has plugged into all of the places it is supposed to go?

Harmony of spirit and action. Two worlds, one purpose. You are blessed.

But I'm not a seeker. I'm just a guy trying to do good work in a world that needs help, and have a good time, too. I'm not really that dedicated. I screw up, it falls apart sometimes. I can't even pray or meditate for more than thirty seconds without TV jingles playing in my head.

It's not conscious on the unconscious level. You are on your own path. Be well. POW!

Tears stream sideways to the pillow. My mouth is a petri dish full of Drano. That cannon blast must have awakened the dead. Yet the same steady murmurs and chants seep in from the veranda. Now some birds chirped and clucked. It was morning.

No breakfast, thanks. Just water. Dani looked worse than I did, but we both wore sheepish grins. We had to leave so early to catch the ferry and power our way eight hours to the airport that there were no long goodbyes. Rosie looked genuinely sad.

You are not supposed to fly for twenty-four hours after scuba diving, in case the nitrogen in your blood bubbles out and you get the bends at 40,000 feet. I wondered if there was a similar rule about flying after a visit to the Mushroom King.

❦ ❦ ❦

Dean Cycon is a social activist, lawyer, and coffee roaster who has been working in the developing world on and off for thirty years. Some of his travels, adventures, and accomplishments can be perused at www.deansbeans.com.

⪼ ⪼ ⪼

A Fine Kettle of Fish

Love and chaos are one and the same for a dramatic Kurd
and a mid-life Los Angeleno in Istanbul.

KAZIM WOULD TAKE A CAB FOR ONE BLOCK IF HE could; I thought he was lazy and grandiose and that may have been true, but later I realized he had only one pair of shoes and they hurt him. I was in Istanbul with about three words of Turkish, following this Dionysian satyr into eternity.

I drew him many times. I drew everything: crumbling Byzantine bricks, swinging Ottoman lanterns, smiling street vendors. All my life I had been haunted by guilt, thinking always, "I should be drawing." Now I drew constantly, filling page after page: old men in the bazaar, backgammon players, domes, decayed stone and boats and minarets. My sketchbook was my passport, opening doors I hadn't known were closed. The Turkish Tourist

Office, always glad for good press, had commissioned me to produce pen-and-ink line drawings of Turkey. After years of building computer art for Disneyland and Silicon Valley, I was drawing by hand again, from life, and I was on fire with creative joy. A whole new life at fifty, all because I had become entranced with both the Turkish culture and with Kazim, whom one friend called a careening festival of a human being, another an alcoholic Kurdish carpet salesman. I called him a catalyst. There was just something about him apart from his beauty, some compulsion to engage with him that made me want to hit or hump or dance with him. At thirty-four, he had more life force than anyone I'd ever met. He wasn't nice; he was the farthest away I could get from the pleasant successful life that was killing so much of me. I felt compelled to engage with him, violently, passionately, and we would go for days and nights fighting and making up.

Thank God I met Mona, an American with North African roots, smack in the middle of Sultanahmet, the oldest district of one of the oldest cities on earth. Our friendship was my little lamp of comprehension in a dark night of dim bars down twisty cobbled streets, taxis plunging off into mystery, tilting tables in tiny shabby cafés thronged with dark arguing men, all in incomprehensible Turkish.

Tonight we'd walked down the hill to Kumkapi, once the Sand Gate in the massive seawalls protecting the Byzantines from Marmara Sea invaders, now a long row of fish restaurants with tables set outside on the cobblestones. Everyone along the way wanted to feed us. Mona has these Black Medusa looks; from Tripoli via New York. She looks like she stepped off an ancient vase, and all the men were in love with her. All the restaurant touts were touting, and one said, "Excuse me, but are you not Mister Kazim's friend?" So we ate there. They must have phoned him; he called and asked us to meet him later.

When we arrived at his nearby hangout, Mona muttered, "A fake English pub in a Ramada Inn, for Chrissakes." Kazim was at the dart throw, dark in his pale gold suit, a big fleshy man with his slacks worn high. He paused, dart poised, and looked up at us with his diamond-shaped face. "Ah, Sweet," he said over the music. "Welcome." He threw the dart. He ushered us to a table cluttered with beer steins and carrot sticks in lemon juice and little plates of finger food. I think the Turks invented finger food. There were a lot of them sitting around the table eating and drinking. It was clearly his party.

With Mona he was downright courtly, and demonstrative with me. Soon he was kissing my hand and saying to her, "I *love* this woman! And *you* are like my sister, because My Sweet is like my *wife*!"

Many were the nights I'd sat drawing Kazim and his friends while the waves of Turkish rolled right over me and he never gave me a glance. When we were alone, sure, but in public—"Why won't you *look* at me?" I'd said. I could never look at anything but him.

"Sweet, you must know I no look at you because you are part of me."

"That sounds romantic as hell, but I still want you to look at me."

Tonight was different. Like many men, he was at his best and sexiest when there was another woman around to appreciate it. A small boy appeared loaded with roses.

Kazim bought them all and presented them to me, taking one out for Mona. When fruit arrived, drizzled with honey and powdered pistachios, he fed me gently, holding a banana slice speared on the end of a fork, cupping his other hand under it to catch the drips, his eyes slumberous, looking into mine as he sang softly in Kurdish.

Mona and I went to the ladies' room. I got in there and fell backward against the door. My eyes crossed. She said, "*Oh* my *GOD.* He's like a...*sultan,* or something."

"Thanks, I'm just getting my breath," I said. "I'm so nuts about him, I just don't trust my perceptions."

"Well, you're not crazy," she said, "he's larger than life. Geez, if he had money and an education there'd be no stopping him."

"He *had* money," I said. "He threw it away." From his first wife, a Belgian attorney who gave him 3 million dollars. They opened a hotel and some restaurants, he bought a BMW, and gambled it all and lost it all and that was a few years ago. Mona would hear all this from Kazim in the next twenty minutes. He carried his glorious past around with him like a credit card.

When Kazim ordered gin, I knew our time was limited. Soon he would be someone else. I remembered from my own drinking days, how I would feel great, and keep drinking, and then awaken with no memory from the night before and a vague sense of unease. Now, suddenly Kazim was gone. A black-jowled, flat-eyed goon grinned vacantly from his place and toasted us with the gin. Mona looked at me in consternation. "What happened to him?" She didn't bother to lower her voice. I pantomimed a drink going down a gullet. She looked at me, her eyes growing enormous. With dawning comprehension, her hands clasped over her heart, she said, "You mean, the only thing that's wrong with him, all the meanness and violence and bad luck, is just that he's *alcoholic*?"

I nodded. "*Ohhh*," she said, "I *get* it."

She left when Kazim announced he wanted to dance. We reeled up onto the floor. He was draped over me as we staggered around to the music, and he fastened his mouth on my neck. It hurt like hell. I arched my back and threw back my head, and that's when he fell on top of me. We picked ourselves up and I led him outside, huge and reeling, his feet splayed out, my arm in his. Afraid he would pull me over, I leaned into him, taking his weight on my bruised hip.

We lurched across the tramline to the square in front of Ayasofya, survivor of fifteen centuries of fire, earthquake, conquerors, and the Crusades. It is painted red and lit at night. Glowing rose domes and minarets and arches sprawl below a squabble of lunatic gulls, circling and shrieking. And there under the chestnut trees, across from this magnificence looming up in the warm summer darkness, Kazim went insane. He began to scream about his horrible life, this rotten existence, a roaring, gargling litany of strangled frustration and rage. It was about one-thirty in the morning. I couldn't take him back to the hotel, we wouldn't be allowed past the front desk. I couldn't take him back to my hotel; local mores dictated that you couldn't take a drunk to your hotel and cool him out unless you married him first. Shouting, shaking his fist, he took off into the dewy, pristine tea garden, and I took off after him. We stomped through the wet grass toward the silent fountain, over fences and through the flowerbeds—one of us in high heels—and collapsed on one of the benches. His arms were flailing. One of them walloped me on the cheekbone. My earrings flew off and skittered on the cobbled path, my ears rang. "You *hit* me!" I said to nobody. It was the first time. In my life. I sat stunned, trying to comprehend it—*violence!*—while another part of me, urbane and amused, drawled, *How very Tennessee Williams of you.*

He was crying now, slamming his fist against the bench. I grabbed his ears, put his head in my lap, stroked his hair and talked to him. He was shuddering, and finally quiet. I bent over him, and that's when the police arrived. Four of them stood us up and quick-marched us back across the wet grass to Ayasofya, Kazim protesting all the while. They twisted his hands behind him and cuffed him. One officer deliberately slapped him, hard, back and forth across the face. I had wanted to do that myself, but it sure wasn't any fun to watch. A cop shoved me hard into the patrol car. We racketed down the bumpy cobbled hill to the police station at the bottom, all in Turkish.

I love being arrested now that I don't drink anymore. I haven't done anything and I know it. I assumed we were there because of drunken screaming in the park in the middle of the night. I was wearing black slacks and a long shirt, tied up tight around my waist and low on top. In the dark patrol car, I untied and shifted it so that when I got out, I was in a conservative black tunic.

They hustled us into the station, bleak with yellowish light. They slammed Kazim into a chair next to a battered filing cabinet and pushed me toward another. I sat down carefully with my sketchbook on my knees. All this time I had held it. Stalwart in their straps and buttons and buckles, they talked to Kazim as if he were a child, in the patronizing tone people use with drunks. They were reading his business card, the only ID he had. The cop who had shoved me squinted at me. Nobody spoke English. I heard Kazim saying my name to them, but they shut him up. The cop behind the desk looked over at me contemptuously and said, "Your Pass-Port." I handed it over. He looked at it and grunted something. The other one said, lip curling, "Your Pro-Fession." I held up the sketchbook. He came over and got it, an older guy, thick in the middle and bald on top. He walked back around the desk and sat down. Total silence while he looked at every page. Then he got up, walked back over to me, and held out the sketchbook with both hands. He bowed until his eyes looked right into mine. He said distinctly, handing me the sketch-book, "Madam, no problem."

They took the cuffs off Kazim then and offered us cigarettes. He took one. They stood him up and took him out of the room. I started up in alarm. The older cop, very nice now, made calming gestures and panto-mimed face-washing. He offered tea. I accepted. The one behind the desk lectured me in broken English on my choice of companions. I thanked him. They brought Kazim back in, damp around the hairline and a little more sober, jocularly giving them a hard time. They were a little sheepish. Later Mona told me that we'd been arrested because the police thought I was a Natasha.

"—A Russian prostitute. When they saw your pass-port and that sketchbook they must have just *shit*. You could really have gotten them into trouble. Yanking an American artist into custody—didn't even ID you first—treating her like a hooker—"

"I wonder if stuff like this happened to Hemingway or Gauguin?" I'd said.

It was four a.m. when the policeman called us a taxi, and twenty minutes later we were precisely where we had been two hours before when Kazim went crazy, and he was still drunk. At this point, all I wanted was to take him to bed, any bed, a flowerbed!—and sleep. It was very quiet. I wanted to keep it that way.

But Kazim was hungry. "I want fish," he said, as I looked up the dark street, ghostly tramlines in the night, thinking: fast food. "Give me 30 millions, I buy fish."

Thirty million Turkish *lira*, that was almost fifty dollars U.S. at the time. But this was Kazim. Sometimes he couldn't think of the English, and sometimes he didn't care to explain himself to a woman, yet it seemed that when he wanted something there was often a good reason. I said yes to him for the rollercoaster he provided. I wanted to stay on it, any way at all. It never stopped. His recuperation from dead drunkenness was awesome. When *I* drank that much I'd had to go to a 12-Step program and had become so respectable that now I positively craved a little chaos.

So I gave him 30 million and we careened back down the hill past the police station and out onto the highway, Kazim in the front seat with the taxi driver in rapidfire conversation all the way. I clutched my sketchbook. I wanted to see this fifty-dollar fish. I would draw it. We tooled up the highway in the silent darkness and stopped beside a jetty. He told the driver to wait. There was a strong smell of the sea.

Still in our nightlife clothes we walked through a gate in a chain-link fence, down a corrugated metal catwalk, along a splintered wooden pier, and through an open door in a metal wall. We were suddenly in a noisy cavernous warehouse of metal and scaffolding and spotlights like stars. It was lit up like day and full of shouts and echoes. Trucks were backed up to the open far end. Crowded with hundreds of men in rubber boots, ponchos, work shirts, and caps, the wet cement floor was also covered with boxes of fresh fish, every conceivable kind: shellfish and finny fish and flounder fish. Men walked between the boxes, looking down, talking. The air was damp and full of haggling, and I was drawing like a demon. The fish, the men, the building, Kazim. He strolled between the boxes, all shoulders and draped gold suit in contrast to the lumpy plaid and rubber around him. Drawing, I watched him. He walked gracefully, with complete assurance, stopping here, there to glance down and comment. Men fell in with him like iron filings. They deferred, gestured, smiled. I remembered he'd owned restaurants. I thought, *No wonder people have given this man millions.*

I had gotten what I wanted: a completely new experience, and the drawing to keep it. As the sky paled I saw we were across the highway from the restaurants in Kumkapi. Kazim came back with a white plastic grocery bag dangling heavily from each hand, clearly happy with himself. He was excited about the fish. I would see! He would cook for me! He went over to a little stand and gestured to a sleepy boy who, it turned out, sold vegetables. We rode back up the hill past huge rosy Ayasofya into the Sultanahmet. The sun was coming up.

It was the best fish I ever ate, and he made enough to feed the army. Hours later when I had eaten myself into a stupor with prawns, he brought in the platters of bluefish, sautéed and lightly breaded, with an enormous platter of chunked fresh vegetables. The suave carpet

salesman, the ruined remorseful millionaire and the
drunk were gone. Here was a happy, complete man. He
ate voraciously and with joy, pulling out the bones for
me.

"Sut...see?" he said, parting the flaky fish with the
fork, "Sut...means milk...flesh like milk." I went back
to my hotel glutted with fish, fell into bed, and woke up
very happy.

But earlier, in the dawn, tired and gleeful with our
fish still in the bags, we walked in our rumpled ritzy
clothes down the damp silent pale street to the carpet
shop, pounded on the metal door, and woke up the guy
who lived in the shop and guarded it. The shop had a
kitchen about the size of a teakettle, and Kazim wedged
himself into it. The wall slanted over the stove, barely
clearing the top of the dented double boiler steaming upward into the curling patches of peeling paint.
Kazim wielded the knife amid the garlic and the but-
ter, humming a little song. His hair looked like a black
pelt and he moved like he was dancing. He was cleaning prawns as big as my hand. I was standing outside
the kitchen alcove, drawing him so cheerful after our
night of mayhem, when he set down the knife, washed
his hands, leaned out the door and kissed me intently,
passionately for a long time, his lips and tongue very
strong, with a little scratching of beard, one huge hand
wrapped around the nape of my neck and up into my
hair. I stood there holding my sketchbook with both
hands, kissing him back for all I was worth. When he
returned to his cooking I said, gasping a little, "What
was *that*?"

He said, "That was love."

❧ ❧ ❧

Californian Trici Venola is a Los Angeles visual artist with a background in digital art. She fell in love with Turkey when it reawakened her talent after a bad case of computer burnout creating art for a slew of video games, such as the Super Mario Brothers. Drawing from life in pen and ink, she has completed an illustrated memoir of her experiences in and about Turkey over the past five years. Her tale here is adapted from that memoir. She lives in Istanbul's Sultanahmet neighborhood.

❦ ❦ ❦

The Ring

A symbol of long-ago dreams surfaces, and finds a home.

SHADOWY BROODING POSSESSES MY SOUL. CLOUDS hover over the rose garden. Where does promise dwell? A story overshadows me, invades. I move aside uneasily. What will this story tell? Tightness grips my stomach. It spreads upwards, hits between the ribs. I am back in constriction. Back behind the Iron Curtain, back in my hometown. I have just returned alone from the mountain village to which my father packed us off in such haste this summer. I am back from the Mountain of Wolves.

It was there one winter, when the village was covered with snow, that my father was out with his first two daughters. It was there, when the berg was white with snow, that the rabid wolf came racing towards them, gnarling with foam. And it was there that winter that my father simply turned to face him, and with his good left arm tightly fisted, bashed him on the nose. (The story was told and retold in our family, of his courageous act, and how he had made the wolf turn and slink away, but how, thereafter, my father had to have twenty injections, straight into the belly.)

In the town below, the foreign soldiers had moved in and were looking for girls. I, a child, was five or so.

One did not get to this village by car; the train went part of the way. But one got there in an open horse-drawn carriage that also served to carry hay. (Three hours were long on the rickety plank that was the seat.) The village was primitive; open drains ran alongside the cottages down the rough stone street. The peasants washed their vegetables and their feet in the kitchen sink (so my mother used to complain) and the water trickled out lazily to the side of the road. Bread was baked in an oval outdoor oven. Cows were hand-milked. Down in the coolness of the cellar the peasants left some of the rich full milk to curdle slowly in deep earthenware pots. Later it became chunky with soft iceberg cubes that floated in whey. (There was a long ladle for this.) Eating was simple; we got a soup plate full of this curdled milk and a chunk of black bread. I loved this. When we were extra lucky we got a slice of bread thickly spread with goose fat, crystal-topped with sugar. In those days I would think, this is wonderful.

There were several small children; we made a little band, in fact. We ran around barefoot like mountain goats. Town-child, I stepped gingerly at first, as on jagged glass. But by the end of the summer I skipped along tough-soled and agile as the others over the rough, sharp stones of road. The village children were clever, I thought. Especially Peter. He taught me how to make a boat. We sent the paper boats with their straw masts down the open drains. They had shorn my hair that summer and put me in rough-cloth shorts. The boys were lucky in that outdoor way; a tree was all they needed. But I had to lag behind and hide. I was the only girl.

Something had happened between us up in that mountain village, something deep and true.

"Papa," I told him excitedly, back in my hometown. "Papa, I am going to marry Peter. But he has no shoes. Will you buy him a pair, from me?"

My father was very thin and tense. He looked at the floor; then said something or other.

But something had happened deep inside me that summer; something for which I have—as yet—no name. In the shadowy past of a little girl's knowing resides a memory that now bolts out of my esophagus, too long held captive. A memory that now wants to be owned.

Outside, the soldiers trampled the streets, hungry for something. The world was then in War II.

Fee, Fi, Fo, Fum!

But where had all the lasses gone?

Inside, I followed my own dream.

"Mama, I need a ring," I told her urgently, back home alone.

Mama was very beautiful and had many necklaces and rings in those days, a whole box full of them. Surely she could give me one?

"I need a ring, *for me*, my Mama," I repeated, and did not think this was a problem.

"So you want a ring?" had said my scraggy middle

sister back there in the village, when I first dared to put it into words.

Then, in those war days, she was just fourteen.

"A ring, you say? Just come with me!"

And she took me out to the road where the home-coming cows were crossing. A few paces behind them walked a peasant leading a thickset bull with a long pole. The clip on the end was hooked into a ring in the bull's nose.

"See that bull?" said my sister sharply, while I stared at her, unable to grasp the point. She glared at me from above her too-thin neck, while her forehead puckered into a desperate frown.

"See that bull?" she insisted. "See his nose? Right? Well, you can have a ring just like his!"

Her jibe sank down my esophagus as I drew in my breath sharply, and slipped deep down inside me like an icy, king-sized marble, that has lain there ever since.

When I got back home, I bothered my mother and I bothered my father, till despite those jibes, I got my ring. We went to the big polished jewel box and my mother and my father and I bent over it. Mama's fingers pushed the rings this way and that, till they rustled and clinked against each other. At last, she picked one up—too big for me by far—and held it up to the light.

"You can have this one," she said.

It was Papa who had the ring remounted, little-girl sized. It took what seemed a long, long time, but then, at last, it encircled my left fourth finger.

But no sooner was it given, than again it was taken: for the time had come to leave, with only a suitcase or two.

Papa said, "You can't take that ring with you. It's quite out of the question!"

And that little-girl's embodiment of dream was left behind, though the icy, king-sized marble slipped out with her.

Fifty years passed. Inhabited again one day by that strange, uneasy brooding, I set out on foot along the tram-lines into Geneva's city center, dreaming of a ring, without knowing why. It was not my birthday, not an anniversary, not even Christmas, but something was simmering inside me. The sun shone brilliantly as I, a woman, followed the solitary trail, heart set on a fire opal.

I had pursued that trail tentatively ten years before, then, too, without knowing why. It had led me to a wholesale jewelery shop whose large showcase displayed a rich array of rubies and sapphires straight from the owner's own private mine in South America. But that was where my adventure ended, then.

Now, a decade later, I wanted to go back there. A faint memory drove me to the wrong passage and up two flights of stairs, only to bring me to a halt in front of a closed door with a drab sign: *MOVED*. But the scrappy, handwritten address beneath it led me to another jeweler's shop altogether, one I had never seen before: small and discreet, with very little on display. There was just enough room for one man behind the counter, and a leather chair in front. I lingered outside long, looking in. Two heads were bent over a necklace; then the client left.

I entered, slow motion, as in a dream. Timidly, at last, "Do you have a fire opal to show me?"

"No, but what do you want it for?"

I could not say, really. I did not know, exactly. But he began to talk to me passionately. "I believe each stone has its own vibration and its own power. Some gems can raise one's energy; they can even heal. Don't you think so, too?"

I only smiled.

He stared past me into space, then added: "You want it for its vibration, too. "

So he knew. A fire opal, I had heard, could increase one's energy.

I opened my heart to this stranger. We talked about good vibes and bad vibes and about how to get through it all. He fished a chain out from under his collar. "Look, I wear a square of jade and an amber dragon. They protect me, keep me healthy, and bring love and victory."

"Where are you from?" I asked him.

"Italy," he replied. Then he looked at me intently. "So you're after an *opale de feu*! Is it for a pendant? No! For a ring?"

"For a ring."

"What do you want to pay for it?"

"I don't know."

The Italian in him rose to the occasion: "Just leave this to me."

Seven weeks passed and I forgot that trip into town. Then one day, at the office, my phone rang.

"The opals you ordered are here."

"The *opals* I ordered? But I only asked for *one*!"

"Well, I got you three."

"*Three?*"

"A young woman brought them in for you today. They're free."

"*Free?* This is Geneva! What do you mean by free?"

He laughed. "I mean," he said emphatically, "you don't have to pay for them!"

I could not wait to get to the jeweler's shop after work. The Italian looked exceedingly pleased with himself and welcomed me with a broad smile. He brought out some crumpled tissue paper and unwrapped three rough fire opals, like orange shards. The fierce summer sun lit them up, revealing flashes of color that rippled and changed. Their orange glow filled me with warmth, brimful. But I felt perplexed.

"*What* young woman came in?"

"Actually," he began, "a young man came into my shop first. You know, the traveler kind with a rucksack. Laid his grubby handkerchief on the counter and unwrapped a fire opal. Brought it back from Mexico. These kids come in here all the time. But I told him one wasn't enough; I had a client for whom I need three. So I turned him away. Half an hour later his girlfriend walked in. Same kind—long dress and rucksack. 'I'm giving you these,' she said, 'for the lady who needs them for their vibrations or something.'"

The jeweler grinned impishly.

"So you see, I wouldn't dare to make you pay for them!"

I said I needed to think it over, and took the three fire opals home. The next day I went to see an elderly dowser and asked him to measure them with his pendulum. He found that one of the gemstones vibrated at a much higher intensity than the others. That is the one I picked for the ring. It was also the most beautiful.

The next day I went back to the jeweler and told him which opal I had picked, and how. There was suddenly a lot to discuss: the shape, the cut, the setting, to polish it or not. Then he sent it off to the workshops: first to the lapidary, genuine artisan of the old school (not many left now, he said); then to the setter for mounting.

"Keep these for earrings," he concluded, handing me the two remaining gems.

It took another seven weeks before he summoned me: the ring had arrived. Oval now and translucent, orange fire danced in the sun as I held it up to the light. Its burnished glow suffused me. Then I, half-century woman, slipped it on my finger, and instantly turned six.

"What did you really want the ring for?" the jeweler asked quietly.

But I had already slipped out.

There had been no promise, but what life had once taken, it now restored. And the memory was made beautiful.

☙ ☙ ☙

Rozalia-Maria Tellenbach is a freelance writer and a member of the Geneva Writers' Group.

TOM HAINES

～ぇ ～ぇ ～ぇ

In the North Woods

Nature is our great teacher—we do well to listen to her.

BEYOND THE TOWN OF ALLAGASH, TREES PRESS HARD against wide dirt roads until, around a bend or over a slight rise, they disappear with a silent pop into open air framed by the stark borders of clear-cut land.

Then, rumble and bump, truck wheels churning and land flying past, the trees are back again, a second generation or third, tall, tight, and true, or young and already tired, thin, and struggling in the soil of stronger spruce, fir, and aspen cut years before, the earliest by men with axes.

Now, though, things move fast and nearly always. Steel timber trucks with claws hanging from their long arms and blades hidden up their sleeves push in to grip and grab the biggest trees standing. Other trucks with flatbeds strong enough to carry a quarter-million pounds charge over those same dirt roads, whether hot and dusty or locked beneath ice, at speeds up to seventy-five miles per hour to mills where their cargo is turned into planks, pulp, and paper.

This relentless rhythm slows only rarely, for a few weeks each spring when the snow melts, low stretches of road gunk up, and the forest calms.

It was during this time, on a Tuesday in May, that I climbed into a pickup truck with two guides and a photographer for a ride over some of those empty roads—the Michaud Farm Road, the Maibec-Blanchette, and the Depot, specifically—to a low bridge over the fat, full waters of the Big Black River. Our plan was to canoe with the strong spring current down the seldom-run river to the confluence with the St. John River and its wide ride back to town. This journey into the relative wilderness would provide a chance to measure the present, recall a more rooted past, and consider, amid the rush of spring runoff heading for the sea, the acceleration of our technological times toward an uncertain future.

A few miles east of the Canadian border, a low, single-lane bridge delivers the Depot Road across the Big Black. Like many of the tributaries that feed the upper St. John, the Big Black weaves through Quebec farmland before flowing into the northwest corner of Maine's 10.5-million-acre woods, part of the largest swath of forest east of the Mississippi.

We paddled downstream from the bridge, where the high water ran easily between banks lined tall with evergreen and still-bare hardwoods. Occasionally, pairs of ducks took flight, or a bird of prey circled above the trees. Then, after three miles, a bend opened to a sweep of river and, on the left bank, an A-frame cabin.

Two women were bent over, cleaning gas lamps.

"*Bonjour!*" one called to us.

She turned to her friend: "Are they Canadian?"

A man with heavy shoulders, a gray beard, and an easy voice joined the women, then pointed the way to a dock and stairs that led to a sprawling cluster of buildings in a backwoods bear-hunting camp.

Inside one sturdy cabin, its beams cut from the surrounding forest, hung pelts of bobcat, otter, and black bear. On the side of a nearby outhouse, a collection of weathered tools—ax blades, a pulp hook, a scaling hammer, a peavey for rolling logs, among others—served as a rustic logging museum.

The owner of it all, Rod Sirois, stood before the cabin and spoke earnestly about the lifetime he had spent in northern Maine, including some twenty years as a game warden.

"The woods is different to me than when I was a young man. The trees were like this," he said, his arms arcing out wide before him, with four feet open between his hands. "You couldn't get your arms around 'em."

As he locked his hands to close the circle of his arms, he said, "Now, it's hard to find one like this."

Timber companies now take nearly twice as much wood from the forest as they did a half-century ago, feeding a greater demand for lumber from spruce, fir, and cedar.

The land north and south of the Big Black, privately owned by several companies, is checkered with a tight grid of logging roads. Some stretches, particularly downstream from the bear camp, are heavily cut to within a few hundred yards of the banks. In winter and spring, slopes and ridges, once an evergreen blanket of spruce and fir, are now the leafless brown of more aggressive hardwoods.

I asked Sirois about balance, about how a wild place can be kept healthy while taking away the strongest things that live in it.

After ticking off the status of big game in the area—the deer population is hurting without the cover of more fully grown forest, while black bear and moose are more plentiful than decades past—Sirois posed a question of his own:

"Can man toy with stuff without changing it?"

Wood, whether standing in the trunk of a tree, or stacked neatly in a pyramid of twigs, branches, and logs, is fuel ready for an oxidizer. Add oxygen, the most common of those, then raise the heat, to about 4,000 calories per gram of wood, and flames begin to leap.

On our first night on the Big Black, we stopped at a clearing on the northern bank, flat and gravelly from its days as an active logging road.

One guide, Don Merchant, a calm, solid man from southern Maine with a passion for building wood-and-canvas canoes, spotted a dead cedar, fallen at a 45-degree angle a few hundred feet from camp. Another guide, Tim Smith, a former prep school hockey star turned wilderness skills and survival instructor at his base in New Hampshire, used one of Merchant's handmade bow saws to cut through the cedar's six-inch trunk.

We took turns sawing the trunk to short, stout logs, and Merchant split those with an ax.

Finally, after the strike of a match—its own head a chemical mixture including sulfur, a fuel, and potassium chlorate, an oxidizer—first clumps of dried grass, then twigs, and the split cedar began to burn.

Smith set dollops of sourdough batter to bake in a camp oven. He wove alder branches into a tight grill to hold steaks at an angle against the fire.

Later, the surrounding air cooled as the cobalt sky darkened and flames brightened the night.

"There are so many things in this world that are superfluous, a construct of society," Smith said, "and a campfire just isn't one of them."

Then, after a pause, he continued: "I guess it is what got our species where we are."

Early humans' ability to produce and control fire made it possible to migrate into and settle colder regions—places, for example, such as the forests of New England.

Into the Middle Ages, fire was such a mystery that it was considered one of the four basic elements of matter, as if it simply existed. But creative minds cracked the code of combustion and harnessed it to drive modernization. Coal, gasoline, natural gas, and nuclear fusion came to fuel our figurative fires: cars and ships, houses and factories, ballparks and strip malls.

The forest, no longer needed to provide ship masts branded with a king's cross, has become a more diverse woodpile. Hardwood is ground to pulp to make paper for news and noses. Wood chips fuel mills that produce more paper to flow through printers in skyscrapers and office parks. Lumber is cut from the trunks of spruce, fir, and cedar to frame apartment buildings and homes.

It is all the more remarkable, then, that at certain bends along the Big Black, it can feel as though none of this ever happened.

By our second afternoon on the river, the photographer, an experienced birder, had spotted dozens of birds, the ruby-crowned kinglet, yellow-bellied sapsucker, and hooded merganser among them. He saw a pair of merlins mating high atop a spruce.

As Smith and I paddled through the calm of a nine-mile deadwater, we slowed to collect clamshells and study the tracks of muskrat and beaver. We floated idly near one wide, low dam, its wall packed tight with well-chewed branches.

At our second camp, we walked into dense woods that traced a brook northward. Smith grabbed a chunk of spruce pitch, a powdery backwoods chewing gum, and popped it in his mouth. He stopped near a mossy log rubbed bare by passing deer, then stooped to study a freshly sprouted fiddlehead fern. He pointed out a black ash, then a cedar.

Forget that caribou and wolves have disappeared from the region. Forget that only 5 percent of the Maine north woods is thought to be old growth—not virgin forest, of course, but "old" in that it was last cut more than 100 years ago.

It was as though this hidden stand near a wide bend in the brook had never felt the press of progress.

We turned back to camp, and I took a detour around a thick patch of saplings. There, on rotted roots, a stump leaned to the southwest. Its rings, huddling closely near the center, showed the tree had grown for ninety, maybe one hundred years. The trunk was sixteen inches wide when it met what looked, judging from the trunk's surface, to be the rugged teeth of a cross-cut saw.

Last year, 25 million people flew from the United States to Europe. Hundreds of passenger jets make the trip each day. Inside the United States, an estimated 30,000 planes depart daily on domestic routes.

The sky is full of little villages with powerful jet engines and video games and tight tubes with twin props and vomit bags, moving, moving, moving.

On our third evening, while the riverbanks drew tight in shadow but the sky still opened in the wash of a soon-to-set sun, a shimmering airplane moved west to east. As it passed the midpoint in the sky, a crisp, steady roar chased it onward.

The jet was one of more than a dozen I had seen since arriving on the Big Black.

Binoculars sharpened the splash of red on the airplane's tail into the logo for Swiss International Air Lines. Later, a check of the schedule would indicate this was probably the Montreal-to-Zurich daily, departing 5:10 p.m., arriving 6:20 a.m., local time.

Two days before, paddling downstream from the bear camp, Smith and I had talked about the velocity of modern life, about the demand for fuel and resources to keep us all comfortable, mobile, and entertained.

Smith has traveled the world, and keeps a well-designed website for his guiding business.

"I'm not a doom-and-gloom type of guy," he said, "but something has got to give. And I do wonder what it is."

We took up the conversation on our last full day of paddling, shortly after we had merged from the Big Black onto the St. John. The distance between the St. John's banks was twice that on the Big Black, perhaps 120 yards across. The current pushed more quickly, but a steady headwind battled back.

I asked Smith why he spends so much time study-

ing the nuances of edible plants and fire-making tech-
niques.

"We're so quickly becoming overspecialized as a
culture," he said. "I think there's some value to hanging
on to how people used to do things that wasn't so input
intensive."

Most days, I live in that disconnected, overspecialized
culture, in which food is harvested more from shelves in
a store than from rows in a field, in which heat comes
from adjusting a thermostat more than chopping wood.

I cannot identify all the trees growing in my backyard,
but like many in today's long-distance, high-energy society, I have new skills: deftly navigating airport security
checkpoints, dozing fitfully during a red-eye flight in
coach, waking to function in a foreign land.

I know that out there, on the edges, are many people
who gather around fires of wood or charcoal each night.
In stretches of Africa, Asia, and South America, they
huddle with family and friends to cook, talk, and sleep.
Many need medical and economic advantages that technology can bring, but they are vulnerable, too, to the
sense of disconnection that comes with it.

On our last morning, we idled at a campsite on the
more heavily traveled St. John. Earlier visitors had left
cans of Budweiser and Milwaukee's Best beneath a
nearby alder. A resident snowshoe hare scouted beside
a picnic table in the hope of finding scraps. The coals of
the fire, tucked in the cover of a rusted barrel pit, glowed
hot against cold gusts.

"The trouble is," Merchant said, "the world is too
big."

He touched his extended hands together, not to fashion an imaginary tree trunk, but the earth.

"It used to be like this," he said. "A kid had purpose, within a family, or on the homestead, or in the village that supported it."

He threw his arms open and up, skyward.

"Now the whole world is out there, and a kid doesn't know how to get there."

After paddling a few final miles to the town of Dickey, we would begin a new journey that afternoon. A ten-hour drive south, past a lumber mill and rows of gas pumps outside Dysart's Truck Stop in Bangor, would accelerate toward Boston.

First, though, after conversation had wound down and canoes were loaded on the riverbank, the campfire flames weakened. Then, with a dousing of cold river water, the coals cracked, spit, and died.

≈≈ ≈≈ ≈≈

Tom Haines is the staff travel writer at The Boston Globe. *He has written about plummeting pesos in Argentina, guns and cricket in Guyana, and trumpets and nationalism in rural Serbia. In 2003 and 2005, he was named the Lowell Thomas Travel Journalist of the Year by the Society of American Travel Writers. Between journeys, he throws stones in the Ipswich River with his son Luca and daughter Colette.*

❧ ❧ ❧

Reading Between the Arches

You too can have it your way.

I N A SMALL, FLY-CHOKED FOOD STALL IN THE COUNTRY-
side of Burma, I met a pudgy ex-hippie pontificating
on the purity of culture. He stroked his bald head and
scraggly gray ponytail as he held court with half a dozen
backpackers. "I know I speak for all travelers when I
say we don't want Burma to go the way of Thailand or
Japan, with a McDonald's or Pizza Hut on every corner.
Totally destroyed their cultures, you know, just turned
them into a couple of American colonies."

But if he had simply stepped into a McDonald's
in Japan and ordered a Coke, as I did, he could have
learned a lesson in the strength of 2,000 years of culture,
a lesson he apparently missed in his politically correct
tour of the local Shinto shrine.

Although the exterior of a typical Osaka McDonald's

is identical to that of any in America, its uniqueness literally shouts out to you upon entrance: "*IRRA-SHA-I-MA-SEY!!*" The staff, wearing their regulation McDonald's uniforms, blurt out the traditional Japanese shopkeeper's greeting: "I humbly recognize your arrival, honorable sir!"

As I entered this McDonald's and approached the counter, the staff members eyed me and nudged one another, pointing subtly at the foreigner, not to mock or leer, but to alert someone to find the most English-competent member of the staff to wait on me. The chosen one rushed forward from the french fry vats, beaming with pride at being the English soldier of the establishment.

He pulled two laminated English language menus from beneath the counter, one for me to read, one for him, the teacher's version with all the Japanese answers on it. He held it low, to show he didn't really need it, but carried it just in case I came up with some really bizarre order, a Shamrock Shake out of season, or an apple pie on my burger. He knew English, but he also knew foreigners could be wildly unpredictable, and it would be best to have back-up.

I ordered a burger and a Coke. "Coke Lite?" he asked hopefully, using the Japanized-American name for their diet drink.

"No, regular Coke."

"Ahhhhhh," he replied, nodding his head slowly, squinting at me with a pained expression. Normally I would have thought him slow, a teen confused about my language, or what button to press on the cash register. But I knew Japanese retail stores taught their employees never to use the word "No." It was too negative, too confrontational, a violation of traditional Japanese culture.

I figured there was a problem, perhaps they were out of Coke, and he was subtly trying to convince me to change my order. I was going to play along, ease his discomfort, but it was too late. "Coke! *Hai!* Yes!" He walked past the soda machine and into the back room. I thought he was going to change the canister which supplied the fountain.

As I stepped away from the counter to wait, I saw a yellow flash out of the corner of my eye. The counter boy, in his full McDonald's uniform, was sprinting across the street. He disappeared into a convenience store for a few moments, then ran back through traffic.

Upon his return, he hesitated a moment behind the counter, bending over as if he had a cramp. I heard the pop of a can, the fizz of soda on ice. Like a magician using classic misdirection, he turned to grab my burger as it was presented from the kitchen, and spun back to me holding both the burger and a medium Coke on ice in a standard McDonald's cup. The poor kid had dodged cars and used his own money (the register never opened) to fulfill those most traditional Japanese cultural traits: avoiding confrontation, saving face, and doing his duty.

In Malaysia, McDonald's offers comparable cultural insights before you even meet an employee. Like Japan, Malaysia is an industrialized and history-rich Asian country awash with McDonald's. To gain even a partial understanding of the nation's interwoven threads of culture, religion, and economics, you would have to traverse the country, visiting their National Islamic Museum, the old trading port of Malacca, and the agricultural Cameron Highlands at a minimum. Or, you could just go to the McDonald's in Langkawi and read the featured menu item: "The Prosperity Burger."

"Prosperity Burger" is a name that speaks volumes. The majority Muslim populace in Malaysia with their prohibition of pork would no more eat something called a hamburger than Americans would flock to order something called a "Shitburger," no matter that beef was the main ingredient of each.

Like the national character, the burger isn't Muslim, it isn't Christian, it just focuses on good times. The menu isn't in Hindi, Chinese, or Malay, but in English, the language of international business. I couldn't wait to get to the counter and tell them that I, like the Malaysians around me, also wanted to get a taste of Prosperity. Sure, it was a transparent McDonald's marketing ploy, but to understand why it was good marketing is to understand a small but essential bit of Malaysia.

Even the absence of McDonald's provides a lesson in politics and culture. The aging backpacker's McDonald's-free cultural paradise of Burma was largely the result of the oppressive military junta ruling the country, and the subsequent world economic embargo meant to knock them from power.

Huge red propaganda billboards loom over city intersections in the capital cities of Rangoon and Mandalay. They list ten-foot-tall commandments in English and Burmese: "Oppose Foreign Nations Interfering in Internal Affairs," and "Oppose Those Relying on External Elements, Acting as Stooges."

Only blocks away from one billboard, a strangely familiar "foreign stooge" beckoned to me. The sickly cardboard cutout clown pointed upward to a skewed set of golden arches announcing Rangoon's own "MacBurger" restaurant with its standard yellow-and-orange décor. Neither a total trade embargo nor international copyright laws could stop what seemed to be an innate human desire for fast food.

Or perhaps it is something that the franchise represents, something recognizable, something safe, a breather from the battleground of Burma, outside of its constant political, ethnic, and economic strife. In America, we may consider McDonald's restaurants to be a rash of neon pimples in a blight of strip malls. But for a weary traveler in a foreign land, the restaurant transforms into the most welcome of safe havens.

Even on internet travel bulletin boards, where backpackers use mocking references to "McDonald$" or shout "keep them out!!", travelers confessed their guilty visits to the clean bathrooms, air-conditioned interiors, and even the purchase of a "vanilla shake to re-energize after six weeks of *roti*."

In Burma, our group including the self-righteous backpacker later debated politics and the trade embargo with a prominent Shan dissident. This local leader told us "democracy is about the right to choose, even to make foolish choices, like to eat at McDonald's. I only wish we had such rights here."

Above the Shan's house in the hills surrounding the village stood a Buddhist temple, the walls painted with the life of Buddha. The mural included the scene where Buddha's disciples had gathered to hear the secrets of the universe from him. In response, Buddha silently held up a flower. He later explained: "If one keeps one's eyes open, one will see the teaching everywhere, and so one's opportunities for enlightenment are endless."

In the same way, when traveling, it isn't so important what you look at, but how you see. You can understand the universe in the contemplation of a single flower, or a country through a fast food joint if you just look at it right.

Bill Fink is a freelance writer based in San Francisco. His travel writing has been published in a variety of publications including The San Francisco Chronicle, Frommer's Guidebooks, *and* Travelers' Tales What Color Is Your Jockstrap? *More of his world adventures can be read at www.geocities.com/billfink2004.*

❧ ❧ ❧

Raven

They went to Mexico to live.

DAVID, RICHIE, AND RAVEN WERE ALL TOGETHER IN San Miguel de Allende, Mexico, because Raven lived here now, and Raven was dying. I met David and Richie one night at Tio Lucas bar about halfway through their visit. The next day Raven drove past the three of us out walking in town and asked them later, "Who's the babe?" It had been a while since I'd been called a babe, and I liked it. We had one week. This created a glow around us, intensity to our time together that was a miniature, more frivolous mirror of Raven's urgency. At the same time we felt no hurry, the days were long.

I was attempting to create a version of a schedule while I was here because back home I led a life of routines. I kept busy writing but the unfamiliar freedom of being away left me wandering streets or sitting in restaurants at odd times of day. Gradually I learned the pace of the place: write early, Bellas Artes for cappucino around ten, walk the hills, visit in the *jardín* around noon, back to Posada de las Monjas for siesta: nap or read on the balcony, meet the neighbors, until at least past seven. Then slowly the nighttime streets of the cobblestone town come to life. Everyone gathers at the *jardín*, walking through the plaza square or sitting on benches to watch people go by and listen to the grackles chatter. College students were here studying Spanish, art, or Mexican culture. Worldly retired Americans and Canadians came to escape winter or empty love lives, to stretch dollars, or possibly, become someone else once more. In their midst: me at midlife, newly unwed, traveling alone, for one week.

The night I met David and Richie I had been to a poetry reading (per schedule), was invited to join the poets for dinner but couldn't handle the group dynamics and slipped away to Tio Lucas. I sat at a table in the bar where David and Richie were waiting to be called for dinner and they didn't notice me. They were here for Raven and each other, plus (I later learned) they had wives at home and were practicing being faithful men, after many lost marriages and failed relationships.

They paused from their dialog and found me there, trying not to eavesdrop.

"New Jersey? I'm from New York!"

"Jews from New York? I married a Jew from Long Island!"

"You dance salsa? Let's go dancing!"

We had all been at the same Ravi Shankar/George Harrison concert at Madison Square Garden in the '70s. It was like I'd known them for years! I didn't know which one to like more. Then their table was called and they politely went off to eat. But Richie returned to invite me to join them, and so I did.

We discussed the menu, jazz, San Miguel, Raven....

"Where'd he get the name?"

"Not from his mother."

"Raven was the first Green Party mayor of Point Arena."

"I was there once...where is it?"

"Near Mendocino."

"Raven's a writer, wild man, activist..."

"...who moved to Mexico to die."

They reminisced about women all three of them had dated, told me all about their ex- and current wives and I described Dearly Beloved's "mental pause" so we started analyzing the midlife crisis.

One said it's real; the other, not.

David called it "road not taken."

Richie blamed "insatiable desire."

I asked, "Forbidden fruit?"

David said, "Jung's shadow...."

I told the story of Ricardo, the married Mexican Texan I'd met two nights before. "He's forty years old, has a two-year-old, a pregnant wife, and came knocking on my door at midnight, begging: *Abre la puerta* (Open the door). Good thing, *no* is the same word in English and Spanish."

After ceviche, more margaritas, *arroz con pollo, carne y verduras, huitlacochtle* (rich, dark, tasty fungus/mushrooms), and one shared ice-cream dessert we agreed to meet in the morning for cappucino, at Bellas Artes, at ten.

The whole next day we walked the cobblestones, up and down steep hills and stairs, studying the map and

views, a museum, shops, eating, laughing, serious banter. We kept meeting every day, falling in love with the
place and each other.

On the fifth day Richie had to drive Raven to the
hospital. David and I sat out the afternoon and twilight
on my hotel rooftop, chatting, sipping *damiana*, and
smoking, close to an increasingly starlit sky, listening to
music all over town, church bells, dogs barking, dialogs
on streets below, hotel guests coming and going. Inside,
we talked on opposite twin beds until three in the morning. Raven wasn't the only one dying, it was happening
everywhere, just not to us, not that night, and we were
sweetly conscious of our healthy bodies, gratitude and
guilty indulgence our aphrodisiac.

The air was charged with talk of death and all the
days and hours of languorous, revealing, verbal inter-
course. Tonight we had covered (among other things)
erotic poetry, the clitoris, David's first fumbling experience with his college girlfriend, how it "didn't work"
and he went to the library to study up and they took
their time and talked themselves through it until they
were mutually satisfied.

"I now consider myself a pretty good lover," he admitted, and described his wife's body to me. "She's not
the type of woman I usually go for. They'd be more like
you."

I contained my longing, as he debated his "moral
dilemma."

With no more talk he moved us into a standing-up,
very tentative hug-then-kiss where our bodies sensed
each other, what it would be like, and our lips reached
and searched and also held back before he pulled away,

then I said, "I'll step back and make it easy for you to leave, how's that?"

I took the step. And he left.

I went to bed with our desire: desire alone, pleasing, mutual, alive.

On my last afternoon in town I finally met Raven. The four of us found an outdoor table at the edge of the *jardín* and watched the people pass.

Richie said, "Ever heard the phrase, 'man with many hats'?" and pointed to a young Mexican selling straw hats, stacked on top of his head, reaching all the way to the sky. A marionette clown wheeled by on his little bicycle, mariachi music drifted around a corner, bells clanged forth from the *parroquia* tower, sun rays penetrated wispy clouds like spread fingers from divine hands.

Throat cancer made Raven's voice quiet, his head bowed into his neck as if surgery had reduced the distance or his ability to stretch up. David, Richie, and I ordered beer; Raven couldn't join in because he must consume everything through a tube. But he begged to taste and did so with a spoon then dribbled and reached for a napkin to wipe his mouth. When he spoke he was the local, and we leaned toward him to hear him better, the knowledgeable one with wisdom at hand, even as his body was slowly, as he spoke, deserting him. "Enjoy this," he was saying.

The old hideous guitar man strolled by our table and handed us a card with song titles: "Cielito Lindo," "La Bamba," "Guantanamera," and so forth. I handed the card to Raven: "You choose." But he couldn't seem to focus on the hand-printed words. All during our time together I watched him struggle to remain in the world with us, as he contemplated leaving it, still in his body, coughing, dribbling, uncomfortable in his posture. He knew he was dying, while David, Richie, and I fancied ourselves in the middle of life, and savored the scene, the sun, beer, good company, blissful in our bodies' passions, hungers, and thirsts. So we were able to pay attention to the ugly old troubadour as he sang through his stained, crumbling teeth:

> *que bonito el cielo*
> *que bonita la luz*
> *que bonito es el amor.*

in memory of Raven

❧ ❧ ❧

Marianne Rogoff is the author of Silvie's Life *and numerous short stories, essays, and book reviews. She teaches creative writing and literature at California College of the Arts in Oakland and San Francisco.*

~≈ ~≈ ~≈

West Meets East

Venice is not just beautiful—it is a doorway
between civilizations.

IN 1869, WHEN HE WAS TWENTY-SIX YEARS OLD,
Henry James visited Venice for the first time. Like
many New England grandees, James sought in Europe
the monuments of Greco-Roman antiquity and the
Renaissance. However, Venice seems at first to have disappointed him. "I can't for my life surrender myself to the
genius of Italy," he wrote to his brother, William. He said
he felt "more and more my inexorable Yankeehood."

James was not much impressed by either St. Mark's or
the Ducal Palace, which the English critic John Ruskin
had called the "central building of the world" for having combined the Roman, Lombard, and Arab styles
of architecture. "Travelling Companions," a short story
James published a year after that first trip to Venice,

seems to express its author's attitude to the strangeness of
St. Mark's Square when the main protagonist describes
himself as a "half-stupefied traveller to the age of a sim-
pler and more awful faith. I had left Europe; I was in
the East."

James probably didn't know that he had stumbled
upon an essential historical fact about Venice: its intimacy with the East. The city had been raised, as the
British politician and novelist Benjamin Disraeli put it,
from the "spoils of the teeming Orient." Venetians pursuing Asian goods undertook long journeys centuries
before the European age of exploration that began with
the Renaissance. It was the wealth created by this trade
with Asia that turned Venice, which began in the sixth
century as a straggly settlement on the island of Torcello,
into the greatest city of the Mediterranean, and gave it a
maritime empire that reached as far as Cyprus. A colony
of Venetian merchants existed in Alexandria from the
fourteenth century. Turks, Arabs, Armenians, Greeks,
and Africans traveled to the city, and even established
permanent outposts in it.

To modern sensibilities, the city does not appear to
have changed much over time. With its beauty and
glamour, it now serves as a consolation, however tem-
porary, to those of us who live buffeted and bewildered
by the modern world. But the city also embodies a long
and complex history of cultural encounters between
East and West. This history describes another way of
living in an economically and culturally interdepen-
dent world—something that takes us beyond the buzz-
words we now use (*globalization, clash of civilizations*)
to understand the troubled state of our own linked
societies.

I knew vaguely about Venice's Eastern connections when I first visited it in 1998. I was under the spell of Thomas Mann's symbol-laden novella *Death in Venice*. The first place I went to then was the Lido, on whose desolate beach, amid the Moorish extravaganza of Hotel Excelsior and the art deco elegance of the Hotel des Bains, Mann's refined writer-protagonist plays out his passion for a young boy.

The Lido, with its broad avenues and promenades, was recognizably of the West, like the cities I had seen since I left India in 1996. The spacious baroque palaces and grand boulevards of Paris, the Renaissance town houses of London, and the mock-Roman grandeur of the Mall in Washington, D.C.—they all conformed to my idea of the modern West, whose immense achievements in science and technology from the Renaissance onward seemed to have reached an apotheosis in the grid-glass canyons of Manhattan.

I wasn't prepared for the traces Venice still displayed of its connection to the East. Being in Venice itself was to be taken back to the premodern world of my childhood: the small medieval towns in India, the labyrinth of alleys where an occasional decaying mansion stood amid buildings of old exposed brick, and the gloomy houses in whose cramped, often windowless, rooms I had dreamed of escape.

The dappled light on the water and the stones, and the cool damp of the alleys, brought back memories of mild winter afternoons in Benares. Emerging onto St. Mark's Square, facing the strangely familiar jumble of domes, columns, and capitals, I felt myself back in the arcaded courtyards of the great mosques and *madrassas* (seminaries) in India to which shop-lined alleys led, dark passages suddenly opening out into expanses of light and color.

I didn't know then that other travelers to Venice had felt the same. Visiting in 1782, the English author William Beckford had written, "The variety of exotic merchandise, the perfume of coffee, the shade of awnings and the sight of Greeks and Asiatics sitting cross-legged under them, make me think myself in the bazaars of Constantinople." In 1850, the French writer and aesthete Théophile Gautier had described St. Mark's as an "Oriental dream." Beckford had been more explicit: "I cannot help thinking St. Mark's a mosque."

My own sense of déjà vu was partly explained when I read Ruskin on St. Mark's in *The Stones of Venice*: "It possesses the charm of colour in common with the greater part of the architecture, as well as of the manufactures, of the East; but the Venetians deserve especial note as the only European people who appear to have sympathized to the full with the great instinct of the Eastern races ... while the burghers and barons of the North were building their dark streets and grisly castles of oak and sandstone, the merchants of Venice were covering their palaces with porphyry and gold."

It had been easier to notice and understand Moorish influences in Spain and Sicily, which the Arabs ruled for centuries. But how had Venice absorbed its Eastern influences? And how had they managed to be so concealed?

For the first seven centuries of its existence, Venice had looked toward Byzantium for its trade, security, art, and identity. But as the Byzantine Empire weakened, and the Arabs quickly spread across the Mediterranean, Venetians developed stronger links with the Levant and then, even farther, with the spice markets of India and Central Asia, becoming part of a global network of trade. The Venetians finally proclaimed their independence by sacking and looting Constantinople in 1204.

Over the next three centuries, they came into even closer contact with the sophisticated urban and multifaith civilizations that had developed in the Islamic world. Few people had believed the tales of the East told by Marco Polo, who had been nicknamed Marco Il Milione (of the million lies). Now, many Venetians saw for themselves the fabulous cities of Baghdad, Damascus, and Cairo.

Just as the household gadgets of middle-class Americans define many people's aspirations in our newly globalized world, so the luxurious lifestyles of the elites of Muslim cities once inspired imitation all over the Islamic world. The nouveau-riche Venetians, too, sought to adopt Eastern habits of conspicuous, if elegant, consumption. Oriental silks, carpets, ceramics (especially Chinese porcelain), and glass were much in demand among the feudal nobility and the rising bourgeoisie—they helped give Venetian painting its sumptuous colors.

The Venetians expressed their political power, too, in terms inspired by or borrowed from Muslim lands. The Gothic façade of the Ducal Palace, which was begun in the mid-fourteenth century, emphasized the city's lucrative trading links with the East. Its pink-and-white lozenge pattern was common in Muslim mosques and tombs along the Silk Road in Central

Asia, where Venetian merchants traveled frequently. The crenellations on the roof of the palace were probably inspired by similar decorations in Cairo. The marble grilles on St. Mark's Basilica were modeled on those of the great Umayyad Mosque in Damascus. The Venetian ruling class adopted Arabic words: *sikka, tariff, arsenale, sofa*.

Traces of that medieval world of traders and merchants survive now in the area around Campo Dei Mori in northern Venice. Decay here, unlike in much of Venice, is more than a patina; it hangs mournfully in the air. On the Palazzo Mastelli, there is a bas-relief of a camel, dating from the fourteenth century. Not far, on the Fondamenta dei Mori, the statue of an Oriental merchant with an oversize turban stands guard on the façade of the house where Tintoretto once lived.

You can only wonder whether Tintoretto, the son of a silk dyer, had any connection with Muslim merchants when you look at his 1562 painting *St. Mark Saving a Saracen from Shipwreck* at the Academia. In the same overwhelmingly rich gallery, Moorish slaves lurk incongruously in Veronese's version of *The Last Supper*. A marble throne with Arabic inscriptions sits in the church of San Pietro di Castello, which was Venice's main cathedral until 1807, when St. Mark's took its place.

Unlike much of Western Europe, with its sword-happy Crusaders, Venice often chose the way of compromise with the Islamic world. Its reluctance to fight Muslims often annoyed the pope in Rome. Religion was important to Venetians, but not as much as trade and coexistence. In 1454, Venice signed a peace treaty with the Ottoman Sultan Mehmed II soon after he conquered Istanbul and ended Christian rule in the East.

Twenty-five years later, the Doge of Venice sent Gentile Bellini to Istanbul, where he painted, memorably, the Sultan and a boy scribe. Bellini's two years among the Turks may explain the preponderance of turbaned merchants in *The Procession in St. Mark's Square*.

Two years after Bellini finished this large canvas, the Portuguese discovered the sea route to India and Venice's importance as a center for trade with the East diminished. The explorations of the New World and the renaissance in art and architecture began to give Venetians as well as other Europeans a sense of belonging to a large continent called Europe.

If the city had looked away from Europe as it rose to unprecedented wealth and power, soon it was slowly being drawn, by conquests and conflicts, into the Italian mainland. In 1797, it was finally invaded and defeated by Napoleon. After the opening of the Suez Canal in 1869, Venice became a stop on Britain's imperial highway to India. The East now began not in Venice but in Suez.

Reabsorbed into Europe, Venice offered convenient metaphors to novelists seeking to define the new worlds conquered by fellow Europeans. Venice "was not Europe" to E. M. Forster, but unlike India, it had "beauty of form." Keen to escape his dull ancestral burghers in Germany, Thomas Mann in his famous story identified Venice with the rational and Apollonian West, threatened only by an East of uncontrollable Dionysian energies.

Shorn of its Asian associations, Venice became part of the nineteenth-century European and American religion called "culture." Only such rich and influential visitors as Henry James enjoyed the privilege of travel then. These Grand Tourists created a sentimental and romantic image of Venice as a city outside time and history that has survived to this day.

This is unfortunate. For the image obscures Venice's extraordinary contemporary relevance. It makes it harder to remember that the city is where East and West met, mostly amicably, in both commerce and art, and where multi-culturalism was an unself-conscious, everyday reality, embraced by almost all its inhabitants, rather than a political slogan of ethnic minorities. For the city's most resonant message today is surely this: that a civilization flourishes most when it is open to external influences, when it ceases to be a fortress and lets itself become a crossroads, a place of chance encounters and unexpected minglings.

I was in Venice not so long ago when I read in a newspaper one morning that Pope John Paul II, clearly distressed by the state of the world, had appointed an envoy for a "dialogue" he wished to conduct with religious figures in the Islamic world. The press in Italy seemed full of reports of such grand and seemingly meaningless gestures. But I didn't turn the page of my newspaper to read on, and as I lingered expensively in Caffè Florian, a long and vain letter to the pope began to compose itself in my mind.

I thought of exhorting him to begin his dialogue with the Church's old adversary, Islam, in Venice, the city that had often ignored his predecessors' call for a crusade against the infidels. Of course, I never wrote to the pope, but now I can't help thinking that Venice's record of disobedience probably offers some lessons in diplomacy to all of us. Even more: the city's pragmatic cosmopolitanism may be an antidote to the ideological deliriums of a world losing touch with its past.

✤ ✤ ✤

Pankaj Mishra, a contributing editor for Travel+Leisure, *also writes for the* New York Review of Books *and* The New York Times. *His latest book is* An End to Suffering: The Buddha in the World.

TIM WARD

❧ ❧ ❧

Lady with an Ax

It is good to pay homage to the Goddess.

W HILE TRAVELING IN INDIA, I NOTICED THE MYRIAD
goddesses worshipped in temples and shines.
As I traveled farther in Asia, I found many more. In
China: Kwan Yin, Bodhisattva of Compassion. In Japan:
Amateratsu, Goddess of the Sun. In Tibet: the Taras, a
set of female Bodhisattvas. So when I returned to North
America after six years living in Asia, it seemed downright weird that we in the West *don't* worship the feminine divine.

Of course it was not always so. In pre-Christian times,
each ancient civilization had their own pantheon of
gods and goddesses. Goddesses appeared as primordial
creators, protectors, and powerful forces of nature and
fertility right back to the dawn of writing. Only in the
past 1,600 years has Western civilization embraced the

religion of the Father as the one and only God. What have we men lost, I wondered, when we turned our backs on the feminine divine? And in particular, how has this affected our relationships with flesh-and-blood women? I believe we men have a deep need to connect with women, which for most of us feels profoundly thwarted. I feel it personally. All four of the long-term relationships I had before the age of thirty-five—including one marriage—ended not just badly, but wretchedly. Was there a spiritual link between our rejection of the goddess and our problems with women?

I decided to find out for myself. Over the course of three years I traveled to the cradles of Western Civilization, to Greece, Crete, Turkey, Israel, Romania, Bulgaria, Ukraine, Yugoslavia, France, Cyprus and Malta. I wanted to walk the ruins of goddess's temples, to gaze at her statues and icons. I wanted to see if they held a resonance for me. Just as a harp string will vibrate if another instrument strikes an identical note, I hoped the images created by my ancestors could bring to life a corresponding echo within me.

I encountered literally thousands of representations of the feminine divine. Facing the goddess allowed me to unleash emotions so threatening and painful I never could have imagined expressing them directly to a real woman. It opened doors that I had long nailed shut. It's one thing to contemplate the goddess as metaphysical idea or a psychological archetype, but when the feminine divine took shape inside my psyche, she often terrified me, evoking desperate longing, hostility, fear, shame—and also incredible beauty.

The first place I visited was Crete. Many archeologists who have excavated "Minoan" Crete's great Bronze Age temple palaces have waxed eloquent about the culture's graceful, feminine character. Nicholas Platon, a former superintendent of Crete's antiquities wrote that "the whole of life was pervaded by an ardent faith in the goddess Nature, the source of all creation and harmony. This led to a love of peace, a horror of tyranny, and a respect for the law."[1] Feminist scholars such as Riane Eisler called Minoan Crete the "last civilization of the goddess," and described it as embodying the "essential difference" between patriarchal and women-centered societies of long ago. I wanted to examine the evidence first hand, and make up my own mind. What would it have been like? I wondered, growing up male in a non-patriarchal society that worshipped the name inscribed upon so many offering tablets—"The Lady of the Labyrinth."

Who was she? Images of an elegant, sublime woman are everywhere in the ruins of Minoan Crete: painted on palace walls, on pots, as statues, even engraved in miniature on signet rings. She wears an elaborate, many-layered Cretan skirt tied tightly round her slender waist and her open bodice reveals full breasts. Long black hair curls in many ringlets around her face and winds like dark serpents down her back. Throughout the island etchings on golden seals depict women bowing to and dancing around a single exalted female whom they appear to worship. Was she a goddess, a dynasty of divine queens, a lineage of high priestesses? On the entrance wall of the great temple-palace of Knossos, also known as the Labyrinth, a huge mural depicts some three hun-

---

[1]   Riane Eisler, *The Chalice and the Blade*, p. 36.

dred and fifty life-sized figures, all turned towards a woman who is the center of attention.[2] In the temple treasury there are statues of women holding snakes in their arms, their eyes wide in trance. Whatever her exact role may have been, the image of the Lady of the Labyrinth arose on Crete, the southernmost island of Greece, around 2000 B.C. and held sway on the island for over five hundred years.

Teresa, my lover, traveled with me to Crete in mid-November, just past the tourist season, when the skies are often overcast and swept with rain. On the plane ride across the Atlantic, she read aloud my horoscope from a *Cosmopolitan* magazine.

"Leo: Now is the time to start saving for that big engagement ring..."

I looked at her, fighting back shock.

"Well," I said curtly, "this shows how seriously to take magazine horoscopes. I'll remember that, next time I'm tempted to believe in astrology."

Teresa still teased me about my refusal to consider marriage. I had been through a messy divorce five years earlier, and I had told her many times I never wanted to get married again. But I could tell she was hurt by the blunt sarcasm of my reply. Of course, what she didn't know was that at that moment I had in my pocket an engagement ring. I'd had a strange change of heart prior to this trip, and had designed and made to order

---

[2] This fresco has mostly crumbled to dust except for the bottom portion which shows the feet, which are all facing the white feet and ankles of the central woman figure. We can be sure she is a woman because the Cretan artistic convention was to paint men red and women white.

a gold ring for her. I planned to surprise her with it on Crete—if I found the right moment. I fiddled with the ring in my pocket. If I didn't ask, she'd never know. No, I wanted this. Or was I already resenting her, afraid of sticking my head back through the noose? Damn horoscope.

After spending our first morning in the Iraklion Museum, we drove inland through the rain to the Labyrinth of Knossos. A million tourists come here each year, but this rainy day only two or three small clusters of visitors wandered through the temple-palace ruins, hunched beneath their umbrellas. We hired a sullen, unshaven Greek named Stephanous to be our guide. He marched us along the grand procession where the fresco of the Lady had stood 3,500 years ago. The entranceway leads to a great central courtyard the size of a football field. Beneath its paving stones and along the downward slope of the hillside there were hundreds of chambers.

"So many rooms!" Stephanous gestured with a sweep of his arm from a vantage point. "Perhaps a thousand! Is like a maze, a labyrinth! You see, they build this way, that way, so confusing, so you can't find the rooms of the king and queen. It is defense from invaders."

But he was making the case poorly. Knossos was far inland and had never been attacked, so there would be no real need for such an elaborate defense. Plus, the floor plan was not at all confusing, just so large it was overwhelming. The building was well laid out, with distinct quarters for artisans, functionaries, larger receiving rooms, smaller intimate rooms for rituals, workrooms, storage vaults, and a few well-appointed chambers presumably for those who ruled. Searching my books, later, I could find not a single depiction of a

maze in Minoan art. It seems the later Greeks made up
the myth of the winding labyrinth—how it housed the
dreaded bull-headed Minotaur who killed sacrificial
youths in its dark passageways. Though the word *labyrinth* originated at Knossos, it did not originally mean
a winding or confusing pathway, but rather, "Place of
the Double Ax."

The myth of the Minotaur probably originated on
the huge Knossos courtyard, where in Minoan times a
ritual was performed that could be the ancestor of the
Spanish bull fight. A bull was released among near-
naked athletes in the courtyard. They danced around
the beast, avoiding the deadly horns until he tired.
Then they grappled with the great head, holding it still
while one of the athletes leapt from a stone platform
and somersaulted between the horns and over its back.
It was a dangerous act. The bones of some Cretan skeletons show clear signs of goring, and some works of art
depict a young body tossed in the air by a maddened
bull's horns.

The clearest depiction of the rite comes from a large
fresco painted on the labyrinth's walls, now on display at
the Iraklion Museum. It's a perfect snapshot of an athlete
in mid-leap, the bull beneath him, legs bucking, huge
and powerful. A young catcher waits at the tail to help
the bull-leaper land, and a grappler clings to the horns in
front. It's a heart-stopping moment of danger and exquisite grace. It brought to my mind the youths and maidens
sacrificed to the Minotaur—all the more so because two
of the three athletes in the scene are women. A lithe
young woman in a loincloth stands at the front of the bull,
her white arms wrapped around a horn as long as her leg,
the curve of it wedged under her elbow, brushing the side

of her exposed breast. Both her hands grab hold near the base where horn emerges from skull, the heat of the bull's breath hitting her full in the belly. She smiles, her grip firm, her eyes focused as the leaper completes his vault.

What kind of a culture celebrates such intimacy between a teenage girl and a wild bull, I wondered? The Lady's culture: elegant and graceful: a strong-wild feminine unlike anything I had ever seen.

The fate of the bull can be deduced from the many ritual vessels for pouring liquid offerings, probably blood, which were made in the shape of a bull's head. At the edge of one bull-games courtyard in eastern Crete we found a stone slab with a hole drilled through it so that spilt blood would funnel through to where it could be collected in such vessels from the underside. One Cretan sarcophagus actually shows a bull sacrifice in process. In this case, a calf on an altar has been bound by the feet and bled at the neck. Its blood is carried away by priestesses and poured out at a shrine of the double ax.

The double ax! What we think of as battle ax was the single most common religious symbol throughout Knossos and all of Crete. In Greek, it's called the *labrys,* and from this the name of *Labyrinth*, "Place of the Double Ax," is derived. Hundreds of giant double axes in bronze stood on poles throughout the chambers of Knossos, and palace frescos depicted it in sanctuaries. The *labrys* was worn as jewelry, carved on walls, painted on pots and ritual vessels, and etched in gold in miniature scenes of the goddess's epiphany. Like the crucifix in a cathedral, the double ax was everywhere, an image repeated a thousandfold; and like the cross, it represented both bloody sacrifice and spiritual transformation. Minoan double axes were often made of gold and copper, materials too soft and flimsy to have made practical implements for war or sacrifice, and the symbol's origin may have more to do with its resemblance to a butterfly (the ultimate metaphor of transformation) than to a blade. Yet the *labrys* is definitely connected with the sacrifice of the bull, for some Minoan bull-head statues have the double-ax inscribed on their foreheads, right between the horns.

Bull horns were another important symbol at Knossos. The outer walls of the temple-palace once were lined with hundreds of stone horns so that the ramparts bristled with them. At the far end of Knossos on the uppermost floor, a great bas-relief of a red bull was also found, its head down as if ready to charge, its horns a perfect sine curve. Revered, respected, the subject of Crete's highest art, most brutal rituals, most enigmatic myths, the bull seemed to me every bit as important as the Lady to the Minoans: a raw, masculine force made tangible in flesh and horn and blood.

To the east of the great courtyard stands an area which Sir Arthur Evans (the Brit who excavated Knossos in the early 1900s) labeled the "Royal Chambers." These were spacious quarters decorated mostly with frescos of flowers, dolphins, and other natural subjects. One distinctive feature, first of its kind anywhere in the world, was a small private room with two clay footpads. Between the pads ran an open sluice that connected to clay pipes for sewage. With a pot of water by its side, this was obviously a 3,500-year-old flush toilet. Another room held a decorated bathtub, so that the Lady of the Labyrinth plainly possessed what may well have been the world's first full-fixture private bathroom.

"Aha!" said Teresa, "This proves that at Knossos a woman was in charge!"

In a small repository behind Knossos's central shrine the most extraordinary treasures of all Knossos were unearthed: a collection of foot-high faience statuettes of women who seem to be either goddesses or high priestesses. Two of them survived more or less intact among the broken pieces in the repository, and these now sit on display in the Iraklion Museum. When I first saw them, they pulled me into their world, these goddesses incarnate, their white breasts exposed, elaborate full dresses flouncing down to cover their feet. Snakes twine the length of the arms of one, coiled around her headdress, while the other, a girl in the first flush of womanhood, holds two writhing serpents aloft in her hands. Her eyes are wide, as if fixed in trance. She's hypnotizing, powerful, her snakes and breasts and wild eyes erotic, strange, confusing.

Religion to the Cretans surely involved this sense of passionate transport to the spirit realm. Roused by beauty of the human form, excited by the bull sports, living in a culture brimming with sacred, living symbols, the divine Lady of the Labyrinth in their midst, it seemed to me the Cretans knew full well how thin the veil is between this world and the world beyond. Nowhere did I see this Cretan spirit realm more vividly than in the gold seal rings on display in the Iraklion Museum, many of them etched with scenes that could have been made by Salvador Dali. Naked to the waist, women sway and dance, their arms raised, or they kneel before a larger woman as if in worship. In the background hover strange and potent symbols of the invisible world made manifest: bees and eyes, a dagger, a *labrys*, the sun and moon, birds, snakes or bull horns that seem to be flying in mid-air. There are hideous creatures, too: weird hybrids of insect, animal, bird, and human. A language of the spirit, visions, light, and dark, all hammered into gold like no works of art I've ever seen before or since. These were the inner realities of the makers and wearers of these rings, the ecstatic psychological landscape, joyful yet shaded with the demonic, in which the Minoans dwelled.

When I gazed at the dazzling figures on the seals and frescos, they seemed so familiar, like those moments in the middle of the day when one sees a bird or a face or some object and it triggers a forgotten dream that remains just out of reach. One grasps at its fleeting shadow, struggling to remember. It reminds me of the Australian Aboriginal concept of the Dreamtime of the Ancestors, preserved in song and art and landscape so that with the right rituals one can re-enter the collective myth of the ancient past. For the Aboriginal, the Dreamtime is still present, still a part of them. It is only we in the West who have put the time of our ancestors at a distance. Our minds are like a room that has been covered over with wallpaper, layer upon layer: Greek over Minoan, Roman over Greek, Christian over Roman, rational-scientific over Christian. All we see with the conscious mind is the surface. Yet our modern intellect has been built upon these earlier layers, like a coral reef, the living coral but a crust upon the bones of the previous generations. Perhaps on encountering Minoan works of ecstatic art, something resonates, strips away the layers between us and them. For fleeting moments, I felt I could catch a glimmer of their world, not in its precise details, but something of its essence, the fragment of the Dreamtime we share with them.

Leaving the Labyrinth behind, Teresa and I drove south through rolling hills of olive trees. I pondered whether or not the Lady and her priestesses actually ruled on Crete. The problem is, the only Cretan script that has been translated so far is a version of early Greek, known as Linear B, which the patriarchal Mycenaean Greeks brought with them when they invaded the island around 1450 B.C. These texts are mostly lists of offerings, and not very helpful. Linear A, the Minoan script from the time before invasion, has so far defied translation.

I asked Teresa what she thought.

"Well, you certainly can't prove that women ruled on Crete based only on the drawings they left behind."

"Don't we say a picture's worth a thousand words?"

"It's just not convincing." she shrugged.

"But look, everywhere else in the Bronze Age world kings and queens were also gods, and in every other civilization, the king and his male warriors are immortalized in art, usually far more than the women. In Crete, it's just the reverse, in fact, even more extreme. Hundreds of Minoan images exalt female figures and mostly depict men either bowing before them, carrying vessels, engaged in rituals, or as spectators of events at which women are the focus. There's just a tiny handful that show men in anything that could be taken as positions of authority, and none that show women in a secondary role to men."

"These other cultures, they all had pictures of women and goddesses, didn't they?" she replied. "Maybe the women ran the religion and the men ran the government, and for some reason they only made art of the religion?"

"Well, then Crete would have been the first nation to invent the separation of church and state. The institutions were one and the same in the Bronze Age. That would be harder to explain than the straightforward deduction that the people depicted in the art are the ones they turned to for leadership—the women."

"It's still just speculation."

"O.K., yes, but it is *solid* speculation, based on real differences between Crete and other kingdoms."

"What difference does it make to you though, in terms of how you see the goddess?" Teresa continued. "I mean, you make such an enthusiastic case for women having leadership roles, as if you really want it to be that way."

She was right, of course. Why was I taking sides? For a while I drove quietly through the hills and thought about it.

"I guess I want to imagine what this civilization might be like if the Lady really ran it," I said at last. "The kings of the Near East, they had armies to back up their power, while here on Crete, the palaces are unfortified. There's little trace of weapons of war or garrisons, at least until the Mycenaeans arrived. Sure, Crete had a navy. But how did the Lady rule the thousands of residents of Knossos, not to mention the rest of the island? I remember that line of Nicolas Platon, the former superintendent, who talked about the Minoan's love of peace, horror of tyranny, and respect for the law, how this all sprang from their ardent faith in the goddess Nature. But these people weren't flower children. There's fierceness here, together with the beauty. It was savage yet feminine. I've never seen anything like it."

"So how do you think these women ruled?"

"By awe, by religion, by training, by sheer force of beauty . . . I'm trying to picture myself among these red-skinned men for whom the line between divinity and the elegant priestesses was perhaps not clearly drawn. Standing before such women, their clothes a brilliant plumage, eyes black, cheeks red, dark hair winding down their graceful necks, I can imagine how overpowering their presence must have been. There's a certain submissiveness men feel in the presence of a great beauty. With her breasts open and exposed, what could a Minoan male do but willingly obey?"

"And even if a man were to hesitate or argue," Teresa jumped in, "then she could always say 'Gee, it's getting a little chilly in here, don't you think?' And start to tug her bodice closed..."

She grinned at me mischievously.

"'No, no! O.K., O.K., whatever you want!' the poor men would blurt out, and rush to do whatever it was the priestess desired."

I laughed, knowing well that if I were a Minoan man, this would be all too true of me.

Teresa and I traveled south to Phaistos, the second city of Minoan Crete, and then on Kommos, an ancient port on the southern coast. Out in the water we could see the squared broken stone blocks of the prehistoric docks. Up a sand cliff, we found extensive excavations, but the site was closed for the winter and surrounded by a barbed-wire fence. Along the cliffs a bit we noticed where others had bent the wires apart, so we ducked inside the excavations grounds for a closer look. Ancient streets led straight up from docks at the water's edge. Large warehouses gave way to scattered suburbs up a hill. We found a stone bench beneath an enormous tree that overlooked the ocean. It smelled fragrant, like rosemary. Silence surrounded us, but for the wind in the branches.

This was the moment.

"Sit here," I told Teresa.

She caught something serious in my tone, and fell silent. When I began to speak about our love, and what it meant to me, she became convinced, so she later told me, that I was breaking up with her, but trying to do it gently. She sat still in quiet panic. I saw the paralyzed look on her face. Unsure of the reason for her distress, I hurried to dig out the gold ring in my pocket. She held it in her hand, uncomprehending.

"It's beautiful," she said, eventually, and fell silent again, gazing down at it.

"Um, I need an answer," I said, unsure now what it would be. Was she disoriented by so sudden a proposal from the man who vowed he would never re-marry, or discomfited that I had actually asked her? I remembered then her stories of previous unwanted engagements, how it was difficult for her to say no to a proposal, because she hated to hurt a man's feelings. So she would just say yes, then leave town without a forwarding address.

"Yes," she nodded, though I was sure that at that moment she did not have a clue what the question was that she was answering. . . .

In the days that followed we traveled east to the Lasithi Plateau, and walked deep into the belly of Mount Dikti, named after an old Cretan Goddess. This was the place where Zeus was raised as an infant. Minoan rites were once carried out in the deepest, darkest depths of its interior. It amazed me to think of the courage of these people, their willingness to embrace the darkness.

We drove down the east side of the plateau to the coastal Minoan ruins of Gournia, perhaps the best site on the island for seeing how ordinary Minoans lived. Stone houses clustered all around a small central courtyard of what might have been a modest local temple palace where bull-games and sacrifices had been made. The foundation stones came about waist-high. Each house had three or more rooms and a hearth on the main floor level, and here and there a stone staircase survived which once led to a second story. The outer walls adjoined to their neighbors like town houses, so that it seemed like a comfortable little community with narrow, cobbled streets. The lack of walls or any kind of fortifications, despite being only a ten-minute walk from the sea meant the people of Gournia enjoyed a sense of security that has eluded much of the human race for much of history. Allowing communities like Gournia to thrive in peace for hundreds of years seemed to me a greater achievement of the Minoan civilization than building a thousand-roomed palace. We left feeling strangely content.

Looping back around the island's northern coast, we visited coastal towns and cave sanctuaries along the way, until we passed Knossos once again and took the road south to Mount Juktas—our final destination.

While most of archaeology is like putting together a jigsaw puzzle with more than half the pieces missing, every now and then a fragment of the past emerges that provides a complete snapshot: a single moment perfectly and unambiguously preserved. One such moment occurred in a Minoan sanctuary near Juktas' peak. We drove to the modern town of Arkhanes in the shadow of the mountain. Arkhanes overlies a Minoan settlement and palace. On a nearby hill Crete's only unplundered Minoan royal tomb was found. The woman inside, known as the Lady of Arkhanes, was probably one of the city's lineage of priestess-queens. Along with rich ornaments and 140 pieces of gold jewelry buried with her, archaeologists found the decapitated head of a bull.[3]

We ended up driving along a precarious gravel road that climbed and climbed until we could see the blue line of the sea. Eventually we found what we were searching for: a plot of scrub strung round with barbed wire with three empty stone foundations in the middle. Around 1700 b.c. a human sacrifice took place here. It was probably performed by people from Arkhanes in an effort to appease divine powers during the initial tremors of an earthquake. The full force of the quake hit at the very moment of the sacrifice. It shook the shrine to pieces, killing those inside and freezing them in the act of ritual murder. Though the city of Akrhanes was soon rebuilt, the shrine was left untouched until it was found by archaeologists in 1979. The macabre details it disclosed shocked those who had idealized the peaceful, nature-goddess worshiping Minoans, and provided a glimpse of the dark side of their religion.

On an altar in the first of three chambers lay the skeleton of a young man about eighteen years old. His ankles had been tied together and a bronze dagger lay on his chest. From differences in the color of his bones on one side, forensic scientists could tell the blood had been drained from the upper half of his body while he was still alive. His carotid artery had been slashed, and he had been bled on the altar in the fashion of a sacrificial bull, exactly as depicted on the side of a Minoan sar-

---

[3]   Michael Rice, *The Power of the Bull*, p. 217.

cophagus from the Iraklion Museum. Two other human
skeletons were found in the room with the victim: a tall
and slender man wearing an iron ring and a woman
who had sickle cell anemia. The man had his arm up
as if to ward off the falling roof and the woman was
crouched in a corner. A fourth body was found crushed
beneath the doorway of the adjoining chamber, in which
the clay feet of what must once have been a wooden idol
remained. That fourth person had been carrying a ritual
vessel similar to the ones depicted in scenes of bull sacrifice. Having poured its contents out to the idol, he or
she was likely heading back to the bleeding boy for more
blood when the quake occurred. The top half of the
broken blood-carrying vessel survived; it was decorated
with a picture of a bull.

Perhaps in such a time of crisis, a slaughtered bull was
not enough to appease the powers that shook the earth,
so the Minoans reverted to an older practice of human
sacrifice. Standing on the windswept, desolate slope, the
green valley and the sea spread out before me, I gazed
at the shrine and thought about what a long and desperate walk it must have been up the steep mountainside
from Arkhanes. Hard to imagine carrying the boy so far.
Could he have walked willingly, side by side with the
priestess, the tall man and the libation bearer with the
bull-vessel in her arms? It must have been obvious what
was happening. Did the youth lie down on the altar, put
his feet together calmly, and gaze trustingly into the eyes
of the woman as they slit his throat? I think so.

I tried to imagine myself on that altar, waiting for the
knife, suffused with the ecstasy of knowing I have become
the man-bull sacrifice for my town. I turn to the priestess,
my goddess. She bends over me, opens her bodice, spilling

out her breasts, and so transfixes me. Who holds the knife I cannot tell. But in my vision, the Lady brandishes the double ax, Her eyes full of love for me, the bull to whom She gives life and death. The scratch of cold bronze at my throat pleases Her. The rhythmic pumping of my blood from my heart is my offering. The red magic that flows from my neck into the vessel will soon pour out before Her idol's sacred feet. Will it save the city? It doesn't matter now. Golden images flash from signet rings. I see visions of Her dancing, breasts swaying, welcoming me to Her eternal dream. The snakes, the griffons, the flying double ax fill the sky, surrounded by waves of rippling light. The sacred bull thrashes his mighty head on this boy's body, and then lies still.

Before flying back to Athens, I bought a statue of the little snake goddess from the palace of Knossos, the one holding twin serpents in her hands. I wanted to place her on the mantelpiece in my bedroom. I took her out of the box and gazed at her on my lap. I was convinced now that Minoan Crete was not a patriarchy like other Bronze Age kingdoms, and pointed to an "essential difference." That essence valued refined beauty, yet it was also wild, ecstatic, savage, and capable of ritual murder. What was it like for the men? Through the bull images and sacred horns all over the Labyrinth, I did feel the symbolic presence of the masculine as a powerful and protective force. I turned to Teresa beside me on the plane, and asked what she thought.

"I still think it's impossible to say what really went on in Minoan Crete," she replied, ever the skeptic. "The question you should try to answer is, how did your experiences on Crete change you?"

"Well, for one thing, I do believe there was a vision of the goddess and the feminine here that's different from elsewhere in the region. I feel some of it touched me. I don't know exactly how."

Teresa was looking at me with a stupefied and pained expression on her face.

"What?" I asked.

"Tim, when you came to Crete, you were completely closed to women. You had vowed never to get married again. You kept all women, including me, at a safe distance behind your walls. You were the very antithesis of the sort of man who should be looking for the goddess. How you were ever going to find out anything about the goddess when you had vowed never to be open to a woman, I had no clue. Do you see what happened to you here? On Crete, Tim, you became engaged. Engaged to me. And because of that, for the first time—"

Her meaning dawned on me: "Yes, for the first time, I've become genuinely *engaged* with the goddess."

❧ ❧ ❧

Tim Ward is the author of four spiritual travel books, What the Buddha Never Taught, The Great Dragon's Fleas, Arousing the Goddess, *and the newly released* Savage Breast: One Man's Search for the Goddess, *from which this piece was adapted. To find out more, and to view his photographs of ancient goddesses, visit www.timwardsbooks.com.*

꙳ ꙳ ꙳

In Jerusalem

A pilgrim sees the ancient place for the first time.

Adwenty LATE, AND A SHEKEL SHORT. THAT'S HOW I FELT, at first; overwhelmed by the old, walled city. The historic air of Jerusalem will never vanish, but how one longs for the days before honking taxis, halogen lamps, and teenage soldiers with automatic weapons slung over their backs.

People hurried by, racing the sunset, as my beer captured the last rays of daylight. The western entrance to Old Jerusalem is an extraordinary place; you can nod to the black-cloaked Armenian priests, watch the Hasids trot by in their huge fur hats, smile at the dark-eyed girls hurrying home to help with the Sabbath meal, salaam the elderly Palestinian with his checkered kaffiyeh and worry beads. And all the while you're fending off shifty-eyed touts, wolfish guides, taxi drivers, and other

319

tomcats, all orbiting past your small wooden table, just down the cobblestones from Jaffa Gate.

I left a few coins on the table and wandered into the labyrinth. The long flight of steps down King David and a sharp left brought me into the Muslim Quarter. El-Wad was crammed with a steady stream of Arabs, flowing toward the Dome of the Rock. Both sides of the path were lined with stalls, a frenetic Middle Eastern bazaar offering halvah and gummy bears, jeans and watches, perfumes, prayer beads, and PC peripherals. Ahead was Damascus Gate, where the coffee was cheap and strong.

Walled cities are worlds unto themselves; outsiders can take away only the barest notion of life within their borders. I walked miles and took as many pictures as I could, but never felt like more than a flat stone, skimming the surface of profound antiquity. It was like being handed a copy of *Anna Karenina* or *Catch-22* or the Bible, and asked to write a review based on one or two randomly chosen sentences.

Another hour of wandering brought me to the fringe of the Jewish Quarter, at the intersection of Western Wall Road. I hesitated. If I followed the path, it would take me to the Kotel, the foundation wall of the Second Temple, an immense synagogue built by King Herod and destroyed by the Romans in about a.d. 70. The Western Wall is the most sacred site in Judaism—but was I prepared? I had neglected to bring, on this first foray into the Old City, the satchel of prayers that I'd solicited from friends back home. Such missives, rolled up and tied with string, are pressed into cracks between the ancient stones of the Western Wall. Approaching the Wall without them felt awkward, like attending a housewarming without a bottle of wine.

Yet here I was. How could I resist?

I'd seen so many pictures of the "Wailing Wall" that I was surprised by how exposed, how stark it appears. My sense had been that the wall was in a grove, or on a platform, free-standing. But the single remaining section of the Great Temple is not an interior wall, but part of the building's foundation. It is enormous, and continues on well past the area where a sea of men in black skullcaps were bowing and muttering prayers with a rapid rhythm.

My single wish was to experience a moment in this holy place alone. But I was given no peace. From the moment I arrived, weary- and wild-eyed devotees competed for my attention. Some demanded I leaf through albums of their charitable deeds and make a generous contribution; others insisted that I receive a blessing from their reb and make a generous contribution. A dozen more, in fluent English full of zeal, tried to kit me out in *tefillen*: small prayer boxes that, tied to the head and arm with leather straps, affirm one's covenant with God.

The one place offering respite from these spiritual remoras was the Wall itself. I made straight for it and pressed my hands and head against the timeworn stone. The crevices were stuffed with bits of folded paper, all prayers, some many decades old. It took a few moments for me to find the wavelength, but after a few moments, the power of the site began emanating through the sandstone and into my skull. When I pulled back from the bricks, my face was streaked with tears.

No visitor to Jerusalem, Jewish or otherwise, should spend Shabbat, the Sabbath, alone. Seeking to avoid this fate, I strolled into the heart of the Jewish Quarter.

I found the flyer tacked outside the Jewish Student Information Center. A crude photocopy, it showed a scene from *Seinfeld*, with Cosmo Kramer leaning hilariously into the door of Jerry's apartment. "Drop in for a Shabbat meal," it said, and gave the number of Jeff Seidel, the social and spiritual ringmaster for visitors to Jerusalem.

Seidel's mission is to place every person who so desires with a local family for Shabbat dinner. I called his cell phone and was told to be at the drinking fountains near the Kotel at precisely 6:10 p.m.

"How will I find you?" I asked.

"Ask anybody," he replied.

Arriving at the Wall, I approached the first person I saw. "Do you know Jeff Seidel?"

"Of course. He was here a minute ago…there he is!" Seidel is a short, bespectacled, action-packed figure. He was nearly hidden, surrounded by dozens of men and women. Most were in their teens and early twenties. I was told the drill: one stands directly in front of Seidel so he knows you are there. He appraises you for a moment, then assigns you to a family, apparently at random.

I assumed the position, waiting beside a young yeshiva student named Adam. After a few moments Seidel pointed to us, and fished a slip of paper out of a skullcap. He handed it to me, then leaned over with great curiosity. "So who did you get?" He read the tag. "Oh! The Helbfingers. They're very good. Very good. You're lucky!" Adam and I nodded gamely; he must say this to all the prospective diners.

Some of the families in Seidel's hat were a fair distance from the Old City, requiring a long taxi or bus ride. Ours—great luck!—was just around the corner, not two minutes' walk from the Wall. One of Seidel's colleagues escorted us, and we soon found ourselves rapping on the Helbfingers' broad wooden door.

It is impossible to overstate the rush of comfort and delight I experienced as Mrs. Helbfinger—a clear-eyed, kind-looking woman wearing a blue head scarf and modest white dress—invited us into her home. The large flat had been occupied since the Crusaders took Constantinople. It was 800 years old, with arched ceilings and simple white walls. The bookshelves were lined with religious volumes; Mr. Helbfinger, I learned, was a retired cantor from a Cleveland synagogue. The table was dressed with white linen and set for twelve. Besides our hosts, their son, Yaacov, and their daughter, Chaiyet, there would be eight guests as well.

"It's our pleasure to do this," said Mrs. Helbfinger, who made aliyah—the immigration, or "coming up" to Israel—in 2002. "Back in Cleveland, there were so few Jews passing through town that people would fight to host them on Friday evenings."

Dinner began with the candle-lighting prayers, but nothing resembling a formal service. The event was meant to welcome the Shabbat, the holy day of rest. For this, there was sweet red wine and dense, homemade challah. The other guests—all of them either friends of Yaacov's or local students of Judaism, steered to the Helbfingers by Seidel—knew the words and melodies by heart. Reb Helbfinger, a delightfully solicitous host with porcelain skin and a long gray beard, looked much older than his olive-complexioned wife. I was placed in the seat of honor, on his left. He frequently and eagerly leaned over to explain exactly what we were reading, and why.

Jewish prayers are unusual, he explained, in that they rarely actually ask for anything. They are not petitions to improve the circumstances of the devotee. The blessings over the wine and bread, for example, are simple statements of gratitude for the fruits of the vine and the earth. Even the somber and personal yahrzeit, recited when mourning a loved one, is a universal prayer for peace.

The meal was served. Our bread and wine, which begins every Sabbath diner, were followed by olives and hummus, tabouli, gefilte fish with horseradish, chopped salad, falafel, pita bread, and many other small plates. I ate well, acknowledging that this easily prepared meal—a dozen courses of Middle Eastern *mezze*—was sensible, given the number of people the Helbfingers fed each Friday.

Imagine my astonishment when Chaiyet cleared off the table, changed our cutlery and brought out our actual dinner: a fragrant roast chicken, steamed rice with Persian bean stew, roasted potatoes, green beans in curry, and the most delicious noodle kugel I've ever tasted. Then followed dessert: freshly baked banana bread and cardamom cookies.

No payment was expected for this feast. All the Helbfingers asked was that we share our impressions of Jerusalem. Our host began, speaking about the joys and foibles of life in the city. Helbfinger described how worried he was when, on renting this flat, he had learned it had once been a prayer room. "This meant, technically, that I would have to perform all sorts of elaborate rituals before making love here with my wife." Fortunately, various loopholes in conjugal law were discovered.

Adam, my companion at the Wall, was a sincere

and open-hearted teenager, discovering his affinity for Judaism after a year in Israel. The other guests faded more or less into the background, but Reb Helbfinger was thrilled to learn that one of them—a painfully shy young man with handsome eyes, jet-black hair and an unmistakably Semitic nose—was the great-great-great grandson of Reb Zushya from Anapoli, a beloved Hasidic rabbi of the late nineteenth century.

(Zushya gained great fame with a single anecdote. "I won't be worried," he once told his students, "if, when I die, God asks me, 'Why weren't you a Moses, or an Aaron, or a Joseph?' I will worry if He asks me, 'Why weren't you Zushya?'")

After half a dozen glasses of the nectar-like wine, my own tongue was loose. I told the story of my 1999 visit to Iran, and how gracious and generous the Persian Muslims had been. On one occasion, I recounted, I found myself held against my will in a Teheran diner, surrounded by fierce-looking locals. I was certain I was being taken hostage. True enough, I would not be permitted to leave—until my hosts treated me to an elaborate buffet.

As the most recently arrived guest, and as an American, I was asked my views on many other subjects—including the Palestinian situation.

I found it difficult, in this Orthodox company, to express my empathy for the Palestinian cause. Still, I had to. Earlier in the day, walking through the Arab sections, I'd watched as elderly women selling fennel and sage from baskets were forced off the streets. I had seen Ariel Sharon's arrogant loft in the center of the Muslim district, the sharpshooters on the rooftops, the checkpoints and the armored security cameras. It was difficult to view the workaday Arabs, most of them Israeli citizens, as anything but second-class citizens.

But the truth was that, after four days in Jerusalem, I found it impossible to fix blame anywhere. Every effect can be traced back to a cause, but every cause was in itself an effect. The cycle seemed endless, a cord running far back into the past and disappearing into the future.

The Helbfingers and their guests listened patiently. Everyone was amazed that I had spent part of the afternoon on the steps outside Damascus Gate, reading a newspaper among the pigeons and Palestinians. It was no mystery, I discovered, why so many Jews in Jerusalem do not fathom the Arab mentality. They have no Arab friends; they do not enter the Muslim areas, except to hurry through or do some quick shopping. An especially telling moment came when Yaacov, the Helbfingers' son, described in amazement how his Muslim classmates at Haifa University had refused all social invitations, clinging without compromise to their routine of daily prayers and forgoing the consumption of alcohol.

"Are they brainwashed," Yaacov asked, "or are they simply made differently?" It was an impossible question for me to address, of course—but it spoke volumes about the rift between these intertwined people, and illustrated how difficult it will be, in the context of such bewilderment, to achieve peace in this part of the world.

There is a certain hubris to voicing almost any opinion in Jerusalem. At dinner's end, I begged my hosts' pardon for any presumption I may have betrayed. But the Helbfingers seemed grateful for my honesty, and invited me to return whenever fate might allow. Our evening ended, I think, on a note of mutual respect.

It was now past nine, and the Old City was dark. I

walked back the way we had come, returning to the now virtually empty Wall. A dozen men sat at the Temple's foundation, reciting blessings from large-type prayer books. This time, my cloth satchel of blessings was in my pocket, but inserting them into the Wall turned out to be more difficult than I had anticipated. Every single crack and cranny was crammed to capacity with prayers, scraps of every size and shape. It took me many minutes, and much studying of the Wall's crumbling architecture, to find resting places for my hopeful missives.

The final piece of paper in my cloth satchel was blank. It was meant for my own prayer, but I hadn't yet written one. Writing is forbidden on the Sabbath, and although I don't abide by this back home, it seemed best to be discreet while standing at Judaism's most sacred shrine. So I pressed the scrap of rice paper to my forehead, and conveyed my wish by direct transmission.

It seemed to take. I rolled the paper up tightly, found a narrow opening, and pressed my prayer so deeply into the wall that nothing short of an earthquake could dislodge it.

The traditional Jewish Sabbath begins with the blessings known as the kiddush. It ends with the lighting of a braided candle, in a ceremony called *havdalah*, the passage from the sacred back to the profane.

Twenty-four hours after my dinner with the Helbfingers, the three stars signaling the end of Sabbath appeared. I walked along the outer wall of the Old City and made my way to the Triangle, the tiny, lively district bounded by King George, Ben Yehuda, and Jafo streets. There, I found myself in the middle of a huge outdoor party, as if every teenager in the Holy Land had converged on this one spot. Hundreds of kids milled between the ice cream parlors, cafés, and falafel shops, while young Hasids whirled to the accompaniment of an electric piano. Everyone was talking to everybody else; nobody seemed left out. Kids with cell phones and hamburgers, girls in tight pants, boys with earrings and braids, and on every corner boys and girls with A-3s slung over their shoulders, smoking and laughing as if the deadly weapons were just part of a party costume. The military presence was welcome; just one week ago, right down the block, a bus had been struck by a suicide bomber.

The Jewish State is still, essentially, a state of mind, and the reverence of the Helbfingers' Sabbath night dinner found its perfect complement in these defiant, celebratory *havdalah*. There were no Arabs in evidence, as if this weekly ritual was a reassertion of the Jewish claim to Jerusalem—not just as a holy city, but as a place for cell phones and sundaes, glitter and raves. The scene seemed to embody the ironic, passive-aggressive motto on the country's tourist materials: Israel: No One Belongs Here More Than You.

It had been a long time since I'd encountered any-thing so familiar, yet so strikingly alien.

~≈ ~≈ ~≈

Oakland-based Jeff Greenwald is the author of several books, including Scratching the Surface, Shopping for Buddhas *and* The Size of the World. *He is also the director of Ethical Traveler, an international alliance uniting travelers to help protect human rights and the global environment (www.ethicaltraveler.com).*

≈≈ ≈≈ ≈≈

Mestizo

Race, culture, religion: reality is more
complex than our imaginings.

I<small>T'S SWELTERING IN NEW YORK, NOTHING LIKE THE</small>
dryness of the Lhasa summer. The music on the CD
must be kept low, because it's long after midnight; even
the gloomier stretches of Upper Manhattan don't like
noise at night. I might as well let Streisand sing. About
women. About where it's written what they are meant to
be. About letting her imagination float across the mountains and the seas.

And can she sing. What richness, what purity of
sound, what shaving of the quarter tones . . . an aesthete's
ecstasy, a nostalgic's prophylactic against misery. Forget
that indulgent orchestration. Just revel in the woman's
tone, her passion, her reach.

Her reach. Her global reach.

❧ ❧ ❧

"Is that the religion which women cannot practice?"

It was the third time we had met in her apartment. Past the Potala, right at the fork, across the roundabout, and into the Chinese part of Lhasa. Left at the second alleyway after the Golden Yaks.

"Is that the what?" I said. It wasn't very good English, and I was only there on the pretext that I spoke English well. Even with it, meeting in her place seemed to be stretching the borders of safe risk. Once a week, Thursday nights. It had taken me a while to find my way there. No one seemed to be watching and I always waited until night, but tourists rarely visited this part of town, west of the Yaks, so it made no odds; I was conspicuous anyway.

There was a door in the wall across the courtyard, across a sward of splinters left by the glasscutters who worked there during the day. Probably Chinese, I thought viciously, who knew all about hard work and private enterprise but hadn't discovered the broom.

Beyond the door in the wall was a second tiny courtyard leading to two rooms cut out of a former outhouse. The first was lined with gilt knickknacks and kitsch calendars. What I could see of the second was lined with books.

"Youtai religion," she explained. The Chinese term for Jews and Judaism. "Women cannot practice."

There is only one place I know where that statement has been formulated. She can't have seen it. They don't show that sort of film in Tibet. They show Hong Kong martial arts films and Hindi movies and dubbed action films with Sylvester Stallone. Nothing too troubling for the mind. Mostly about violence, mostly about men.

And endless twenty-six-part TV marathons about their liberation from feudal landlords by fresh-faced youth dressed in the plain, faded green of the PLA, so popular that on Thieves' Island on the south side of the city you can now hire a private room in a restaurant and be served by girls in the same 1950s uniforms, only newly creased, without the fadedness, and wearing revolutionarily bright-red lipstick.

And anyway all the cinemas in town except for two have closed now, because some smart planner in the Party worked out that wealthy people don't stage demonstrations and tripled all the salaries. So now everyone has bought a VCR, even the Tibetans. But she still didn't have one. So she can't have seen it. And she clearly didn't know that the ban on Jewish women studying had passed by most communities fifty years ago. This was a one-source piece of knowledge, and that source could only be . . .

"*Yen-tel*," she said. "*Yen-tel*."

She came back from the other room with *A Collection of the World's 1,000 Best Films*. At least I think it was called that, but I can't read Chinese. But there, under 1982 or 1983, it was: Directed by Barbra Streisand, Produced by Barbra Streisand, Starring Barbra Streisand, *Yentl*, the story of the Jewish girl who won't accept that the study of the religion is not allowed for her. The girl whom Bashevis Singer had told of, in his wicked, impenetrable, and subversive way, the girl who had disguised herself as a boy in order to study, and who in her desperation to maintain the illusion had ended up in a wholly fabricated sexless marriage. And who after years and years had been turned into a sepia-toned Hollywood epic for which, even for this, they still hadn't given Babs a copper Yak, let alone an Oscar.

My Thursday evening pupil was not far off Barbra's age. Once, I had heard my pupil sing, a spiritual she had learned in its entirety from a Japanese film in which a Negro, as she put it, had died falling from a cliff for some reason I couldn't grasp, singing. She had sung divinely, and I had sat there on her sofa amongst the nylon cushions and the plastic flowers and discreetly cried. But she didn't have a film star's looks. The horn-rimmed spectacles, the scraped-back hair, the asexual garb, the absence of adornment, severity of appearance. At first, three weeks before, in the Snowlands Restaurant where she had asked if I would teach her, she had seemed more like an Asiatic Rosa Klebb. She embodied the Chinese puritan, the ones who were already too committed to abandon woolen stockings for skin-tight polyester suits and nylons when the market had arrived, or, rather, had been pushed in. Or the ones who gambled that the state bureaucracy was a safer bet than the main-street stores and nightclubs that they maybe had realized even then were sure as spring tide to come.

She didn't only look like a stern-faced Chinese cadre: she was a Chinese cadre. A very high-up Chinese cadre. In my very last lesson I finally dared to ask, "What do you do?"

"You would not understand," she said, "I have seen films. I know what Americans in offices do. Especially New York. They work, all the time. It's a different system here. We do nothing. We play mahjong and we do nothing. It's different here."

Her gamble had been right, of course: she did nothing all day and still got paid. Handsomely by local standards, 2,000 kuai a month, I'd bet. Of course she had been right: the Party wouldn't dare to break the iron rice bowl in

Tibet, the life-long social safety net. Tibet is one place where it doesn't mind paying for compliance, at least among officials. Anyway, she had placed her bet both ways: she had long since told her husband to leave, and had paid her way into part-ownership of a high-class nightclub, in which Sichuanese migrant girls in scanty outfits—Tibetan girls, she said, just don't know how to do it—served liquor to Chinese soldiers and office staff drinking up their altitude-allowances and remoteness-bonuses, but still left with plenty to squander in brothels on their way to their bare and lonely one-bulb rooms in China's western outpost.

That's a smart cadre. Play both ways.

She served more tea. Chinese leaf tea, almost color-less, bitter but refreshing in the intense cold now that the sun had long gone down. I was still trying to exonerate my religion. It was just a custom in some communities, I stammered hopefully, it has no written basis. "They were the ones who killed Yishu," she declared. The Chinese word for Jesus. So now I knew from whom she had learned her English: it must have been the officially sanctioned foreign English teachers, the same covert Protestant evangelists who had told me that all Tibetans were damned to hell. I had killed Jesus, so I understood why I should go there, but what the Tibetans had done I wasn't sure. But the missionaries weren't there to ex-plain these things to foreigners, they had more pressing work to do.

She looked through the book and wrote some notes on films we found. *Bullit. Star Wars. Vertigo.* Her pen was lavishly inlaid with fake lapis lazuli, an excess of plastic opulence. "Presented to Tibet's Cadres by the Central Authorities' Representative Delegation on the

30th Anniversary of Peaceful Liberation" it had faintly etched on it. It ran out of ink again. I lent her mine.

"I was in it," I said. "The tailor. The apprentice tailor."

She took no notice, she was writing in her notebook. A long description of her father's life lay across its pages, written in a grotesque cursive that knew no horizontals, and she was copying my corrections to what had been her homework from the week before. He had been a landless laborer in the Yunnanese southwest sixty years before, and had fled to join Maoist guerrillas in the hills after beating the landlord's donkey to death by mistake. But it wasn't his oppressed credentials that had brought him to high office under the new regime: it was the happenstance that he had learned Tibetan in his youth from driving animals to market across the mountains in Tibet. First a translator for the arriving army as it followed the passes he had so often crossed, then some years of education in the cadre's school, and finally a county leader, or as she put it, a district magistrate. This woman ate dictionaries for breakfast.

She reads everything, the Tibetan girl from the Snowlands told me later. All she does is read. No one of us knows as much as her. And she's read all of the Water Margins. And not just the Dream of the Red Chamber, either. Other things too, she said. She hardly goes out, she just reads.

I remembered the Dostoevsky I had recognized amongst the rows and rows of Chinese novels, next to the photo of her taken as a student twenty years ago at college, with the red neck-scarf that marked her party future. It was printed on that lightly plastic-coated paper at that time used for posters, too large for any private photograph, with some caption printed underneath: she must have been a propaganda model distributed across the country. My god, she had been beautiful then. Joyous, gleaming, flush with the promise of revolution. Now rows and rows of bookshelves towered around the dusty memorabilia of a thrilling youth. There were cheap encyclopedias leaning against the empty fish tank, and picture books of other countries stacked beside the songbird's cage. And all across the glass-topped table were ornate cups and boxes filled with plastic flower stems and fountain pens whose bulbs no longer would accept ink.

She passed me the next installment of her homework. This time it was not about her father. It was about her mother. And her mother had been even poorer than her husband, and had become a much higher cadre than either him or their ever-so-accomplished daughter. Something really high, but this was not for telling, not even in the quest to acquire more vocabulary. All I knew was that the mother had been born of poor farmers in the hills just to the west of the Drichu, and had traveled into Lhasa behind the army which her husband was then translating for. Swept up in that great movement she had ended up by the seventies as a leader in Tibet.

That was when I realized. West of the Drichu were the heartlands of Tibet. My pupil couldn't write it, she couldn't read it, she could only speak it with effort, she surely wore no *chupa* and she didn't eat parched barley flour. But her mother was Tibetan. And on weekends and late at night perhaps, or sometimes in her dreams maybe, the daughter was Tibetan, too.

The Tibetan language likes to play with unequal pairings and conflicting negatives: *ra ma lug, lha ma yin*—neither beast nor bird, goat nor sheep, neither god nor human. They do not describe such people as half this, half that, but as *rgya ma bod*: neither Chinese nor Tibetan. I watched her write more new words into her vocabulary list and wondered if I was looking into the mixed, the hybrid, the non-dual, the undivided, the commingled, the neither-being-nor-not-being described in the Higher Sutras. Then I remembered I was looking at the Cadre Who Played Both Ways, who was weaned on Marx, and who graduated on Bashevis Singer.

In the Upper Manhattan apartment Barbra is still singing of her long-lost father and the window from which she can see only a patch of sky. It is nearly day. I wonder what my pupil is doing now. Whether she had to answer questions about the unofficial evening classes. Whether she kept her resolve to sell the night-club holding. Whether she is still writing in her notebook, hoping for some Western teacher to come one day to check the endless pages of cursive confessional. Whether she dreams she is Tibetan. Whether she still thinks Jews are all misogynists. Why she never asked who the tailor was.

Hollywood and Bashevis Singer gave *Yentl* a glorious ending, by having her escape the misery of her homeland and the fiction of her marriage by taking a boat to America. Being great writers of fiction and crafters of dreams, they never told us if she was happy when she got there. Or if she retained the love of her religion and her language after the first few years had passed. Or if the culture left behind survived. They didn't describe the Land of Individual Freedom where men survive by roaming Manhattan streets at nighttime counting coke

cans out of garbage bins at fifteen dollars a day, where
Barbra had in childhood been unhappy.

The half-goat, half-sheep grazes both the pastureland
and the mountainsides; she doesn't run away to sea. The
one migrates in chase of dreams; the other adapts. The
one enchants, the other discards outward charms. With
her the future lies.

≈≈ ≈≈ ≈≈

*Robbie Barnett was born in London in 1953 and first visited Tibet
in 1987. The following year he founded the Tibet Information
Network, an independent news and research service. Since 1998 he
has been teaching at Columbia University in New York, and since
2000 running a summer language program for foreign students at
the university in Lhasa. He started his career as an actor in 1975
and appeared in Roberts Brothers' Circus, Circus Hoffman, Billy
Smart's Big Top, and the Spanish State Circus before going on to
work with the Royal National Theatre,* The Muppet Show, *and
the BBC, as well as on several major films, including* Yentl.

PHIL COUSINEAU

❧ ❧ ❧

The Oldest Road
in the World

We are all walking the ancient path.

ON THIS MOON-FLED NIGHT WHAT I'VE LEARNED while looking up something else—is that the oldest road in the world is in danger of being lost.

I'm hunkered down over a glass of chianti at Mario's, my local North Beach café, riffling through the pages of an old magazine when my eyes bulge under the weight of the following words:

> A project is underway to preserve a ninety-foot-long trail of human footprints in northern Tanzania that, scientists say, provide the only proof that man walked upright as many as 3.5 million years ago.

338

I read on to learn that in 1977, on the barren plain of Laetoli, two archeologists on a team led by paleoanthropologist Mary Leakey were "larking about"—hurling dry elephant dung at each other—during a playful camp fight. One of the scientists tumbled and by sheer chance noticed some peculiar indentations in the dusty ground underneath him. Thousands of years of erosion had exposed the imprints of plants, animals, even raindrops that had hardened to stone through the millennia. Further excavation revealed that the animal prints had been made when they tramped over fresh ash from the nearby Sandiman volcano while the ground was still wet with rain, and over the millennia the ash set like concrete.

Two years later, Leakey herself discovered an even more tantalizing print—a single heel print she was convinced belonged to a hominid. Eventually she uncovered a veritable trail seventy-seven feet across the Laetoli Plain. Two or even three individuals had walked this way millions of years ago. Leakey surmised that the two larger ones were ambling side by side shortly after the violent blast, one slightly behind, unwittingly leaving a few prints behind them in the wet ash. The prints of the third, evidently a child, were laid, in places over the larger tracks.

Ingeniously, Leakey noticed that one of the prints left by the female turned outward, a single stutter step the scientist interpreted as a brief pause when the female looked over her shoulder. To listen to the rumble of the volcano while the ash fell all around her? To check on her child as lightning sundered the sky? To better hear the growl of a predator?

What moves me most about this serendipitous discovery is Leakey's own description of what she saw through the scrim of time, what she read through her own fingerprints when she touched those antediluvian footprints:

"This motion, so intensely human, transcends time . . . a remote ancestor—just as you or I—experienced a moment of doubt."

In the hopes of preserving this eerily human moment—and the compelling evidence of transition from "four-limbed arboreal life" to "two-legged travel"—Leakey's team covered the fossil trail with polythene and river sand. But over time termites have chewed through the plastic. Acacia seeds hidden in the sand have grown into trees. Their roots are destroying the trail. Twenty years later, twenty-nine of the original sixty-nine footprints have eroded. The rest remain buried under river sand. Plans for the surviving roadbed range from surgically excising the tree roots and injecting acrylic into the prints, to covering it over with concrete, or even transferring the entire road to a museum in the shadow of the Sandiman volcano.

I finish the article and am overcome, as if I've swerved back and forth several million years in a matter of minutes. Why am I feeling such a cascade of emotion? Why all the concern over a trail left by unknown ancestors while Africa reels under relentless cycles of famine, slave trading, and warfare? Because "genetic memory." As Richard Leakey has suggested, is the source of our fascination with prehistory? Out of the intellectual pleasure that the "unambiguous evidence for upright walking" means that *locomotion* may be the adaptation that set our ancestors apart? Or is it due to some vague sense of nostalgia for the original home of the whole human race?

I gaze through the red and yellow neon lit window of the café, and across the street to tree-lined Washington Square Park. In one corner looms a statue memorializing the fireman who have saved San Francisco time and time again. In another corner looms a monument to Juana Briones, a woman who fed the hungry after the 1906 earthquake. In a small grove lies a time capsule, not to be opened until 2079. Relaxed by the ruminations, my mind moves slantwise to an interview in which Laurens van der Post asked Carl Jung why we should be concerned about the fate of ancient cultures.

"Everyone has a 2 million-year-old man inside," Jung replied, "if he loses contact with that he loses himself."

Before I can figure out what he meant, I'm riven by strange dislocations of time. I'm back on the beach at Camp Dearborn, a boy of four or five. My hand is in my father's. He is pulling me forward and I try to keep up, walking in his footprints in the hot sand, longing for the cool lake water.

He is pulling me forward.

Then once again time dilates and I'm flung forward forty years, taking my own boy's hand and leading him down to the ocean. I'm pulling him forward. I'm looking over my shoulder and seeing him try to walk in my footsteps. He has to leap from one to the next, but he does, though the sand nearly swallows his tiny feet and his prints disappear into mine. But isn't that the way it's always been?

At the water's edge he looks up to see if I'm watching him. I am. His eyes leap with joy.

It means everything to be able to remember all of this.

≈≈ ≈≈ ≈≈

Phil Cousineau is a freelance writer, teacher, adventure travel leader, and documentary filmmaker. His numerous books include The Art of Pilgrimage, The Hero's Journey, Once and Future Myths, The Olympic Odyssey, *and* The Book of Roads, *from which this piece was excerpted.*

ACKNOWLEDGMENTS

Introduction by Herbert Gold published with permission from the author. Copyright © 2006 by Herbert Gold.

"Music of the Storm" by Judy Copeland reprinted from the Fall 2004 issue of *Water~Stone Review*. Copyright © 2004 by Judy Copeland. Reprinted by permission of the author.

"To Lhasa" by Pamela Logan published with permission from the author. Copyright © 2006 by Pamela Logan.

"Sex, God, and Rock 'n' Roll" by Bob Guccione Jr. reprinted with permission from the August 2005 issue of *Travel + Leisure*. Copyright © 2005 by American Express Publishing Corporation. All rights reserved.

"Japanese Tattoo" by Dustin W. Leavitt reprinted from Issue #47 of *Kyoto Journal*. Copyright © 2005 by Dustin W. Leavitt. Reprinted by permission of the author.

"Sahara Unveiled" by Dar Robertson published with permission from the author. Copyright © 2006 by Dar Robertson.

"Blinded by Science" by Melinda Misuraca published with permission from the author. Copyright © 2006 by Melinda Misuraca.

"Full Moon over Bohemia" by Christopher Cook published with permission from the author. Copyright © 2006 by Christopher Cook.

"The Discreet Charm of the Zurich Bourgeoisie" by Alain de Botton first published in Farflungmagazine.com. Copyright © Alain de Botton. Reprinted by permission of Alain de Botton and Aragi Inc.

"The First Kiva" by Rirchard Bangs published with permission from the author. Copyright © 2006 by Richard Bangs.

"The Place You Could be Looking For" by Thomas Swick reprinted from the *South Florida Sun-Sentinel*. Copyright © Thomas Swick. Reprinted by permission.

About the Editors

James O'Reilly, president and publisher of Travelers' Tales, was born in England and raised in San Francisco. He graduated from Dartmouth College in 1975 and wrote mystery serials before becoming a travel writer in the early 1980s. He's visited more than forty countries, along the way meditating with monks in Tibet, participating in West African voodoo rituals, living in the French Alps, and hanging out the laundry with nuns in Florence. He travels extensively with his wife, Wenda, and their three daughters. They live in Palo Alto, California, where they also publish art games and books for children at Birdcage Press (www.birdcagepress.com).

Larry Habegger, executive editor of Travelers' Tales, has been writing about travel since 1980. He has visited almost fifty countries and six of the seven continents, traveling from the Arctic to equatorial rainforests, the Himalayas to the Dead Sea. In the early 1980s he co-authored mystery serials for the *San Francisco Examiner* with James O'Reilly, and since 1985 their syndicated column, "World Travel Watch," has appeared in newspapers in five countries and on WorldTravelWatch.com. As series editors of Travelers' Tales, they have worked on more than eighty books, winning many awards for excellence. Habegger regularly teaches the craft of travel writing at workshops and writers' conferences, and he lives with his family on Telegraph Hill in San Francisco.

Sean O'Reilly is director of special sales and editor-at-large for Travelers' Tales. He is a former seminarian, stockbroker, and prison instructor who lives in Virginia with his wife Brenda and their six children. He's had a lifelong interest in philosophy, theology, and travel, and recently published the groundbreaking book on men's behavior, *How to Manage Your DICK: Redirect Sexual Energy and Discover Your More Spiritually Enlightened, Evolved Self* (www.dick-management.com). His most recent travels took him through China, Thailand, Indonesia, and the South Pacific.

TRAVELERS' TALES
THE POWER OF A GOOD STORY

THE BEST TRAVEL WRITING 2005 **$16.95**
True Stories from Around the World
Edited by James O'Reilly, Larry Habegger & Sean O'Reilly
The second in a new annual series presenting fresh, lively storytelling and compelling narrative to make the reader laugh, weep, and buy a plane ticket.

IT'S A DOG'S WORLD **$14.95**
True Stories of Travel with Man's Best Friend
Edited by Christine Hunsicker
Introduction by Maria Goodavage
Hilarious and heart warming stories of traveling with canine companions.

A SENSE OF PLACE **$18.95**
Great Travel Writers Talk About Their Craft, Lives, and Inspiration
By Michael Shapiro
A stunning collection of interviews with the world's leading travel writers, including: Isabel Allende, Bill Bryson, Tim Cahill, Arthur Frommer, Pico Iyer, Peter Matthiessen, Frances Mayes, Jan Morris, Redmond O'Hanlon, Jonathan Raban, Paul Theroux, Simon Winchester, and many more.

WHOSE PANTIES ARE THESE? **$14.95**
More Misadventures from Funny Women on the Road
Edited by Jennifer L. Leo
Following on the high heels of the award-winning bestseller *Sand in My Bra and other Misadventures* comes another collection of hilarious travel stories by women.

SAFETY AND SECURITY FOR WOMEN **$14.95**
WHO TRAVEL
(SECOND EDITION)
By Sheila Swan & Peter Laufer
"A cache of valuable advice." —*The Christian Science Monitor*

A WOMAN'S PASSION FOR TRAVEL **$17.95**
True Stories of World Wanderlust
Edited by Marybeth Bond & Pamela Michael
"A diverse and gripping series of stories!" —Arlene Blum, author of *Annapurna: A Woman's Place*

THE GIFT OF TRAVEL **$14.95**
Inspiring Stories from Around the World
Edited by Larry Habegger, James O'Reilly & Sean O'Reilly
"Like gourmet chefs in a French market, the editors of Travelers' Tales pick, sift, and prod their way through the weighty shelves of contemporary travel writing, creaming off the very best." —William Dalrymple, author of *City of Djinns*

Women's Travel

A WOMAN'S EUROPE $17.95
True Stories
Edited by Marybeth Bond
An exhilarating collection of inspirational, adventurous, and entertaining stories by women exploring the romantic continent of Europe. From the bestselling author Marybeth Bond.

WOMEN IN THE WILD $17.95
True Stories of Adventure and Connection
Edited by Lucy McCauley
"A spiritual, moving, and totally female book to take you around the world and back."
—*Mademoiselle*

A MOTHER'S WORLD $14.95
Journeys of the Heart
Edited by Marybeth Bond & Pamela Michael
"These stories remind us that motherhood is one of the great unifying forces in the world."
—*San Francisco Examiner*

A WOMAN'S PATH $16.95
Women's Best Spiritual Travel Writing
Edited by Lucy McCauley, Amy G. Carlson & Jennifer Leo
"A sensitive exploration of women's lives that have been unexpectedly and spiritually touched by travel experiences.... Highly recommended."
—*Library Journal*

A WOMAN'S WORLD $18.95
True Stories of World Travel
Edited by Marybeth Bond
Introduction by Dervla Murphy

———— ★ ★ ★ ————
Lowell Thomas Award
—Best Travel Book

A WOMAN'S PASSION FOR TRAVEL $17.95
True Stories of World Wanderlust
Edited by Marybeth Bond & Pamela Michael
"A diverse and gripping series of stories!"
—Arlene Blum, author of
Annapurna: A Woman's Place

Food

ADVENTURES IN WINE $17.95
True Stories of Vineyards and Vintages around the World
Edited by Thom Elkjer
Humanity, community, and brotherhood compose the marvelous virtues of the wine world. This collection toasts the warmth and wonders of this large extended family in stories by travelers who are wine novices and experts alike.

HER FORK IN THE ROAD $16.95
Women Celebrate Food and Travel
Edited by Lisa Bach
A savory sampling of stories by the best writers in and out of the food and travel fields.

FOOD $18.95
A Taste of the Road
Edited by Richard Sterling
Introduction by Margo True

———— ★ ★ ★ ————
Silver Medal Winner of the Lowell Thomas Award
—Best Travel Book

THE ADVENTURE OF FOOD $17.95
True Stories of Eating Everything
Edited by Richard Sterling
"Bound to whet appetites for more than food."
—*Publishers Weekly*

HOW TO EAT AROUND THE WORLD $12.95
Tips and Wisdom
By Richard Sterling
Combines practical advice on foodstuffs, habits, and etiquette, with hilarious accounts of others' eating adventures.

Destination Titles

ALASKA $18.95
Edited by Bill Sherwonit, Andromeda Romano-Lax, & Ellen Bielawski

AMERICA $19.95
Edited by Fred Setterberg

AMERICAN SOUTHWEST $17.95
Edited by Sean O'Reilly & James O'Reilly

AUSTRALIA $18.95
Edited by Larry Habegger

BRAZIL $18.95
Edited by Annette Haddad & Scott Doggett
Introduction by Alex Shoumatoff

CENTRAL AMERICA $17.95
Edited by Larry Habegger & Natanya Pearlman

CHINA $18.95
Edited by Sean O'Reilly, James O'Reilly & Larry Habegger

CUBA $18.95
Edited by Tom Miller

FRANCE $18.95
Edited by James O'Reilly, Larry Habegger & Sean O'Reilly

GRAND CANYON $17.95
Edited by Sean O'Reilly, James O'Reilly & Larry Habegger

GREECE $18.95
Edited by Larry Habegger, Sean O'Reilly & Brian Alexander

HAWAI'I $17.95
Edited by Rick & Marcie Carroll

HONG KONG $17.95
Edited by James O'Reilly, Larry Habegger & Sean O'Reilly

INDIA $19.95
Edited by James O'Reilly & Larry Habegger

IRELAND $18.95
Edited by James O'Reilly, Larry Habegger & Sean O'Reilly

ITALY $18.95
Edited by Anne Calcagno
Introduction by Jan Morris

JAPAN $17.95
Edited by Donald W. George & Amy G. Carlson

MEXICO $17.95
Edited by James O'Reilly & Larry Habegger

NEPAL $17.95
Edited by Rajendra S. Khadka

PARIS $18.95
Edited by James O'Reilly, Larry Habegger & Sean O'Reilly

PROVENCE $16.95
Edited by James O'Reilly & Tara Austen Weaver

SAN FRANCISCO $18.95
Edited by James O'Reilly, Larry Habegger & Sean O'Reilly

SPAIN $19.95
Edited by Lucy McCauley

THAILAND $18.95
Edited by James O'Reilly & Larry Habegger

TIBET $18.95
Edited by James O'Reilly & Larry Habegger

TURKEY $18.95
Edited by James Villers Jr.

TUSCANY $16.95
Edited by James O'Reilly & Tara Austen Weaver
Introduction by Anne Calcagno